M000096895

HOCKEYTOWN DOC

A Half-Century of Red Wings Stories from Howe to Yzerman

Dr. John "Jack" Finley

TRIUMPH
BOOKS

Library of Congress Cataloging-in-Publication Data

Finley, John, 1928–

  Hockeytown doc : a half-century of Red Wings stories from Howe to Yzerman / Dr. John Finley ; [foreword by] Gordie Howe.

    p. cm.

  Summary: "Dr. John Finley was the team physician for the Detroit Red Wings for more than five decades, and these are the stories of his unique experiences"-- Provided by publisher.

  Includes bibliographical references and index.

  ISBN 978-1-60078-771-3 (hardback)

  1. Detroit Red Wings (Hockey team)—Anecdotes. 2. Finley, John, 1928– 3. Sports personnel. 4. Physicians—Michigan—Detroit. I. Title.

  GV848.D47F55 2012

  796.962'640977434—dc23

                    2012020752

This book is available in quantity at special discounts for your group or organization. For further information, contact:

Triumph Books LLC
814 North Franklin Street
Chicago, Illinois 60610
Phone: (312) 337-0747
www.triumphbooks.com

Printed in U.S.A.

ISBN: 978-1-60078-771-3

Design by Amy Carter

Photos courtesy of Dr. John Finley unless otherwise indicated

To my father, a wonderful and enthusiastic sport fan, a dedicated primary care physician, and caregiver to many scholastic, collegiate and professional athletes.

To my colleagues responsible for medical care of amateur and professional sports teams, who devote untold hours to advance medical and conditioning advice to competing athletes.

To my colleagues in the Osteopathic medical profession who have committed themselves to caring for athletes on every level of sports activity.

To my wife, Genevieve, and our six children, who grew up knowing hockey, the atmosphere of the Red Wings, Olympia Stadium, and Joe Louis Arena, for the sacrifice and commitment of time away from home and practice in fulfilling my duties to the team I was privileged to serve during those 47 years, and to their families— Mike, Michelle, RJ, and Casey Finley; Mary, Gary, and Megan Straffon; Maureen, Paul, Lauren, and Craig Kaplan; Bridgit, Brian, John, and James Hermann; Molly, Paul, and Nicholas Riccio; and to Colleen, my appreciation for your patience.

To the hundreds of Red Wings and NHL players, past and present, who I had the good fortune to have known, cared for, admired, and respected, and for all the many exciting moments they have given hockey fans throughout North America.

To our many friends and acquaintances through the years who said, "You should write a book," and to my family members who encouraged me to start writing years ago and thought I'd never finish it! I'm happy you stuck with me.

And most important to Marian and Michael Ilitch for their generosity through the years, making us feel part of their great organization in the NHL.

CONTENTS

FOREWORD

A FRIENDSHIP—AND HOWE

I have had the privilege of knowing Dr. Jack Finley as a friend, and as my personal physician, for more than 50 years. From a player's point of view, he was a hero. He was our guardian angel, stitching our gashes, casting our breaks, draining our infections, straightening our spines, and easing our pain enough for us to be able to rejoin the battle. He was our psychologist and confidant, helping us navigate the demands of being fathers, husbands, and sports figures.

But Dr. Finley has been much more than that to the Howe family. We have been fortunate to be good friends with the Finleys for more than six decades. Colleen, Genevieve, Jack, and I enjoyed many great evenings together, long before the kids came along. It is a rare friendship, the kind where you know that the answer will be yes, no matter what the question.

We have watched the Finley children grow from infants into successful young adults in their own right. In turn, the Finleys have been there to share in the joys of our family, including birthdays, family vacations, Peewee hockey tournaments, Christmas parties, you name it. Jack and Genevieve's son, Michael, hit it off with our son, Murray, skating together at Howe Hockey School, and later as teammates. Doc Finley's love for his craft no doubt had an influence on both Michael and Murray pursuing medical careers.

The stories Jack shares in this book are more than just sports stories. They are a very personal testament to the powerful bonds forged between players, management, fans—and all of our families. We all needed each other, and still do. I am honored to have been part of this book; it is a tribute to the wonderful career of a brilliant, caring physician and friend.

—Gordie Howe
Mr. Hockey

Standing to my left in 2003 is one of the most remarkable, toughest, and humble athletes of the century, Gordie Howe. (Photo courtesy of the Finleys)

ACKNOWLEDGMENTS

While researching the background of the Red Wings' predecessors, a number of books have been helpful to me. One was the book signed and presented to Genevieve and me by Helen Adams, *If They Played Hockey In Heaven: The Jack Adams Story*, detailing his early background as a player, coach, and developer of the players under the ownership of James E. Norris and the events leading up to the great post–World War II teams.

Two other historic photographic books in the *Images of America* series, written by Bob Wimmer, a photographer whose presence at Olympia Stadium in the Original Six days and presently at Joe Louis Arena, were very informative. Leafing through franchise history recalled many memorable stories of the great days of the 1950s, '60s, and '70s. Many stories came from conversations with team stars and executives who became dear friends, such as Sid Abel, Alex Delvecchio, and Ted Lindsay. And it was an honor to work under owner Bruce Norris, followed by the remarkable Ilitch family that continues to achieve great success for the NHL and the city of Detroit.

The momentous task of reviewing 12,000 pages of carefully written information jarred from memory, accumulated from many articles, communication with select individuals, companions, heirs, and friends to help set the record straight is almost impossible. Together with my incredible wife, Genevieve, our amazing daughter, Colleen, and the tireless Keith Gave, piecing this all together in a manuscript remains even now almost beyond imagination. Recording the events, the laughter, sadness, enthusiasm, wonder, and amazement accumulated during that half-century has been a challenge. The effort of collating this information of a medical sports venture into a serious historic collection and, hopefully, a fun read has been an incredible experience.

I wish to thank Michael and Marian Ilitch, their family, Red Wings management, Ken Holland, Jim Nill, Jimmy Devellano, and the many front office people and other friends connected with the Detroit franchise and Joe Louis Arena who helped instill the memories of 50-plus years to make this task a reality.

To sportswriters Mitch Albom, Nick Cotsonika, the late Joe Falls, as well as others at the *Detroit Free Press* and *Detroit News* and writers in Red Wings publications throughout the years, thank you for your kind words.

To photographers Julian Gonzales, Eric Seals, John Hartman, Mark Hicks, and Jim Mackey for sharing their talents getting the "perfect" shot and revealing the emotions of the subjects and actions.

To our dear friend, Keith Gave, the former *Detroit Free Press* beat writer and columnist, for his countless editing hours and suggestions to take my ideas and dreams for a "book someday" to the completed work you are holding in your hands...our deepest gratitude.

Our thanks to Ingrid Ankerson at Washtenaw Community College and her Graphic Design students for sharing their talents and enthusiasm with this project.

To Dave Agius, Sharon Arend, Rob Carr, and the many others at Ilitch Holdings who answered our concerns with this book.

To our dear friends Janis Irvine and her husband, Lex, a former Midwestern University board member, for their assistance in contacting Mitch Rogatz from Triumph Books.

Many have contributed to this effort. The respected editors and their reviewers, those who sifted through dozens of photographs, the many personal comments about the game, its believers, its characters, its brute force, and all the remarkable people who made this sport an international phenomenon with world recognition are commended.

INTRODUCTION

A Debt of Gratitude

My years with the club have been a timeless legacy, including memories of 47 years of surgically repairing and serving the medical needs of the Detroit Red Wings and players throughout the National Hockey League and assisting Wings physicians while serving as a general surgical resident at Detroit Osteopathic Hospital.

There have been no books by team physicians, related surgeons, and orthopedic specialists such as internists or ophthalmologists that I am aware of, other than related directly to the evaluation and treatment of medical injuries. I made the mistake of thinking that writing a book of this nature was automatic, but only after several years behind my computer's keyboard did I realize how wrong I had been. Writing is hard. But the exercise of just recalling these many wonderful memories has given me immense pleasure.

This book is actually a love affair with a franchise, one that I hope documents my unwavering respect and admiration for several generations of the Red Wings' family—the players, the organization, the owners, and the behind-the-scenes individuals, many of whom I had the privilege of working with, caring for, and sharing their delights and frustrations. It is not the easiest job in the world, but it is very fulfilling, not only because of the results you achieve but because of the relationships you build.

One does not serve a position like this alone. Our hospital and its dedicated staff—and myriad other specialists from various locations— were strongly supportive of this effort and provided the specialty and subspecialty immediate response assistance required to protect the lives and careers of the players and the safety of the team.

We all have our goals in life. Mine was to be a devoted husband and father, and a skilled, sincere, and dedicated surgeon. I inherited from my father not only a love of medicine, its history and progress, but a desire to maintain and enhance my interest in athletics both as a participant and caregiver.

My service to the Wings was spent during the years of the Original Six (starting in the 1950s), the first NHL expansion and the rise and fall of the World Hockey Association (in the 1970s), the influx of European players (in the 1980s), consisting mainly of defecting players and those too old to be of value, and the league's further expansion (in the 1990s) and beyond into the new millennium. I witnessed the explosion of hockey on national television in Canada and in the United States, the labor dispute in the mid-1990s, and the lockout by the owners throughout the 2004–05 season and its temporarily debilitating effect on the players and fan interest in the league.

In many respects this book is also an inside look into the locker room and beyond—into the trainer's room for a unique perspective on the hopes, fears, and anxieties of the game's participants, their families, and interests, the grand old buildings, the front office, and the team activities in which they participated.

I understand and appreciate what a huge step it is for anyone who plays hockey to reach the NHL. It is a whole different game requiring remarkable physical, mental, and athletic skills—speed, strength, talent, dedication, character, exceptional skating skills, the ability to see the ice, stick-handling, taking a hit (or avoiding one) to make or receive a pass, anticipating where the puck is going, and getting there first. And when something goes wrong, as it often does when these special athletes compete so fiercely, an immensely talented team of trainers, doctors, dentists, and other first-responders are there to patch them up and, sometimes, even save a life.

Finally, I feel anything I have done in this life has been an acknowledgement of what my parents gave me during my developmental years and an affirmation of my father, John H. Finley Sr. D.O., a physician trained just prior to the days of the great flu epidemic of 1918–19 who used his medical training and osteopathic manipulative techniques to more effectively manage his patients and develop a sincere ability to improve their care. To this gentleman, a wonderful and enthusiastic sports fan, dedicated primary care physician, and caregiver to many scholastic, collegiate, and professional athletes, and to the osteopathic professionals who continue to care for athletes at all levels of participation, I owe everything.
—John H. Finley Jr., D.O., FACOS, FICS, FACGP Hon.

Father, mentor, gifted physician, and outstanding sports enthusiast, Dr. John H. Finley Sr. (Photo courtesy of the Finleys)

PROLOGUE

WAITING TO EXHALE: WHAT TO DO WHEN YOUR STAR PLAYER CAN'T TAKE A BREATH

Sergei Fedorov lay on his side on the trainer's table struggling for every breath and fighting off the immense pain that came with it. Moments earlier, one of the game's brightest stars, a former league MVP, sustained a severe costochrondral rib injury after being checked by an Avalanche player early in the second period of a critically important playoff game at Joe Louis Arena. What happened as he lay there was something I'd never experienced either before or since in a career of nearly 50 years caring for NHL players—and what followed was something straight out of a Hollywood movie.

With the roar of 20,000 fans seeping into the Detroit dressing room as play continued without one of the Wings' most important players, there, in the doorway to the trainer's room, stood Captain Steve Yzerman imploring his teammate to get back onto the ice.

"Sergei, come on. Let's go," Stevie said.

"I can't," Sergei said, barely able to talk.

"But we need you, Sergei. Come on. We need you," Yzerman said.

"I can't breathe," Sergei said, trying to yell back, but his voice was barely a whisper.

I'd never before seen a player leave the bench and go into the medical room in the middle of a game unless he was injured and needed immediate attention. But this is how important this moment was to this Detroit Red Wings team that was fighting desperately to win its first Stanley Cup title in 42 years. And no one felt the pain and angst of this interminably long drought more than the captain, who had been reduced to tears on more than one occasion in preceding seasons that ended in heartbreak—and with some fans and media pointing their fingers at him.

This was a watershed moment in the history of a franchise trying to restore its pride. It came as two of the best teams in the league—the Detroit Red Wings and the defending Stanley Cup champion Colorado Avalanche—were in the early stages of establishing one of the best, most intense rivalries in all of sports. A year earlier, in Game 6 of their Western Conference Finals series in Colorado, the rivalry turned ugly when Avs forward Claude Lemieux delivered a running hit from behind and knocked Detroit center Kris Draper face-first into the boards. It resulted in one of the worst facial injuries I'd seen in my career.

Ten months later, on March 26, 1997, the Wings got a measure of revenge—and sent a strong message to their rivals that they would not be pushed around—in a melee that erupted in Detroit when Wings enforcer Darren McCarty pounded Lemieux into submission in front of the Detroit bench. It ignited a brawl that included the goaltenders, Detroit's Mike Vernon and Colorado's Patrick Roy, exchanging blows at center ice.

Now the teams were locked in a fierce seven-game playoff series, which was tied at one game each. The Wings' most dangerous offensive player was on his side on the trainer's table gasping for air, and their captain was in the doorway imploring him to get back on the ice.

After quickly evaluating Sergei and realizing this was a severe rib contusion, I said to Dave Collon M.D., the team's orthopedist, "He needs a rib block."

"I've never done one," Dr. Collon said.

That's not uncommon. Many physicians have not, even though it's a fairly common—though very delicate—procedure for certain types of injuries, like rib fractures, nerve injuries to the chest wall, and postoperative pain along the rib nerves (intercostals nerves). An injection of a small amount of local anesthetic can significantly diminish the pain.

Prologue

Although anesthetizing the area is relatively simple, the danger associated with those procedures is that if the injecting needle is passed too deeply, it may easily penetrate the pleural (lung) cavity and cause the lung to collapse. That would confront the involved hockey player and medical staff with a second, more difficult challenge, caring for the dropped lung as well as the problem of the original rib injury.

I had a done a fair number of these procedures in general surgical cases. Each time we had to open the chest or separate the ribs during hiatal hernia repairs, esophageal work, or radical gastric procedures, therefore I was sure this could help Sergei. But there was one small hitch. Most of the patients on whom I performed a rib bloc were sedated—anesthetized and lying still. Never had I performed one on a player who was awake and struggling for every breath. So as Sergei lay there in intolerable pain, he asked about what we could do, and I explained to him that the pain was due to tearing of the tissue where the rib had joined the cartilage.

"Just hold your breath," I told him, explaining that there could be no unusual movement. I prepared the combination short- and long-acting local anesthesia, surgically prepped the involved area, and made a skin weal with some quick-acting local. With Dr. Collon and Wings physical therapist John Wharton holding on to Sergei to steady him, I passed the needle through the weal until it struck the involved rib, slid the needle just inferior to the bony edge of the rib, injecting the previously prepared local (anesthesia) safely into the area of involvement.

Within two minutes, its effect took hold. Sergei was completely free of pain and able to breathe normally.

"No more pain," Sergei said. "I can't believe it. I feel great."

We were able to dress and splint the area, and we could clear him to play. The total time consumed to diagnose and treat the disabling rib contusion was, at the most, 10 minutes. So Sergei was ready by the time the third period began. And he went out and played hard and well, relatively pain-free, with no difficulty breathing. The Wings won the game 2–1 on two goals from Fedorov's winger, Slava Kozlov. Sergei assisted on both goals.

Detroit took a 3–1 series lead with a 6–0 win over the Avs in Game 4. But the Avs returned the favor, winning 6–0 at home in Game 5.

Game 6, predictably, was a tense, titanic struggle, and it was not secured until Brendan Shanahan's empty net goal that made it a 3–1 final. But it was Sergei Fedorov, still nursing badly bruised ribs and still requiring that delicate injection before the game to anesthetize the injury, who scored the goal at 6:11 of the third period that stood as the game-winner.

The Wings were on their way to the Stanley Cup Finals for the second time in three years. With Sergei fairly recovered from the injury and no longer needing the treatments, the Wings swept Philadelphia in four games.

Then Sergei and every Wings fan could finally take a breath—and exhale a sigh of relief.

CHAPTER 1

A Stitch in Time

BORJE SALMING TOOK NEARLY 300 STITCHES TO HIS FACE WHEN IT WAS CARVED OPEN AT JOE LOUIS ARENA.

For years, the word around North American hockey circles was that European hockey players, used to playing in the longer and wider ice rinks, would never thrive in the hard-hitting and checking game played predominantly by North Americans in the National Hockey League.

Borje Salming, a Swedish import known to his legion of fans as "The King," was the first great exception to this way of thinking. Playing most of his career with the Maple Leafs, he suffered more than the average number of serious injuries, scored more than the average number of points, and led the way for future Swedes with his toughness as well as his prowess with the puck.

But one morning, Borje woke up in a Detroit hotel room and was nearly moved to tears by what he saw in the mirror.

"Oh, my God," he said to himself. "Am I going to look like this for the rest of my life?"

It was Thanksgiving morning, and I can assure you that just hours earlier, holding a white towel crimson with blood from a laceration that ran the length of the right side of his face, he looked much, much worse.

Facial lacerations are some of the most common injuries in hockey, and were far more prevalent during the Original Six era and the first waves of expansion, before helmets and visors became more common.

Ironically, Salming had been experimenting with wearing a visor in the days and weeks prior to this injury. He had worn one a week earlier after taking a few stitches above his eyebrow, but discarded it after a few practices.

As he explains it in his book, *Blood Sweat and Hockey*, the incident that led to his horror in front of the mirror occurred during a goalmouth scramble in the Toronto goal. Salming was where he was supposed to be, in the area around the crease, defending his goaltender, when he fell to the ice on his back. In the chaos that ensued, Detroit's gritty left winger Gerard Gallant was pushed from behind, and his skate came down on Salming's face.

"The cold steel sliced the skin above my right eye, then cut deeply into my nose and along the side of my face," Salming wrote. "It's odd, but there was no more pain than cutting a finger with a sharp knife. I knew that something serious had happened, but the cut was so fast and clean, it didn't hurt. I got up on my own and skated off the ice. When I reached our bench, my knees buckled and the other players had to help me lie down.

"The trainer, Guy Kinnear, tried to stop the bleeding with a towel, but the blood soaked right through."

It was a gruesome sight. My family and I had seats at Joe Louis arena just three rows up behind the Detroit bench, and I immediately got up and went to the Toronto bench where Salming lay with a Zorro-like "Z" laceration extending from his upper forehead, down adjacent to his right eye, within a millimeter of the inferior puncta tear duct opening, inferiorly through all the muscles of his cheek to the right corner of his mouth.

"Get more towels," Kinnear was screaming.

Continuing to apply pressure, we took him into their medical room and applied even more pressure with surgical sponges and sterile towels. But the blood continued to soak right through. This is the only injury that I can ever recall dealing with that I couldn't control the bleeding with simple pressure.

Hockey players take immense pride in their ability to sustain a cut, get into the medical room to be stitched up, and return to the ice, sometimes without missing a shift. Borje Salming was done for the night, and—as he would come to wonder for himself—there would be some doubt about whether he would ever even look the same again.

"Let's get him to the hospital," I said, and we alerted the operating room at Detroit Osteopathic Hospital, transported him by gurney to the waiting ambulance while I maintained pressure on the massive facial laceration, and we were at the hospital within five minutes.

On the way, Borje was concerned, and asked how bad it was.

"This isn't serious," I assured him. "You'll be all right."

As hockey injuries go, it wasn't particularly serious because it was controllable and repairable. But it certainly looked bad.

On arrival to the hospital, he was taken to the operating room and given IV sedation by our anesthesiologist, Mark Grant, D.O. Local anesthesia was administered to the entire wound area. The bleeding was now under control, the puncta and nasolacrimal duct probed by ophthalmologist Glen Hatcher, D.O., who found no serious damage. My greatest concern was regarding visible facial nerve branches, so the laceration was carefully repaired in layers, approximating each muscle group.

Borje was awake, but sedated, during the entire procedure. After about 90 minutes, he looked up through the surgical drapes and sutures and asked, "Almost done?"

"Young man," I told him, "we've just passed second base."

Three hours and nearly 300 stitches later, the bleeding was controlled, the laceration closed, and the wound nicely approximated. In the quietude of the operating theater in the early morning hours, Borje asked again about the injury, and I told him I was very satisfied with the closure of the laceration. However, it would take days and weeks before we know the final result because of the potential nerve damage.

We left the hospital, and I drove Borje to his hotel, where he could get a few hours sleep before rising to peek into that mirror. As he describes it in his book, "Black threads poked out everywhere and my hair was matted with blood. I showered for a long time, watching the blood disappear down the drain. The shower made me feel better, I even looked slightly better without all the dried blood. The doctor had done a fine job."

He phoned his wife, Margita, refusing to give her many details about the injury but trying to prepare her nonetheless. At Detroit's Metro Airport, Salming hid behind a newspaper to shield himself against the gawkers.

Salming returned to Toronto the next morning with his team. Dr. Leith Douglas, Toronto's team physician and distinguished plastic surgeon, examined Borje, checking his facial expressions and taking a series of photos. He was very pleased with the result, telling me later he was most impressed that the facial expressions were maintained. Gradually, as the wound healed and the swelling receded, the facial expressions returned, the redness disappeared, and, considering the natural deep furrows in his face, the scars blended well and were barely visible.

"It was difficult for a long time, but eventually we realized that the doctor had done a superb job," Salming said in his book. "The red snake of a scar became smaller and smaller until it disappeared altogether. Dr. Finley, quite simply, had done wonderful work."

So Borje, a Maple Leafs great and favorite with Toronto fans, was pleased with the result—and therefore I was also. And for someone who had been stubbornly opposed to visors because they periodically fogged up, he wore one from that time on.

A few years later, Borje signed as a free agent with our club in Detroit. The first thing I did was to inspect the injury. I was interested in any areas of numbness, which would have indicated a loss of sensation. There was none. Everything was intact. There appeared to no abnormal residual defect.

We also had a chance to take more follow-up photos. I always marvel at the remarkable healing power of these wonderful world-class athletes.

As a bit of a postscript to this story, I ran into Gerard Gallant when he served as a pallbearer at the funeral of teammate Bob Probert. Gerry told me he had no idea that it was his skate that caused that injury until one of his teammates told him it did. He then had to watch the replay to

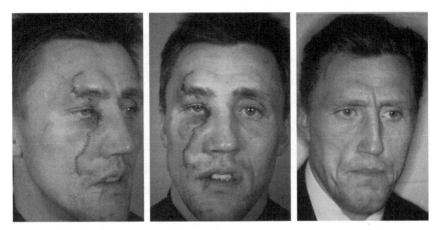

Severe facial lacerations sometimes occur. Grimacing shows intact facial nerves. 1986. (Photos courtesy Leith Douglas, M.D.)

verify it for himself, and indeed it showed another player pushing him into Salming. Gerry recalled a trip to Sweden years later, when he competed in the World Championship tournament. There on the wall of the corridor of the arena in Sweden where they were playing was a poster-sized-picture of the injured Salming—and one of Gerard Gallant, the culprit. But everyone nonetheless treated him very respectfully there.

The team medical staff always has repair materials ready to proceed with suturing the laceration, particularly for gaping wounds. In the 1950s, if the wounds were relatively small, we would repair them without local anesthesia, feeling there was a degree of injury numbness associated with each that remained during the repair. By the '60s, we always had local anesthesia ready and proceeded to localize the wound once antisepticising and surgically prepping the wound were complete. The diagnosis had to be made quickly and accurately. With visiting teams usually leaving right after the game, we would give the trainer a report to present to the team physician back home or, if the injury was significant, we would call the team physician directly. As worries about HIV and bloody exposure of wounds to others occurred, immediate sterile repair was necessary as well as gloved protection of any medical person when examining any injured player.

In many sports, a player sustaining a laceration might be out a day or two. In hockey, it is repair them and return them to play. The number of facial lacerations seen in hockey during the Original Six days until head-gear became mandatory was likely the most common injury seen at that time. It was rare to have a game in which some sort of laceration repair was not required. As a consequence, we always had a sterile covered laceration tray ready to go into action at a moment's notice at every game. One might wonder how safely accomplishing this work in an arena atmosphere without serious complications of infection, hemorrhage, or wound disruption could occur. There are a number of ways to approach that issue, considering the number of unrelated events taking place there, such as circuses, rock concerts, fights, rodeos, and more.

All players who have risen to the NHL level of hockey are aware that because of the physical and violent nature of the game, injuries can and do occur. And undergoing repair and playing over them is commonplace so as not to lose one's place on the team's roster. Players fall in the class of young, healthy individuals who respond quickly to injury. On the average, hockey players shower at least once a day and frequently more than that, so that in spite of their ever-present perspiration, once their wound is surgically prepared and draped, accomplishing effective repair is the rule, particularly when working in concert with competent dental specialists.

Initiating effective surgical debridement and repair immediately, before serious swelling takes place, is usually rewarded with a very favorable result. The surgeon repairing these wounds must have a broad knowledge of the anatomic structures so that any injury more complicated than a superficial repair would need careful evaluation and restoring all anatomic structures to permit effective avoidance of disabling or disfiguring scars.

Not all injuries occur during a game. An example of this was when Greg Smith, then a young defenseman for the Wings, and Walt McKechnie were playing one-on-one before practice. Walt tried to go through Greg and was succeeding according to Walt. So Greg did what all defenseman are trained to do at that moment: he took down his man. The two of them crashed into the goal, which was secured to the ice surface by a 16" lead pipe. Walt's skate flew up and cut Greg's face at the corner of his right eye.

I was in the operating room at the time, finishing a major surgical case. The OR supervisor came into my surgical suite to tell me that Wings trainer Lefty Wilson was on the phone with an emergency. As soon as I picked up the phone, Lefty said, "Doc, I've got a bad one." He immediately sent Greg up to D.O.H., where he was wheeled into a very

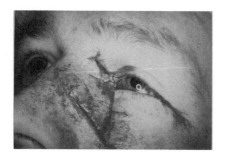
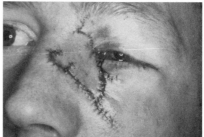

Hockey club team surgeons always have to be ready to serve their players. This 1982 injury occurred in practice. (Photo courtesy of John Finley, D.O.)

hectic surgical ward where the day's busy schedule was interrupted for this emergency.

Like the Salming injury, Greg had suffered a serious laceration close to the eye. His was a stellate laceration at the corner of his eye, passing within an eyelash of the puncta. That area of the injury was examined and probed by our ophthalmologist, Dr. Patrick Murray, D.O., the hospital's Chief of Ophthalmology, who found everything intact. No ocular defect had occurred, and there was less deformity to the muscular structure than the Salming injury. But Greg's laceration damaged the very fragile tissue around the eye, which made it that much more difficult to repair. We used a very fine suture to close the injury. The result was remarkably good in this healthy player.

Repairing these injuries almost immediately after they occur allows careful, precise approximation before much swelling or distortion occurs. We had sequential pictures of his injury on the wall of our office. When Steve Yzerman stopped by our office shortly after he joined the Wings, he admired the pictures, inspecting them closely. The next time we played Washington, the team to which Greg had been traded, Steve made a point to get a closer look at Greg's face to check for himself that there had even been an injury. Greg had healed nicely, with minimal noticeable scarring.

Another gruesome injury occurred early in the first period of an exhibition game against Philadelphia before the 2000–01 season, when defenseman Eric Desjardins took a slap shot from one of his own players directly in the center of his mouth. He came off the ice and went to the visitors' dressing room. We rushed to the room, as well, arriving the same time the player arrived—just in time to see him swing his stick like a baseball bat and hit the 25-gallon Gatorade cooler, causing a flood on the dressing-room floor.

Our dentist, Dr. Chet Regula, and I immediately surveyed the damage—to the player. Eric had suffered a crushing injury to his mouth, losing his four upper front teeth (two of which were artificial) and four lower front teeth. He also suffered extensive soft-tissue lacerations, several through and through. We initially repaired the soft-tissue injury to help control the bleeding and normalize the anatomy. Then Dr. Regula attended to the broken teeth, doing an on-the-spot root canal on one, filing the ragged edges on others, and extracting the broken artificial ones. After 1½ hours of procedures in the visitors' dressing room while the game was still going on, our work was completed.

Remarkably, and so indicative of the classy nature of players in the NHL, the first thing Eric Desjardins did was thank us for our work in a very grateful manner rather than running to the mirror to inspect the injury and the repair. The Flyers were in Detroit again three weeks later for a regular season game, and we had a chance to inspect our work that turned out very well. Again, Eric came to find us to express his appreciation.

Hockey players. They're special people, and they deserve our very best.

The NHL Team Physicians Society has been continuously concerned about the increasing number of facial injuries and is an outspoken advocate for the use of visors. These visors will not eliminate facial injuries, but they will reduce them immeasurably and in many cases, because of the protection they provide, reduce the severity of many injuries like Borje Salming's and Greg Smith's. Though it would require the approval of the NHLPA to institute such a rule, I would urge the league to continue pressing for it to protect these marvelous athletes.

CHAPTER 2

Vengeance Is Theirs

CLAUDE LEMIEUX AND THE COLORADO AVALANCHE WOULD PAY FOR REARRANGING KRIS DRAPER'S SMILE.

Kris Draper is one of the most resilient and popular players I have ever seen. Hockey fans in Detroit have a warm spot in their hearts for most players who wear the winged wheel, but few men enjoyed the appreciation and respect of the fans, the media—and his own teammates—more than Kris.

And perhaps no one played a more pivotal role in the development of a franchise intent on ending a Stanley Cup drought that had entered its fifth decade.

Growing up in Toronto, Kris Draper played in one of that city's great developmental programs, the Don Mills Flyers. In 1986, he was picked to play for the Canadian National Team. He was also selected by the Windsor Spitfires in the Ontario Hockey League's priority draft. But instead of coming to Windsor, Kris favored playing with the Canadian National team until it was time for the NHL amateur draft in 1989. And as an 18-year-old, he was chosen 62nd overall by Winnipeg.

That happened to be an era in the NHL when teams favored size in players over skill. In fact, it was often said that a big player had every opportunity to prove he couldn't play in the league, while smaller players fought for every opportunity to prove that they could. Kris was among the smaller players at 5'10" and 180 pounds, so after three games with the Jets, he was sent back to Ottawa for more grooming in junior hockey and Moncton of the American Hockey League.

Even then, few seemed to notice and even fewer seemed to appreciate the speed, heart, and character Kris Draper brought to his game every single day of his career.

Enter Bryan Murray, the Wings general manager whose right-hand man, Doug MacLean, then assistant GM in Detroit and general manager of Detroit's AHL franchise in Adirondack, discovered Draper. In 1993, the Wings acquired Kris from the struggling Jets for future considerations, which turned out to be $1. Actually, since it was a Canadian dollar, that meant it cost the Wings about 71¢ according to the exchange rate at the time. It might have been the best bargain in Detroit sports history.

Even at age 39 in his last season with the Red Wings, Kris led his team on the ice with an enthusiasm that immediately alerted the crowd that great hockey action was about to unfold. His speed, aggressiveness, and defensive play made him a standout. Because his enthusiasm was contagious among his teammates, he was often the brunt, or perhaps the victim, of many attempts by opponents to impede his movement. And never was that more apparent—and horrific—that on the night of May 29, 1996, with the Wings playing Colorado in Game 6 of the Western Conference Finals in the Stanley Cup playoffs.

Kris was on the way back to the Detroit bench after finishing another intense shift. He was out of the action and slowing up when he was struck from behind by Avalanche right winger Claude Lemieux, who at 6', 220 pounds stood 2" taller than Draper and outweighed him by 35 pounds. Lemieux, the Conn Smythe Trophy winner as the MVP of the playoffs the previous year with New Jersey, skated full speed from 20' behind, driving Draper head-first into the boards, causing a severe facial contusion, black eye, broken nose, and a fracture of the right maxilla. The broken fragment held three teeth. He also suffered a concussion.

Our dentist, Dr. Chet Regula, and I evaluated the damage. There were several facial lacerations that I sutured, requiring about 40 stitches, plus the lacerated gum needed work to temporarily align the fracture. It required wiring his teeth and mouth shut to allow the fracture to heal.

We were able to help stabilize his mandibular fracture by closing the lacerated gum in preparation for his trip home and the inevitable jaw wiring that would ensue.

Coincidentally, Brian Burke, director of hockey operations for the NHL and the league's designated disciplinarian, happened to be at the game, which was played in the decrepit McNichols Sports Arena. As we were finishing our medical work, Burke came into the dressing room and took a look at Kris, whose face was already badly swollen. Burke then interviewed Chet and me. However, he appeared to have a rather blasé attitude about it, which was confirmed the next day when Burke added insult to injury by announcing that Lemieux would be suspended for just one game. In his appalling decision, Burke indicated that Draper had his head down and should have been prepared for the hit, knowing that Lemieux was coming.

The Wings—the heavy season-long favorite to end four decades of futility and finally win the Stanley Cup—lost that game, ending a fantastic season in which they set an NHL record with 62 victories en route to 131 points. Had the Wings advanced to the Stanley Cup finals, there is no way Draper could have played a game. His injuries would sideline him for weeks, perhaps months. In my opinion, Lemieux's paltry one-game suspension was nowhere near equal to the penalty deserved for knocking an opponent out of the playoffs plus the weeks of disability suffered by the injury.

Interestingly, when Burke left the NHL's New York headquarters and moved on to the Vancouver Canucks as general manager at the beginning of the 1998–1999 season, his team immediately became tougher. He brought in Marc Crawford as the coach (who was Colorado's coach when Draper's face was rearranged by Lemieux), and Burke had more than one enforcer on the team. And the dirty stuff continued.

In a game in February 2004 at the Pepsi Center in Denver, rookie Steve Moore, a Harvard graduate, caught Vancouver captain Markus Naslund with a shoulder check to the head that knocked Naslund unconscious. Retribution seemed inevitable. The teams met again roughly two weeks later in Denver. Both NHL Commissioner Gary Bettman and Colin Campbell, who succeeded Burke as disciplinarian and director of hockey operations, were in attendance. The game was tight, ending in a 5–5 tie, and nothing happened.

A week or so later, the teams met again in Vancouver, and the media had built up this game as an opportunity to get even—on home ice. Both teams were battling for first place in the Northwest Division. The Avs took an early lead, and shortly afterward Moore was taken on by the Canuck's enforcer, Matt Cooke, who easily overpowered Moore.

That should have ended any need for further retribution. By the end of the period, the Avs were up 5–0. But according to some media reports, Crawford had written on the game-plan board words to the effect that "Moore must be made to pay the price." There were two more fights in the second period when the Canucks scored two goals to close the gap to 5–2.

It was all Colorado from there, though both coaches—Crawford with the Canucks and Tony Granato behind the Colorado bench—were continually shouting at one another during the game, and both men continued to show poor judgment by sending certain players onto the ice in such a contentious atmosphere in a lopsided game.

By the 8:00 mark of the third period, the Avs held an 8–2 lead, and Crawford sent big rugged forward Todd Bertuzzi onto the ice against Moore's line. Bertuzzi chased down Moore and tried to get him to fight, but Moore kept skating away, figuring any old scores were long settled.

Finally the 6'3", 250-pound Bertuzzi caught Moore from behind and delivered a punch to the side of Moore's head, knocking him unconscious and falling on him as his victim fell face first onto the ice, severely injuring his neck.

Avs players went to Moore's aid, jumping on Bertuzzi, trying to pull him off, and actually the weight of their bodies likely further contributed to the injury. The final analysis was that Moore sustained three fractured cervical vertebra, a mandibular (jaw) fracture, nerve damage, facial lacerations, and a concussion that resulted in post-concussion syndrome and amnesia.

Reaction in the league office was swift and severe. Bertuzzi was suspended for the remainder of the season (13 games and the playoffs), costing him more than $500,000 in salary. The Canucks management was also fined $250,000 by the league and several lawsuits were filed both in Ontario and British Columbia that included in addition to Bertuzzi, Canucks enforcer Brad May, Coach Marc Crawford, GM Brian Burke, and the Canucks owners, Orca Bay.

Moore spent 4½ months in hospitals, wore a neck brace for a year, and never played again. His civil case again Bertuzzi and Crawford was still pending seven years later. Meanwhile, Burke moved on to Anaheim, where he established the same kind of toughness that is characterized not only by intimidating opponents but by hurting them. Sergei Fedorov, who was having a Hall of Fame career in Detroit when he signed with Anaheim, never stood a chance there after Burke assumed control. I'm convinced that Sergei's non-combative style of play prompted Burke to trade him to Columbus five games into his second season in Anaheim.

Eventually, Burke built a team in Anaheim that won the Stanley Cup in 2007. He left the Ducks after a quarter-way through the 2008–09 season to assume the role of GM of the most valuable franchise in the NHL, signing a five-year, $15 million contract with the Toronto Maple Leafs, who had not won a Stanley Cup since 1967. The Leafs have not qualified for the postseason since 2004 and have shown little progress under Brian Burke.

It's also notable that Burke is an American who played college hockey at Providence College, rooming there with Toronto Coach Ron Wilson. Together they were the muscle and brains behind the 2010 USA Olympic hockey team narrowly defeated by Canada in the thrilling Gold Medal game.

As noted, hockey players have long memories, and retribution is not only accepted but expected. And the Detroit Red Wings would have their vengeance on Claude Lemieux. It came 10 months later, on March 26, 1997, in what stands as one of the most memorable games in franchise history. The teams had played three times previously that season, and Lemieux wasn't in the lineup for any of those games. But he played that night at the Joe before a packed house of fans who hadn't forgotten what Lemieux did to one of their favorite players the previous spring.

Tensions mounted with two fights by the midway point of the first period. But it was a collision between Wings center Igor Larionov and Avs center Peter Forsberg that led to a melee that stirs emotions in both

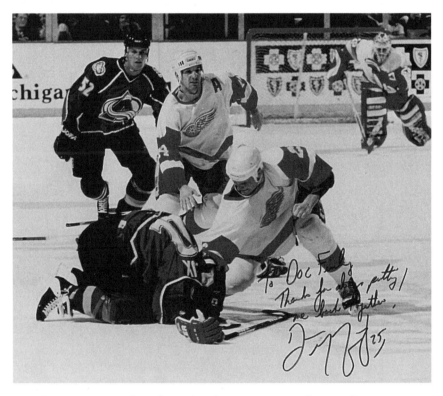

March 26, 1997: Colorado's Claude Lemieux turtles on the ice to shield himself from blows from Wings forward Darren McCarty (right). Coming to the aid of their teammates are the Avs' Adam Foote (52) and Detroit's Chris Chelios. (Photos courtesy of Mark Hicks)

cities to this day. It happened at the 18:22 mark when Detroit Grind Liner Darren McCarty seized his opportunity to confront Lemieux right in front of the Wings bench. Lemieux dropped to the ice after a right hook from McCarty, then the Avs forward covered his head, refusing to fight as McCarty pummeled him until the two were separated by officials.

By then, all five players on each team had paired off, and Avs goaltender Patrick Roy was skating to center ice, inviting Wings goaltender Mike Vernon, who was all too happy to oblige. The two goaltenders dropped their masks, gloves, and blockers, and began trading punches, with Vernon

A melee involving the goaltenders at center ice, Colorado's Patrick Roy (left) and the Wings' Chris Osgood, catapulted Detroit to the Stanley Cup in 1998. (Photos courtesy of Mark Hicks)

pounding Roy until his face gushed with blood. There was more blood on the ice where Lemieux lay beneath McCarty.

There were five more fights in the second period but few incidents in the third, which ended 5–5. It was McCarty who scored the winner against Roy in overtime, assisted by Brendan Shanahan and Larionov. And for the first time, for many, it felt like the Wings might have the upper hand against the defending Stanley Cup champs.

Wings players were almost universal in their belief that this game brought them together in time for a playoff drive that led them to their first Stanley Cup title in 42 years. And no one smiled wider or celebrated harder with the Cup than Kris Draper.

Justice was served, though Draper's career was just beginning to blossom—and he continued to pay a heavy price with some serious injuries throughout his time in the NHL. He suffered three broken jaws in his career, and never did his passion, enthusiasm, and sense of humor wane. He came perilously close to another one in the 1999 playoffs against Anaheim, when he took a high stick from former Red Wings enforcer Stu Grimson. Asked what he might have said to Grimson to deserve that, Kris said, "It's tough to talk with a stick in your mouth." A year later, while we were visiting our son in California, we were at the Staples Center where the Wings were visiting L.A., and Kris took another high stick to the head that caused a transverse laceration of the ear. It was repaired by L.A. team surgeons, and it healed beautifully.

Even though hockey players pride themselves on being able to tolerate all the severe injuries they are confronted with, another incident made me appreciate how the pain and hurt of each event is actually endured and overcome to prove the recipient's toughness and desire to be a player in the NHL. Kris caught yet another high stick from former Wings and University of Michigan star Mike Knuble. It caused a fairly significant facial laceration, which I repaired. After the game I had to check a player in the visitors' room. I knew Mike well from his Red Wings days, and he made a point to inquire about Kris. He asked me to tell him he regretted the incident.

When I returned to the Wings' dressing room, I gave Drapes the message. He disgustedly replied, "Tell him to go [expletive] himself."

Back in 1996, Scotty Bowman and Wings management watched an exceptional defensive performance in Edmonton by right wing Kirk Maltby, and they were able to bring him in at the pre-playoff trade deadline. Having suffered a serious eye injury with the Oilers during practice, Kirk always wore a visor. He immediately teamed up with Drapes at center and sometimes Marty Lapointe or Darren McCarty on the other wing.

When Joey Kocur was sent to Vancouver from the New York Rangers, he retired and came home. But his closeness to Dave Lewis drew him out of retirement and back to the Wings as a free agent—he was signed by Christmas. Drapes worried that Joey might be all fight rather than a defensive force, but Kris and everyone else soon learned otherwise.

Kocur was indeed a very good player, and the great chemistry between them quickly made them a force to deal with. Like all defensive checking forwards, the threatening talk against opponents, and vice-versa, raged wildly and was a major part of their protocol. McCarty frequently replaced Joey, and they were a very effective line—and one that deserved a name.

Naming lines used to be very popular when players stayed with their clubs for more protracted seasons and played longer, sometimes for months and entire seasons, as a unit. But these days that doesn't often happen, and hockey has lost some of its traditional heritage because of it. Due to their success and the shrewdness of their famous coach who put them together, Scotty Bowman knew exactly what the Wings needed and what he wanted—a fast-skating, hard-hitting and relentless forechecking defensive line with a bit of an edge. Draper anchored the unit as a center able to play any forward position and assume many roles on different occasions. He also excelled at face-offs—an important and underappreciated part of the game.

Draper, Maltby, and either McCarty or Kocur always played with an edge and became an integral part of our team, so having a name to go by seemed to be a natural for them. After a great deal of private discussion they came up with the great name that described their role with the team—the Grind Line or better still the Grinders. That was exactly what they were and did, so it fit perfectly.

Everyone in Detroit loved it, but opponents found them to be a huge nuisance. The line not only drove opposing players to distraction, but it contributed timely goals at unexpected and momentous times. McCarty scored the Stanley Cup–clinching goal in the 1997 sweep of Philadelphia in the finals. Malts scored a game-winner against the Oilers in the first round of the playoffs of 2006. Every goal Draper scored in the playoffs seemed huge. The Grinders always were proud of their status with the team, never wanting a bigger role in an effort to get more money. And they carried that banner until they each retired.

After winning the Stanley Cup in 2002, Kris returned to training camp with a big, fat, 35-stitch gash in his lower lip, just another telltale mark of his intense preparation for the coming season. In his final playoff appearance in 2011, Kris was still a major force on his team. He won an incredible 56 percent of his face-offs against San Jose, allowing the Wings to possess the puck that much more in the offensive zone rather than have to fight to get it back.

Off the ice in the dressing room, Kris always had a mischievous streak, often spraying unsuspecting linemates with shaving cream or some equally humorous practical joke. Another major role Drapes took on was that of the voice of reason in the dressing room. He was a go-to guy for the media, and he always seemed to say the right thing on behalf of his team. After Steve Yzerman retired, Kris led by example. His strenuous exercise talents were something that everyone wanted to emulate, and he served as the team's off-ice conditioning and workout expert.

Interestingly, and very likely the result of his intensive exercise program, Kris developed a sports hernia, a small tear in the thickened fascia overlying the groin, prior to the beginning of the 2010–11 season. Repair usually involves overlapping the groin muscles, resecting the fascial defect, and applying a synthetic patch covering the defect, allowing resultant comfort from removal of the diseased tissue. Drapes had the surgery and missed the entire 2010 exhibition season and the first 22 games of the regular season. Like several of his teammates, he sought the help of an exercise trainer during the off-season. After he recovered from sports hernia surgery, on any off-days he returned to his trainer, Mike Knight, who provided an alternate program for him. Rather than riding the bike and bench exercises, Kris did a lot with ropes and kettle bells, employing flexibility and agility exercises to work the same muscle groups in different ways and strengthening them, as well.

He was always very particular in his preparation for the game, so prior to every game shortly before warm-up, Drapes came into the training room to have Tcheky (Sergei Tchekmarev, our very popular Russian masseuse) give extensive last-minute massage. He manipulated and stretched Draper's legs and applied appropriate oils and lotions—I believe from a secret Russian formula—that gave Kris the fleetness that typified his swift-skating defensive ability and prepared him for action with the Grinders.

Since Drapes had his heart and soul in the game and was only interested in winning, his enthusiasm was such that he had the honor of leading the team on the ice with his gusto. The way he headed out on the ice was as though he was shot out of a cannon. He used to follow the goaltender and did one quick spin around the ice. According to the NHL rules, only the guys due to play in the first shift are supposed to go out on the ice, mainly to speed up the movement of players. But with Drapes it was his and the Wings' routine. His technique seemed to tell the team to react in the same explosive way during their battles on the ice, and I'm convinced it often had an adverse affect on the opposing team, too.

Few athletes enjoyed the connection Drapes had with the fans, the media, and the club that he enjoyed for 17 seasons. When Chris Chelios opened his Chelli's Chili restaurant in Dearborn, Michigan, Drapes was one of the first teammates there to help support that effort. The press always knew they could get a good story, or at least a comment that wasn't a cliché, so his stall was a favorite interview stop. He always granted more face-to-face interviews, participated in more charity events, hospital visits, and youth clinics than most other players. He and his family were great supporters of our annual spring/Easter party.

Prior to retiring, to stay in shape Kris worked out with the Detroit Lions at Country Day School in suburban Beverly Hills. He held his own. Several of the Lions joked that the Canadian Football League's Toronto Argonauts were calling, saying he should try out with them.

After the 2003–04 season, he was honored by receiving the Selke Trophy as the NHL's best defensive forward. In 2009, Kris played in his 1,000th game with the Wings, quite remarkably only the fifth Red Wing after Howe, Delvecchio, Yzerman, and Lidstrom to do so. Along the way, Drapes helped the Wings win four Stanley Cups in 1997, 1998, 2002, and 2008.

To reinforce the value of his parent-family relationships, his parents attended nearly every game at the Joe. When Kris retired, the Wings held a press conference attended by a large gathering of media, teammates, coaches, front-office personnel, and family who heard GM Ken Holland say, "Kris stands for everything that's right about people and about the game. He didn't just thank everybody [in the building], but he thanked each of them by name. He was incredibly proud to play for the Wings."

For all of us who knew Kris Draper, that pride went both ways.

CHAPTER 3

The "Heart" of the Problem

WHAT CAN HAPPEN WHEN PLAYERS TRY TO DEFY MEDICAL SCIENCE. For most Americans, September 11, 2001, is a date imprinted on our memories—the day hijacked airplanes crashed into the Twin Towers of the World Trade Center in New York, changing our world forever.

For first-responders at a National Hockey League game, another imprinted date is November 21, 2005, when unspeakable tragedy was narrowly averted. It happened at the 12:30 mark of the first period of a Monday night game against the Nashville Predators at Joe Louis Arena when promising young Wings defenseman Jiri Fischer suddenly collapsed on the bench after a particularly long shift, the victim of an acute, near-fatal heart seizure (cardiac arrest). The urgent action that took place in the seconds and minutes that followed saved his life.

The problem, a congenital hypertrophic cardiomyopathy, was detected in Jiri during the preseason physical examinations at Traverse City in 2002, when a routine electrocardiogram revealed its presence. Once he was further evaluated, the danger of an acute heart stoppage was recognized. Extensive discussions began between Jiri, Red Wings management and owners, the cardiology staff at Henry Ford Hospital, and Jiri's family (who were brought into Detroit from the Czech Republic) with the express purpose of deciding whether this exceptionally talented, elite young professional hockey player could or should continue to play and compete. When all aspects of the condition were reviewed and explained in detail, it was his choice to continue to play.

The medical staff then made sure an automated external defibrillator (AED) was always nearby—in the dressing room, on the players' bench, among the equipment carried by the trainers on the team plane to road games—everywhere that Jiri went with the team. Fortunately, after my retirement, the team physician, Anthony Colucci D.O., was an emergency medicine specialist who was knowledgeable and skilled in the necessity for urgent care of this type of problem. He had assisted in preseason physical exams since the mid-1990s. When Jiri collpsed, Dr. Colucci immediately went to the bench, began cardio-pulmonary resuscitation (CPR), used the AED—and was able to immediately revive Jiri as players and coaches on the bench and fans in the audience looked on in fearful disbelief.

Considering the circumstances, obtaining a normal recovery was a remarkable feat in itself when one considers that players have layers of equipment, underclothing, and jersey to uncover to get to his bare chest to make the appropriate application of the AED and initiate CPR.

Meanwhile, the ice was resurfaced while decisions were being contemplated on whether to continue the game. It did not continue. With the approval of both teams and the NHL commissioner, the game was wisely postponed and rescheduled.

Hypertrophic cardiomyopathy, a hidden cardiac condition that frequently causes sudden death, has been diagnosed with increasing efficiency in hockey players since the Jiri Fischer incident. It is a genetic mutation that causes the cardiac ventricular muscles to hypertrophy, and individuals with this condition are in danger of sudden death when overexerting themselves physically—which is what hockey players do several times each game.

On his revival and stabilization after being unconscious for several minutes, Jiri was taken to the nearby emergency hospital, Detroit Receiving, where his condition was stable. He was conscious and talking to medical personnel. When he realized what had happened, that Dr. Colucci had saved his life, Jiri smiled and said to him, "I guess I owe you a dinner." They both laughed over that. Beaumont Hospital's renowned cardiologist, William O'Neill M.D., however, noted that this indeed was a serious situation. The quick and immediate action taken by Dr. Colucci saved Jiri's life, Dr. O'Neill said, since one has a five-minutes-or-less window to act and effect a response before a fatality occurs. That's why the portable, automated external defibrillator has become such an important supplement not only to the trainer and sports medicine staff's equipment but as part of emergency equipment everywhere—airports, shopping centers, and wherever large numbers of people congregate.

What happened to Jiri Fischer was one of the most unusual and fortunately rare incidents ever to occur during an NHL game, and naturally the incident became a Rosetta Stone for members of the media to put the games and the men who play them at this level into some perspective. Some of the press became very philosophical about the event, explaining that athletes are accustomed to being called warriors. But playing tough and playing over injuries is not the same as going to war—and sometimes players do what they have to because it's their job.

The pressure to perform, often despite injury and illness, is immense. For many players, it's a matter of staying employed. Being out of the lineup for more than a game or two usually finds management bringing up a replacement player who is anxious and trying to stake a claim to a position on the team. Because team chemistry plays a significant role, it usually takes a while for players in this fast-moving game that requires split-second decisions to move in and immediately fit comfortably among teammates who work best together when a certain trust has been established.

Once Jiri's abnormality was discovered, meetings between his parents and heart experts revealed that Jiri's father had suffered from a cardiac event at age 39, so the problem seemed to be genetic in origin. Still, the decision was made to continue playing until that fateful November night.

The Red Wings' organization had such big plans for this big—6'5", 225-pound—immensely talented defenseman. And they still do. At age 31, in what should have been the prime of a long and lucrative playing career, Jiri continued to serve the club as its director of player development, helping young potential Red Wings hone the skills that will allow them to fulfill their dreams and get them to the NHL.

The legacy of the Fischer experience was far-reaching, and it probably led to the early retirement of another player well known to Wings fans.

Greg Johnson was an outstanding athlete at the University of North Dakota, earning a degree in business before joining the Wings in the 1993–94 season. After playing 12 seasons in the NHL with several teams, serving as captain of the Nashville Predators, Greg was picked up again by Detroit as an unrestricted free agent for the 2006–07 season. But his preseason physical exam conducted by Dr. Colluci revealed an underlying cardiomyopathy similar to that suffered by Fischer. Johnson underwent further tests at the Mayo Clinic where consulting cardiologists and other experts advised him that the risks of continuing his hockey career were too great. Greg retired from active play and became a scout for the Wings.

Ironically, Greg found himself credited for scoring a goal before the start of a game as a member of the Nashville Predators against the Red Wings. On that fateful November 21, 2005, game, Johnson had scored the lone goal in the first period of a game that was eventually postponed when Fischer collapsed. The full game was replayed on January 23, 2006, and Johnson's goal was allowed to stand, thus giving Nashville a 1–0 lead before the opening faceoff.

Another former Wing with a curious heart issue was goaltender Kevin Hodson, who played four seasons in Detroit from 1995–99, serving as the third goaltender for the Stanley Cup teams in 1997–98. Nicknamed "Ticker" by his teammates, Kevin developed several episodes of acute tachycardia (excessively rapid heartbeat) because of an abnormal accessory cardiac neuropathway (the heart's electrical system) that periodically would be stimulated and cause his heart to beat between 200–300 beats per minute. This did not permit his heart chambers to fill and empty appropriately, causing sudden lightheadedness.

Typically, it occurred in private, but once it happened during a practice at Oak Park Ice Arena that I attended. We immediately had it checked out and then sent him to the Cleveland Clinic, where neuro-cardiologists performed ablation therapy using a device that electrically burns and destroys the abnormal pathway, allowing only his normal cardiac neuro-pathway to function—and thus ridding him of the disabling condition.

Also Noteworthy

Dr. Colucci reported his complete evaluation, care, and treatment of Jiri Fischer in its entirety at the next NHL Team Physicians Society meeting in 2006.

In September 2007, Darcy Robinson, a defenseman from British Columbia playing in a European League for Asiago in Italy, fell to the ice without being hit at 3:25 of the first period and later died at the hospital.

On October 13, 2008, New York Rangers prospect Alexei Cherepanov, 19, the team's first-round draft pick the year before, died on the bench while playing alongside Jaromir Jagr during a game in Russia for Avangard Omsk in the Kontinental Hockey League. He had scored the first goal of the game.

Dr. Tony Colucci.
(Photo courtesy of the author)

Could these have been incidents of hypertrophic cardiomyopathy, the same condition that nearly killed Jiri Fischer? It's very likely. And that's why the NHL has to increase its vigilance with regard to the heart conditions of every one of its players. An EKG on every player and a thorough evaluation of the medical history of the player and his parents should alert the examiners about who should undergo further testing. Simply put, the medical staffs charged with caring for and treating these athletes cannot be too careful.

CHAPTER 4

A Great and Wonderful Game

BUT IS ICE HOCKEY SAFE AT ANY LEVEL?

All parents of children playing sports worry that their kids are in danger of getting hurt, especially considering variations in size and talent—and the quality of coaching they receive. It gets easier to predict the higher the level of play. Professional athletes playing a high-speed, physical game will get hurt. It's inevitable. The simple truth is, it's impossible to eliminate injuries in a contact sport like hockey.

Which raises an obvious question, especially for parents: Is hockey too dangerous to play? The answer, as always when the discussion involves intense physical activity and medical issues, is complicated.

As it is played at all levels around the world, ice hockey is a game involving speed and technical variability, including stick-handling and puck control by players of varying size and weight—on lethally sharpened skate blades, carrying sticks and competing to put a frozen rubber disk into their opponent's goal—on a playing surface surrounded by flexible glass and boards and movable nets designed to protect players in the event of a collision. Players are also protected by a variety of equipment, including body padding around otherwise exposed joints, padded helmets (preferably with cages or visors for younger participants), well-fitting mouth guards and, of course, good-fitting, sharpened skates, and a stick of appropriate length.

Hockey is a contact sport that requires appropriate policing, preferably by coaches and referees (but sometimes by the players themselves), to keep the game as safe as possible. Important safety skills involve knowing how to avoid body checks or maintaining balance to take a check when confronted or expected.

The game should not involve hits to the head during play, hits to the head while fighting, shoulder or head-butting, and other blind-side cheap shots—though anyone who has watched a game at any level has seen some of these dangerous activities occur.

Obviously, armor-hard and often oversized protective equipment can work both ways. Is it the fault of the player who uses his extra-large, stone-hard shoulder or elbow pads to check—and injure—a puck-handler? Is it the puck-handler who fails to wear a properly fitting mouth-guard or a helmet? Or is it the player who skates with his head and eyes down, failing to protect himself from a violent hit and potentially serious injury?

As we examine the complexities of the game and keeping its players safe, let's review some of the factors involved from a safety and medical perspective.

Skates: It's essential that they're comfortable and durable. It takes time to break them in to assume a satisfactory and safe fit. Also, how the blade is sharpened varies a great deal with the style and skating technique of the player. In the 1940s through the 1960s, every player wore skates that had an unprotected heel. The Wings always had a large knob of white plastic attached to the back end of the skate blade, which was their improvement. Periodically lacerations would occur. The Montreal Canadiens were the first players that I remember who played with a guarded strut from the end of the blade to the heel of the boot.

Occasionally a player would go down and slide into the boards with his feet up to stop his momentum and drive the heel post of the boot into his heel, causing a very painful bruise. The skate companies developed a very lightweight plastic support configuration to hold the removable skate blade. This essentially prevented the injury from occurring and allowed the player the opportunity to select the thickness and curvature of the blade. About the same time, the ski boot manufacturers designed a comfortable, lighter, more protective, and easily identifiable boot with their logo on it, which is what we see today.

With the help of the boot manufacturers, skates have come a long way. Most players say it takes about six weeks to break in a new pair of skates, so they wear them in practice as often as they can to ease the skate into conforming to their foot. Manufacturers who have players under contract often build a boot to the player's specifications.

Another medical problem we see occurs from the way the player wears his skates, whether he tucks the tongue of the boot in and tapes it down or leaves it out, giving him more freedom and allowing him to skate faster. But not tucking the tongue in exposes the lower leg extensor tendon to accidental laceration from another player's skate, severing the underlying tendon, which causes the inability to extend or flex the big toe. This is a fairly common and unnecessary injury.

That accidentally severed tendon is a particular problem since it may go initially unnoticed or undiagnosed during the initial repair at the rink—especially if the player is urging the surgeon to quickly finish the repair so he can return to action. Inability to dorsi-flex the great (big) toe makes the surgeon suspicious of the more serious diagnosis, and definitive operating room tendon repair is required. Therefore, a proper tendon repair must be done in an operating room setting, and after repair the foot immobilized and protected until the tendon injury is healed. The injury appears minor, but in reality if not correctly diagnosed and managed, it may affect the player's career.

Sticks: The skill, control, and handling of the hockey stick are what separate the great from the average players. On the other hand, injudicious use of it as a weapon or instrument of intimidation is the source of many injuries—and penalties doled out by the referees. Wings Hall of Famer Ted Lindsay was small in stature but huge in grit and ability.

Before the days of helmets and visors, when Lindsay and Marty Pavelich played, lacerations of the head and face were commonplace, occurring in almost every game. Because of that, I took every opportunity I could to become skilled in rapid, safe, competent, and appropriate laceration repair. It was important for us to remember that every player we took care of was going back into battle, so the repair had to be secure enough to avoid disrupting in future battles.

I recall Darren McCarty having a postage stamp–sized piece of skin torn off his face, very close to his eye, doubtless the result of an errant stick. Sergei Fedorov found the skin fragment on the ice and brought it in to the medical room, where we were preparing for the repair. We cleansed it antiseptically, defatted the tissue, and performed what amounted to a full-thickness skin graft. McCarty wore a visor during the third period but didn't use it thereafter. It was healing beautifully. Unfortunately, 10 days later he got in a fight and the repair was completely disrupted.

Sometimes the stick is used as a battering ram or spear when a player directs the tip of the pointed blade to hit or slash the opponent. The stick is often used in a cross-checking maneuver by holding it at chest level and thrusting it against an opponent's body, often from behind. When aluminum sticks were developed, we worried about the additional damage they might cause. Also, when broken in half, the fragments could inadvertently cause serious injury similar to a stab wound. That didn't seem to happen, but aluminum sticks have for the most part been replaced by the graphite composite stick—lighter, stronger, and more durable but also many times more expensive. The game's rules state, essentially, that any time a stick is broken it must be dropped immediately or a minor penalty will be called.

The Puck: Made of hard rubber and frozen to permit controlled play and prevent bouncing, the puck can achieve speeds exceeding 100 mph with the slap shot. Defensemen are taught to purposefully block shots with their bodies. Jim Schoenfeld, who spent most of his career with the Buffalo Sabres except for a short stint with the Wings in the early 1980s, was one of the most fearless shot-blocking defensemen I ever saw. When he coached in the '90s for Buffalo, New Jersey, Washington, and Phoenix, I asked him why he didn't teach his defensemen to block shots the way he did. "I tried, but they were smarter than I was," he said. Until the goaltender neck guard was developed, I always worried about the danger of goalies being struck in the neck by a deflected shot.

Ranger defenseman Brian Leetch was struck in the neck at Joe Louis Arena in Detroit during the 1988–89 season while I was in the visitors' room repairing a laceration on one of his teammates. Our son, Michael, an internal medicine resident in Detroit at the time, was at the game with us. Recognizing what had happened, he ran out on the ice to help. The injury caused Brian to have a severe laryngeal spasm, and he couldn't get his breath for a few moments. Typically, these spasms last about 15–20 seconds, but those few seconds are very frightening for any player. Their trainer at the time was David Smith, who later became the physical therapist for the referees and linesmen. He understood what happened and helped reassure Leetch. One of the Rangers equipment people came into their dressing room and notified me. By the time I arrived, the spasm had subsided, and we were able to treat him in the room with ice to the neck and oxygen inhalation.

A much more serious neck injury incident occurred in Montreal on January 29, 2000, when Habs forward Trent McCleary was struck in the throat by a slap shot, fracturing his trachea. McCreary was unable to breathe from the bleeding and immediate soft tissue swelling that occurs in

In March 1989, the author's son, Dr. Michael Finley (left), was called into duty of an on-ice injury while the author (second from left) was busy in the dressing room tending to another injury. (Photo courtesy of John Hartman)

such an injury. Montreal surgeon David Mulder, M.D., immediately recognized what happened, attempted endotracheal intubation at the Forum, but was unsuccessful due to the swelling and the difficulty performing such a maneuver on a patient who was awake. Dr. Mulder temporarily gave him oxygen by mask and quickly transported him by ambulance to Montreal General Hospital, less than five minutes away.

At the time of the incident, their operating room was contacted from the arena. Trent was immediately taken to the OR, given sedation, intubated (a procedure that requires inserting an endotracheal tube into the trachea), and treated appropriately by the ENT (ear, nose, and throat) and pulmonary specialists. Associated with the airway injury was a collapsed lung, so a chest tube was required to re-expand the player's lung.

Dr. Mulder's quick expert action saved that young man's life. The doctor reported the entire event and management at the next NHL Team Physicians Society meeting so all team physicians could be aware of the possibility of this type of injury and its appropriate management.

Facial fractures, lacerations, and mouth and dental injuries occur more frequently from errant pucks. Wings fans will recall when Steve Yzerman was struck in the face by a shot during a playoff game, causing a depressed facial bone fracture, which was expertly managed by a several-hour procedure performed by the oral facial surgeons at Henry Ford Hospital. Failure to successfully realign the lower orbital fracture may result in diplopa (double vision) and force unexpected retirement from the game, as happened to Henry Boucha, a Native American who wore a red headband when he played. He was injured in a stick fight with Boston's Dave Forbes.

Nick Lidstrom, who succeeded Stevie as team captain, was struck in the face by a hard shot during the exhibition season of 2008 in a game at Joe Louis Arena against Montreal. It lacerated the area of the right eyebrow and fractured his nose, narrowly missing his eye.

The above incidences reported and the innumerable ones that, until recently, were rarely documented, strongly support the effort of the NHL Team Physicians Society to mandate a league requirement for players to wear facial protection such as a visor to protect their eyes. However, as of this writing, the league and NHLPA have failed to support such a mandate.

The Goal Net: Made of a metal frame 6' wide and 4' high, the goal's posts and crossbar are painted red, the remainder painted white, with extra-strong fish-netting type of material attached to it. For years through the Original Six era and long after, the goal remained stationary with a 10" metal pipe fitted into a slightly larger pipe embedded 4" into the ice surface and 6" up into each goal post.

Because there was no give or flexibility to the stationary position of the net, repeated serious injury would occur when a player would lose control and strike the net at full-speed or, from a body-check, close-by. To improve the safety of the fixed goal-net position but still allow the goal to come free when hit abruptly, the NHL fashioned magnetic discs under the upright goal posts. They were an improvement but still didn't prevent injuries that occurred when a player struck the net from the side, as Steve Yzerman did after a clean check from Sabres defenseman Calle Johansson. It happened on March 1, 1988, not long after Steve scored his 50th goal of that season. Johansson sent him sliding across the ice into the left post of the goal, causing the rupture of the posterior cruciate ligament of his right knee. That's one of the ligaments that control forward and backward movement of the knee. By the time the net came off the magnets, the injury had already occurred.

Thereafter, the league began using the same idea as the original lead pipes stabilizing the goal posts, instead using 10" flexible rubber pegs. They seem to work well, keeping the net stationary until struck by a player, when it moves off its moorings.

The configuration of the base had been the same throughout the Original Six era and the first round of expansion when the NHL went to 12 teams. It was changed after a serious injury to Mark Howe, Gordie's son, who recently was honored with entry to the Hockey Hall of Fame. At that time, the base of the net was shaped like a huge No. 3, the center projection tapered to a fine point on the ice, and the entire frame beveled to deflect any puck coming up into the netting, allowing it to be seen by all.

While playing for the Hartford Whalers, Mark was chasing an opposing player, rushing toward the Whalers' net, when he was taken down in front of the goal. He slid with both feet raised into the netting to stop his momentum. But the front of the net came off its moorings and rose up, and the sharp center piece of the net mooring impaled him, causing a serious laceration and subsequent infection that took weeks to recover from and could have caused severe permanent injury.

The Boards: Every arena is lined with hard—and often unyielding—boards topped with non-breakable glass. For years, games were conducted without any protection above the boards, and fans used to lean over the boards, almost getting involved in the action. As play became faster and flying pucks more of a danger to fans, wire fencing of varying heights was placed on the boards—at first around the end boards, then later around the entire ice surface. The fans loved it since they could still hear the player comments to one another on the ice. The configuration of Olympia Arena was such that the rinkside seats at each end of the arena were at the level of the top of the boards, giving those fans a unique view of the game.

Before the advent of the glass partitions, wire-mesh fencing barriers permitted fans to harass the referees unmercifully. The fencing allowed the referee or linesman to grab hold and jump up on top of the boards to avoid a collision with the players along the boards during play. This encouraged the referee-jeering-fans to holler at them to "get off the fence, you monkey"—especially if they were calling a bad game.

The battle of the boards occurs every night. Players are constantly battered into them. They are a handy trap, permitting no escape from a check, sandwiching the opponent between the checker and the boards to enhance the impact. Players often hit the boards shoulder first, accounting for the high incidence of acromial-clavicular (shoulder separation) sprains in hockey players—notable among them Bill Gadsby.

Since the sad death of a 12-year-old girl in the Nationwide Arena, the NHL mandated that all NHL arenas protect fans in the end zones with netting above the glass, similar to the screens that protect baseball fans from sharply hit foul balls around home plate.

A word of caution about equipment fatigue—the remarkable advancements in hockey equipment are a testimony to the efforts of companies, trainers, equipment personnel, management, and those who administer the

NHL. They have done exhaustive studies with various materials to determine their fatigability, weight, padding, comfort, fitting, and protection. It's well-documented that the more trauma and abuse on the equipment, the more likely it will break down. As players become accustomed to certain items, they feel comfortable with the fitting and are hesitant to change.

Some players are wearing pads they have worn for years. The companies and team equipment people work very hard to keep everything in playing shape and replace worn items. Occasionally, a company will go out of business or discontinue making certain items, which affects what the player wears. Also the manner the equipment is worn is important. This is particularly true of helmets.

Remember that equipment fatigue is really a double-edged sword. It is very difficult for a player to replace comfortable, well-broken-in protective equipment often modified to the player's particular style. But from a safety standpoint, it must be replaced when it no longer serves the intended purpose. The person in charge of equipment and the trainer should accept the responsibility of deciding when to replace worn pieces as a matter of safety for those playing the game.

In the NHL, as in every professional contact sport, injuries serve as justification for disappointing team performance, and fans favoring the opposition will indicate their hope that the weakened enemy will be easier to overcome since his chemistry and strategy are likely affected. Likewise, absence of injury or avoiding injury, particularly involving its main participants, usually goes a long way in determining the team's success. Avoiding an inadvertent infection or unexpected illness to any one or more of a team's regular players can play a huge role in the success of a team.

The spearing of Wings captain Nick Lidstrom in the groin area by a Chicago Blackhawks player in the second round of the 2009 Stanley Cup playoffs caused him to miss several games, and although the Red Wings defeated Chicago, he was never fully recovered during the remainder of the playoff run when the Wings lost Game 7 of the Finals to Pittsburgh.

Frequently unnoticed, turn-around teams that remained healthy and avoided troublesome injury often became successful over more talented teams that have a disabling injury to one of their stars, weakening their ability to compete at an optimum level. A slap shot that struck Brendan Shanahan's foot, causing a painful hairline fracture and persistent swelling prevented him from being able to tighten his skate just prior to the beginning of the 2001 playoffs. A coinciding broken ankle injury to Yzerman effectively took the Wings out of contention that spring when they lost in the first round to L.A. in six games despite winning the first two games of the series in Detroit.

Experts who appraise the effect of HGL (history-adjusted games-lost average) over several seasons can sometimes predict the likelihood of a successful or unsuccessful final outcome. Injuries or their absence often have a drastic effect on a team's success. They are unexpected and uncontrollable.

HOCKEY-SPECIFIC INJURIES AND UNIQUE ISSUES.
Skate cuts

Injuries from the skate blades occur relatively infrequently but are often the source of some of the most serious injuries ever seen in hockey, like the incident on March 22, 1989, when Buffalo goaltender Clint Malarchuk's internal carotid artery was severed by Steve Tuttle in a goalmouth scramble. Malarchuk thought he was going to die on the spot and frequently said later that all he could think of at the moment was hoping that his mother wasn't watching. Only some fast action by trainers and medical personnel prevented a tragedy.

Frequently, skate cuts involved severed tendons, like the one sustained by Mike Modano who returned home to Detroit to play his 20th NHL season after 20 Hall of Fame years with the Minnesota/Dallas franchise. In November 2010, a player was checked into the boards and his leg flew up as he was falling to the ice, transversely lacerating Modano's wrist, severing flexor tendons, and partially dividing several fascicles of his median nerve. The injury had to be repaired under microscopy, and the arm was encased in a splint and immobilized for some three months. He recovered and resumed play by late February, but played sparingly down the stretch and into the postseason. He returned to Dallas and retired from the NHL after the 2010–2011 season.

Goaltender Terry Sawchuk, while playing for Detroit in a game against Toronto at Maple Leaf Gardens, reached out his gloved hand to smother the puck sliding in front of the goal as another player skated over his outstretched hand, severing the goalie's four extensor tendons. The late Dr. Jim Murray, the Leafs team physician and a plastic surgeon also specializing in hand surgery, called me describing the injury he proceeded to repair. Within 6–8 weeks, it was completely healed, and "Ukie" was back playing like nothing ever happened. Shortly thereafter, Dr. Murray was elected president of the International Society of Surgery of the Hand.

Eye Injuries

The most severe, career-ending injury I've ever been associated with was the eye injury to Doug Barkley, one of the most skilled defenseman of the 1960s. He played right defense, and during a game against Chicago, while battling Doug Mohns along the boards at their blue line, the accidental injury occurred. Mohns was trying to relieve Barkley of the puck by lifting his stick with great force. Unfortunately he missed Barkley's stick, Mohns' stick came up suddenly, and the tip of the blade struck Barkley in the left eye, rupturing his eyeball and causing multiple facial lacerations around the perimeter of the orbit. We carefully took him into our medical room immediately.

There was vitreous (the inner eye gelatinous material) extruding from the eye, and marked soft-tissue swelling was already occurring. Dressing and ice were applied, his head and neck were stabilized, and he was taken by ambulance to Detroit Osteopathic Hospital. Our ophthalmologist, Dr. Patrick Murray, was called immediately from the arena and met Doug when he arrived. Barkley was given emergency care, the eye repaired, and

In spite of losing an eye, Doug Barkley (left) continued to function well. Here, he enjoys a 1976 golf outing with (from Barkley's left) the author, the University of Michigan's Robert Bailey, M.D., and the Wings' Al Coates. (Photo courtesy of the author)

as the nature of the injury was determined every effort was made to save his eye and preserve any sight at all.

He had a badly detached retina and was shortly sent to Charles L. Schepens, M.D., a prominent Boston retinal specialist who had been doing some very creative work with these types of injuries. He performed retinal surgery on Doug while the patient was suspended face down with his body at a 45-degree angle and the surgeon lying on his back. Regretfully it was unsuccessful, and his eye had to be sacrificed. Doug later became our coach and wore unbreakable glasses behind the bench to protect his remaining eye.

Danny Gare suffered a corneal abrasion in one of the first games he played for Detroit after his trade from Buffalo in 1981. The abraded cornea is extremely painful. Taping the eye tightly closed and protecting it with an eye patch allowed time to get to the ophthalmologist for evaluation and further treatment. Hemorrhage in the anterior chamber (hyphema) of the eye usually prevented the ability to visualize the inner aspects of the eye efficiently, requiring a period of time until the blood reabsorbed to allow an adequate ophthalmologic internal evaluation of the eye.

A Surprise Nose Job

Terry Sawchuk had too many injuries to count. One of the more memorable ones caused a circumstance I had never seen before. It was late in the second period of a game in the late 1950s. A shot on net was deflected and struck Terry in the face, lifting the lower edge of his nose away from his face. He was bleeding quite severely from his nose. We only had one goaltender in those days, and there was no backup goaltender there to take his place. Terry skated to the bench. Trainer Lefty Wilson and I evaluated him. The referee, Frank Udvari, came over, as well. I told Frank that the injury could not be repaired in two minutes but required at least 20.

Therefore he blew his whistle, cleared the ice, sending both teams to their dressing rooms while we repaired the injury. The ice was resurfaced as though it was the end of the period. Once the damage was corrected, the teams came back out and resumed the game with four minutes left in the second period. When the buzzer sounded at the end of the second period, both teams went to center ice for the face-off to begin the third period without retiring again to their dressing rooms. Sawchuk completed the game without further incident.

"Gunk" and Worse

Through the years, Dennis Polonich also suffered more than the average number of injuries, particularly to his face—mostly, I believe, because of his height (5'6"). But no doubt, too, because of his feisty nature. Polo was a real team player and always gave out as much as he received. His principal medical problem was the "gunk," as the players had nicknamed it. The medical name is miliaria, a stubborn skin rash.

Dennis was the recipient of a brutal cross-check across the face that shattered his nose and fractured several facial bones. The medical care of the game was being covered by my partner, Dr. Milton Kosley, so when

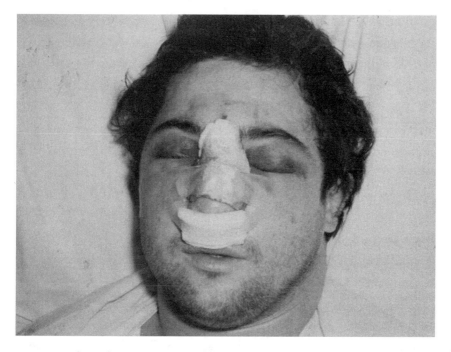

Dennis Polonich was cross-checked across the face in 1978, sustaining nasal and facial fractures. He made a good recovery.
(Photo courtesy of John Finley, D.O.)

listening to the game and heard about the incident, I drove to the hospital to help the eye, ear, nose, and throat (EENT) specialists manage his care.

We also took pictures of the injury, which proved fortuitous because the case ended up in court as a malicious injury suit that resulted in Dennis being awarded a substantial settlement. He hung up his skates professionally shortly afterward but returns frequently for special games with the Red Wings alumni. He became a players' agent.

Spittin' Chicklets

Kevin Miller was a very dependable forward who played for about a third of the NHL's teams (nine in all). He was acquired by Detroit from the New York Rangers with Jim Cummins and Dennis Vial near the trade deadline in 1991 for Joey Kocur and defenseman Per Djoos. We were in the playoffs, I believe in St. Louis, when Kevin sustained a fracture of the maxilla that took three of his upper teeth with it. Dentist Chet Regula calmly asked Kevin to bite down on the tongue blade he had placed on his lower teeth on that side. That nicely forced the fracture back into normal position, after which I merely sewed the gum closed with dissolvable sutures, allowing us to send him back to Detroit with the fracture reduced, only requiring his teeth to be wired together to stabilize the fracture with no further work required.

Diabetes

A number of hockey families have endured the difficulties of diabetes, but the only diabetic hockey player I have known was Bobby Clarke of the Philadelphia Flyers. While the 1969 Entry Draft was going on, I received a call from Jimmy Skinner, asking for my opinion about the wisdom of drafting a diabetic hockey player. I told him of all the prominent diabetic athletes I knew who played major professional sports, but I also cautioned him that they sometimes heal more slowly or have more serious infections complicating their injuries. Skinner chose to bypass Clarke and chose goaltender Jimmy Rutherford instead. Both players went on to have great hockey careers.

Steroids

About the same time hockey players were troubled with inexplicable skin rashes (gunk), the sport of football encountered the complex problem of some of its players bulking up using steroids to make them stronger. Soon some experienced various complications, the most serious of which was the development of aggressive and fatal liver neoplasms. Fortunately for us in the NHL, bulking up was not as important as speed, and for those interested in gaining weight, increasing their caloric intake generally took care of it.

Steroids frequently cause a crusty demeanor and an aggressiveness that is exacerbated by its use, particularly by those attempting to overcome pain or excessive training and not otherwise seen in younger players. While steroid use was rarely a problem for hockey, it did become a hot topic in sports medicine because of what was happening in some of the other sports. Our trainers were constantly on the watch for its use. To the best of my knowledge, it has never become a problem in the NHL.

AIDS/HIV

The human retrovirus HIV–1 was first identified in 1984 as the cause of a widespread epidemic of immuno-suppression infection called AIDS. It is the most severe manifestation of a spectrum of HIV-related conditions. The danger related to athletes and athletic activity particularly in punishing contact sports is that its transmission requires contact with any body fluid or exudates (specifically blood, semen, vaginal secretions, breast fluid, saliva, or wound exudates).

A widely publicized sports concern involved an Italian soccer player who developed the HIV infection after playing in a soccer game against an unknown (at the time) HIV-infected opponent, I believe from Africa, who had a bleeding open wound. His disease was apparently diagnosed weeks later. No one was sure that event was indeed the incident where the Italian player contracted the disease, but sports teams everywhere were aware of that possibility.

Most if not all sports teams quickly educated their training and medical staffs relative to the importance of rubber-gloved handling in dealing with athletes for their own protection and to avoid transmission of any infection. Although the NHL Players Association and some teams prevented us from universally testing players—some players privately asked to have the test. None we checked ever came up positive.

It was interesting to note that sports medicine orthopedic specialist and L.A. Kings team physician, Steve Lombardo, M.D., who also cared for the L.A. Lakers NBA team, had the occasion to perform a physical exam, for life insurance, on Earvin "Magic" Johnson, which required an HIV test. That test was positive. Lombardo then was called upon to explain the disease to Johnson and to arrange treatment for which Magic has responded well for more than 20 years.

Team Physicians: Ethics and Attitude

Team physicians are concerned and interested in doing everything possible to try to avoid, prevent, or minimize all hockey injuries. Concern related to playing techniques and protective equipment rank high on their attention list. As an example, many of the older players from the Original Six and early expansion eras feel that the widespread use of high sticks today is directly related to the wearing of face masks and half-shields, called visors. With that protection, the players today feel fearless. The respect players formerly had toward high body hits and shots has disappeared. Some even feel that wearing helmets has increased the tendency for neck and cervical spine trauma.

Another question frequently arises regarding the doctor's allegiance. If the team physician is a fan, can that person perform independently for the best interest and safety of the player, not otherwise for the benefit of management or the team's owner? Hockey evokes some of the strongest reactions in its fans. It is incumbent on any physician accepting the role of team doctor that the safety, health, and welfare of the athlete are their primary missions.

Obviously, that also includes aiding in developing and supporting conditioning programs that assist in preventing or reducing injury or its severity. Being a fan and interested in the success of the team can affect the physician's objectivity in managing medical conditions and injuries. In my experience, the most difficult aspect to overcome is the player's desire to return to play in spite of warnings that it might further compromise an injury.

Usually, having the trainer advise management of any potential danger to a player immediately brought their assistance in restricting the player. Infrequently, a coach would appeal to us to allow a player, particularly if that individual is one the team depends on every night to dress so the

46

opposition might think he was back to his usual full-strength status even though the coach planned to use the player only on the opening faceoff or some brief instance. I found that to be a mistake. Usually, if the player dresses for play, in spite of promises to the contrary, the coach often uses that player the entire game. Therefore, I found it was always better not to have a borderline-recovered player dress if he was not ready or able to play the whole game.

Finally, the team physician must detach himself from the emotion of the game when precise medical judgment is needed to analyze and diagnose the problem, completely avoiding any status as a fan. This type of behavior always communicates clearly to the athlete and coaches that the team physician can remain objective in medical decision-making. The NHLPA also has a list of trusted consultants available for a second opinion if a player or management feels that option is necessary.

Malpractice liability has always been the curse of all sports medicine physicians. Many very competent medical people have been cited and have discontinued care of athletes for that reason alone. A team physician first has to love the game. Secondly, he must be willing to give up a great deal of private time to care for these elite individuals, their families and friends, management, and often arena personnel.

Physicians affiliated with major medical centers and working under their malpractice umbrella usually have a little less concern since most often the system has a reputation of quality care of great athletes as well as the general public and cherishes the notoriety gained from being known for providing care to those individuals. For the individual practitioner or limited medical group, there is greater concern. Not only is any malpractice action a disturbing distraction to a physician's daily workload, the notoriety in the media, frequently promoted by the player's attorney, compounds the dilemma.

For years, the hockey physicians in Canada received blanket coverage under the national medical program. Then, a decade or so ago, they were informed that the program would not cover their care of those hockey-related athletes. It created a crisis situation for them. Some imme-diately left. Others developed some type of coverage, often through Lloyds of London, known for covering high-risk groups, or through arrangements with their individual NHL clubs.

Those who have been involved in selected cases have found that some player representatives have used innuendo, improper suggestion, and over-emphasizing of an injury or treatment to seek the sympathy of the media, fans, and sometimes a jury to sway opinion to their advantage.

CHAPTER 5

Getting a Good "Head" Start

THE NHL's CONCUSSION CRISIS MUST BE ADDRESSED.
Headshots are the bane of all sports and a challenge approaching epic proportions for those of us charged with caring for athletes. Their sequela do more to affect, endanger, and limit the bright futures of talented young men and women playing contact sports than any other single injury entity.

The legendary football coach of Michigan State University, Duffy Daugherty, had his trite but favorite description of football: "It's not a contact sport but rather a collision sport." That aptly describes any fiercely traumatic sport, including hockey. I'm reminded of two comments regarding this type of injury made by two entirely different styles of NHL players. The first, Gordie Howe, always said how when he was playing it was an unwritten rule to keep the puck low and avoid blind-side hitting of the unprotected head. It was a matter of respect among players in his era. Another was made by Red Berenson, the longtime University of Michigan hockey coach, when helmets were made mandatory by the NHL. "Now we have to worry about all the wide-open neck and head injuries created by leaving the head better protected," Berenson told me. And he was right.

Of all the classes of athletic injuries in hockey, the most concerning to individual players and management at every level of play are cerebral concussions. A cerebral concussion is characterized by post-traumatic loss of awareness or memory lasting from seconds to minutes without causing gross structural lesions in the brain and without leaving serious neurologic residual. Head injuries have short and long consequences. Some years ago, the criteria stated that if loss of consciousness was involved, the player was felt to have a concussion. Evaluation by a neurologist or neurosurgeon followed, and the decision of when to return to play depended on that specialist's opinion and the player's required compliance follow-up.

Currently, that isn't the case since brain impairment is the determining factor. Short-lived consequences such as temporary loss of memory or awareness lasting from seconds to minutes, confusion, dizziness, nausea, sensitivity to light, vacant staring, and slow or garbled answering of questions are some of the cardinal signs of a concussion. If associated loss of consciousness has also occurred, then we know there has been a serious head injury. The following Cantu guidelines are commonly used to classify the seriousness of a head injury and the time it will require to recover:

Grade I—No loss of consciousness, post-traumatic amnesia lasting less than 30 minutes, or post-concussion signs lasting less than 30 minutes.

Grade II—Loss of consciousness lasting less than one minute and post-traumatic amnesia lasting longer than 30 minutes but less than 24 hours, or post-concussion signs or symptoms lasting longer than 30 minutes but less than 24 hours.

Grade III—Loss of consciousness lasting longer than one minute or post-traumatic amnesia for more than 24 hours, or post-concussion signs or symptoms lasting longer than seven days.

When attempting to determine the degree of injury, we would ask questions such as, "Where are you playing? What period is it? What is the score of the game?"

Players have undergone preseason psychological testing that is used as a baseline. After an injury, individuals are removed from play until they are retested, and resumption of play is based on their return to their preseason status and all symptoms have disappeared. Several factors need to be considered. Is the team doctor getting all the history from the player, or is that individual holding back information to avoid being taken out of the lineup? The effect of sustaining a second head injury prior to recovering from the first is paramount to safe treatment.

The NFL is frequently regarded as the leader in North American sports when it comes to such issues as diet and conditioning and sports medicine evaluation and care. But there is one area where it lags behind the NHL, and that is the medical protocol regarding when to clear players to return to play from cerebral concussion injuries.

Since 1997–98, the NHL has made great strides in cerebral concussion management. It requires that each player have a neurologic assessment taken during training camp or before NHL play as a baseline, including an assessment of each player's focal assessment findings and his reaction and response time. If a concussion occurs, he is required to rest and be free of symptoms before he is allowed to be retested.

Then the results are compared to the baseline, and upon passing that hurdle he is allowed to resume working out but must remain free of symptoms during and after the workouts. He is not allowed to return to game action until the results fall within acceptable limits, and he passes a physical exam including further neuropsychological tests and a review of test results by the team and by independent physicians—the decision is made jointly by the player and the team. If the player is still concerned, he can consult with the NHLPA's consulting physicians to arrange a second opinion from a concussion expert.

Nevertheless, the list of elite players prematurely retiring because of head injuries seems to be increasing each year. Former Red Wing Keith Primeau, Detroit-area native Pat LaFontaine, former MVP Eric Lindros and his brother Brett, and Paul Kariya are among the better-known players who have done so. More recently, Pittsburgh star Sidney Crosby's career appears threatened after a series of head injuries.

There is nothing more sickening than watching an elite player being carted off the ice on a stretcher after a blind-side hit to the head, often from a player known for that type of play.

Primeau, playing with Philadelphia in 2006, suffered a concussion when he was hit in the jaw by a defenseman's shoulder. After failing to recover satisfactorily, he retired. In 2009, New York Rangers center Chris Drury, a skilled gritty player both offensively and defensively, suffered a serious concussion after a blindside hit by Calgary's Curtis Glencross. It was Drury's third concussion, and he never regained the form that made him one of the game's most clutch performers. Drury retired two years later after just 12 NHL seasons.

Simone Gagne, the delightfully talented center, suffered a series of concussions, as many as three in five months according to some reports, when he was playing for Philadelphia during the 2007–08 season. The most serious came in a collision with Panthers defenseman Jay Bouwmeester. After sitting out for two weeks, Gagne was permitted to play, but post-concussion symptoms returned and he went on injured reserve, missing 26 games. A month after his return on January 10, he collided with Pittsburgh's Gary Roberts and did not return for the rest of the season.

Paul Kariya was a wonderfully skilled center who spent most of his career with Anaheim and later played with Colorado, Nashville, and St. Louis in a 15-year career cut short by post-concussion syndrome. He was outspoken regarding the culture of the league and its excessive physicality as well as the lack of deterrence. "There's too much of a lack of respect players have for one another," he once told *The Sporting News*. "If the league wants to stop that kind of conduct, it will have to punish players.... Ten-game suspensions...and more have to be brought back to help wake up players.... There probably isn't a player in the league who hasn't had a concussion."

He's right. The NHL has a real dilemma on its hands regarding head injuries, and much of it has to do with the culture of the sport. All through a hockey player's preteen and teenage years, he is urged by parents, coaches, and others to develop and exceed at all levels of play, learning to acquire increased speed, endure with more grit, and perform despite bruising encounters that include the "play at all costs...play through the pain" attitude that permeates the sport and exists largely for players to maintain their status on the team.

Parents or people close to the player must learn and be aware of the symptoms and effects of concussions and be part of the solution for their care rather than being part of the cause by failing to appreciate their danger and urging the player to return too soon. The result is the acceptance of much of the stress and pain, while admission of such might be seen as a sign of weakness by teammates, opponents, and those in charge. Even the proper wearing of equipment, especially a helmet and mouth guard, does not guarantee a player the prevention of a concussion.

That individual must develop the ability to know the situations when a head injury is likely to occur, avoid as much as possible the danger of becoming involved in those events, and learn how to protect oneself from the severity of the collision to minimize its effect.

The number of players having retired or having been advised to retire has increased immeasurably and typically involves key team personnel—often the ones the fans pay to see. The post-concussion syndrome that often occurs has to be evaluated and followed very carefully. When that condition persists beyond an acceptable period of time, as determined by appropriate experts, the player must cease competitive play to avoid the danger of permanent disability.

More evidence is being developed by medical experts related to studies of NFL players and the development of diminished cognitive acuity at rates earlier than average for their age. The ravages of prize fighting left many participants severely disabled with what used to be called being punch drunk or the medical term dementia pugilistica.

Actually, a bevy of syndromes fall into that category. The advantages in ice hockey are the skill, talent, conditioning, and lightning reaction time exhibited by elite NHL players, plus appropriately worn helmets and mouth guards, that allow them to, in most cases, minimize the danger present in today's game.

This is particularly true when one evaluates the conditions that are currently occurring in the game—the speed, the players' size, their strength, the surface they play on, the frozen disc they propel, and the formerly wood but now graphite or lightweight composite sticks employed, all of which contribute to the overall danger of the game and increase the risk accepted by the participants.

The one parameter that hasn't changed is the size of the ice surface that could accommodate the changes described above. There is less hitting, less bruising play, and rarely fisticuffs on the international rinks essentially due to greater elbow room of the larger surface. Putting larger ice surfaces in the current North American arenas would be costly. It would reduce the buildings' seating capacities and likely be discouraged by owners and management and, to some degree, the fans who appreciate being close to the sometimes brutal action.

Since some owners have facilities both in North America and Europe, the advantages of larger arenas may be recognized by them. The loss of an elite player can be costly in terms of a team winning or losing, and could prompt owners' interest in putting controls in place to minimize such losses. The size, strength, and speed of participants in all professional contact/collision sports have increased immeasurably while the playing surfaces have remained the same. Consequently, the risk of concussion has also increased—especially in hockey, where targeted players cannot seek refuge from danger out of bounds.

Medicine has progressed remarkably in the last 50 years, and I believe the NHL has been a leader in diagnosing post-concussion disorders. When a player gets his bell rung, as the press agents are likely to describe it, or is stunned from an event, the typical team physician seriously considers the magnitude of the trauma. His evaluation and the neurosurgeon's neurologic examination are next, followed by a most important neuropsychologic evaluation.

The latter is a follow-up of one taken at the beginning of the season before any chance of trauma that includes everything from memory to reaction time, cognition, concentration, amnesia, dizziness, headache, and all sorts of tests peculiar to that specialty that allow the examiner to make a reasonable decision when that person can return to play. They are always withdrawn from play, practice, and exercise, returning gradually in reverse order once the okay is given.

The medical condition called a cerebral concussion in contact sports is clinically known as Chronic Traumatic Encephalopathy (CTE), a degenerative brain disease. It triggers a number of different symptoms that can only be evaluated by undergoing appropriate neurologic evaluations exactly the same as those taken prior to beginning play and comparing the results of both. If each is similar, then return to play is allowed. If triggering symptoms remain, the return to play is postponed until they disappear. The testing must be within its pre-play test level.

When CTE occurs, especially repeatedly, it looks like dementia—but it affects players in their forties, fifties, and sixties. The classic symptoms are associated with gradually worsening behavioral and cognitive difficulties characterized by short-term memory loss, attention difficulties, and short temper outbursts. A 2009 report from the University of Michigan's Institute for Social Research concluded that NFL players are 19 times more likely to develop Alzheimer's or other memory-related diseases than other men between the ages of 30 and 50. To some degree, I believe this may be true of NHL hockey players, especially those who have sustained some type of head trauma.

Unlike football, the concussion caused by a hit or head-trauma incident in hockey is easily seen not only by the players but on the TV replays. Only a small number are caused by fights, but they are certainly one of the causes—as evidenced by the trauma sustained by Wings former defenseman Andreas Lilja in 2009. Repeat events particularly at close intervals are more worrisome. If the avoidance of this injury is so vital and important to each player, why wait for the GMs and the league to legislate something? The players themselves, both the hitter and the recipient of the hit, must take some responsibility for concussions.

Most coaches were developed through systems in which bruising hits, checking, and some aggressive stick work were all employed as ways to relieve an opponent of the puck. This is part of the game. But so are blind-side hits, hits to the head, and hits from behind, and that's what general managers, owners, and league executives—along with the players and their union—must somehow rid from their game.

The late referee Art Skov, a frequent visitor to the Red Wings Alumni Room at Joe Louis Arena, would occasionally say to me that his greatest worry was that professional hockey players were trying to seriously hurt one another. Intimidating opponents by a forceful hit to take them off of the puck is acceptable as long as one is not also trying to injure.

Hockey is their livelihood, so bumps and bruises are expected and inevitable, but creating serious injury is not, and players must accept some of the responsibility for that. Gordie Howe told me that when he was competing against the Canadiens, he once caught Jean Beliveau unprepared for a hit and could have badly hurt him. But regarding the kind of player he was, the Big Guy merely brushed Beliveau a little bit, coming away with the puck. After they both retired, Jean said he appreciated his concern by avoiding injuring him. Respect doesn't get any better than that.

Penalties related to headshots or infractions that caused head injuries such as hitting from behind, boarding, high-sticking, and players leaving their feet for a check have to be clearly enforced and appropriately punished by referees and league officials. In the meantime, the league has to regulate and require other means of protection, like appropriate headgear and more. Helmets have greatly improved and new variations are offered each year.

On the other hand, it is necessary to educate and seek the cooperation of the players to wear them appropriately by using ones with a liner of proper thickness and using a chin strap that is fastened securely in order to minimize an injury. One other very important device that can protect players from concussions is the expertly fitted mouth guard. No prize fighter would enter the boxing ring without one, but some hockey players have played much of their careers without one.

They take some getting used to, and in many cases they are hard to wear and easy to avoid wearing, but without exception mouth guards do a remarkable job of minimizing or avoiding concussions. The dental support people during my era, Drs. Chet Regula and his associate Joseph Gandolpho, always fitted all players with properly adjusted mouth guards, not necessarily to avoid dental injuries, which they did, but more importantly, the mouth guards had the ability to avoid or reduce the danger of cerebral concussions.

Toward the end of my career as a team physician for the Wings, Dr. Regula told me that on average only 35 percent of players wore the mouth guards that had been specifically made for them. It would be interesting to do a study of players who have had to leave the game due to concussions to see if they were wearing mouth guards when the injury occurred.

Players who have suffered from the long-term effects of head injuries are left with permanent disabilities, so early detection, treatment, and minimizing or avoiding them in the first place is of utmost importance. Banning hits to the head won't stop all such hits or the concussions that often result.

As Steve Yzerman and other elite players have acknowledged, head-shots are difficult to define. It's a physical game, and guys skating with their heads down are going to get hit. A clean body check should not be a reason to penalize a player. Guys have to be courageous, and going into dangerous areas to make great plays differentiates the timid players from the great players who make exceptional plays. Courage and skill are the hallmarks of elite players.

But somehow, some way, this amazing league must find a path toward reducing the number of injuries and the early retirements of so many elite players. Retraining coaches and management in the strategy of their play in a game of hitting and bumping is long overdue. Employing the safety equipment of helmets and shoulder pads as weapons to be used in checking needs to be seriously evaluated and corrected.

"Concussions are the NHLPA's top priority right now," said Mathieu Schneider, the former defenseman of 21 NHL seasons and now a special assistant to the NHL Players Association's executive director, Donald Fehr. He added that players "have to feel they can play and perform at 100 percent and be safe out there. There's a lot of work to be done over a short period of time, but we want to make the game as safe as possible as soon as possible."

Schneider is leading the way in a multi-pronged approach to the problem by changing the culture of the game as it relates to concussions. It includes a mini-documentary to be shown to players. The film features former players in their post-playing-career lives dealing with the debilitating consequences of head injuries.

It's a good start.

CHAPTER 6

A Major-League Problem

DRUGS AND OTHER PERFORMANCE-ENHANCING SUBSTANCES.
All professional sports have to be on guard for players deviating from the traditional standards of honesty and fair play, particularly related to the danger of using prohibited substances or medications. The International Olympic Committee, for instance, has very strong rules and techniques to both regulate and randomly check players who earn the honor of representing their country in the competition to be sure they have not enhanced their performance by use of prohibited substances. This is specifically related to using "prohibited classes of drugs, medications, or related substances."

Many such drugs and medications are perfectly legal, even found in over-the-counter (OTC) products, but nevertheless have small amounts of banned substances that could unwittingly disqualify an athlete and result in the loss of earned medals. Therefore my advice to any candidate for Olympic play was to just avoid taking anything—OTC or prescribed. For team physicians, it is not possible to prevent players from obtaining substances privately beyond the limits of the training room. Sometimes a trainer or team physician can become suspicious of that activity and randomly test the individual for both the player and team's benefit.

Professional football was confronted with the problem in players in the 1970s who found that by taking certain hormone-related substances they could bulk up and become stronger. Soon some of those players began to develop tumors in their livers or elsewhere, and some quickly jumped on the bandwagon to admit their mistake and promptly cautioned others not to repeat it. This did not seem important to hockey, but the NHL began to worry about the use of other substances that would speed up or enhance their ability to react quicker, have more endurance, or otherwise improve their performance.

In 1979, before team physicians had begun to meet, NHL President Clarence Campbell asked all the existing team doctors to gather during the league's annual June meetings held that year in Buffalo. Although we talked about a number of issues—preseason physicals, blood work, cardiac evaluations, and more, league management was especially interested in the evolving sports-related drug problem.

Prior to the meeting, Don Murdoch, a talented young Rangers forward, was found to have prohibited drugs in his possession when going through customs. He was suspended on July 6, 1978, by the league for the entire 1978–79 season for a substance-abuse violation and put in a required rehabilitation program. The suspension was ultimately lifted after 40 games, but at that time it was the league's best way of handling the situation.

As the NHL's position regarding drugs matured, a specific instructional program was born. The NHL started treating drug abuse as an illness and put in place a Substance Abuse and Behavioral Health Program led by Ph.D.'s David Lewis and Brian Shaw. In addition to their instructional and advisory program, they were available at any time should anyone need counseling or emergency intervention. Considering the magnitude of the stress and danger a player in the NHL is exposed to, it's easy to understand how easy it is to fall into the trap of using prohibited substances.

But even legal and properly helpful substances must be carefully monitored. For as long as I can remember, athletes in general and hockey players in particular have been interested in taking vitamins and minerals of various kinds. Their interest was to supplement their own diets in a healthy manner to minimize the many bruises, strains, and sprains that are a daily occurrence in professional hockey and make them heal faster once an injury occurs. Most players look to their trainers or team physicians for help in this area.

A Major-League Problem

Back in the mid-1970s, a reporter from *Sports Illustrated* interviewed me in our office next to Detroit Osteopathic Hospital. He was interested in learning more about my interest and love of the game of hockey. He inquired about what we, as fans and team physicians, would do to enhance the care and performance of our players. I explained that the prime premise in our office was to be immediately available. When I first met Gordie Howe, he told me how our predecessors often kept them waiting for up to three hours to be seen for any medical problem. From that time on, I instructed our office personnel and the residents and support people at the hospital to alert us the minute a player came in for care. We had a system with the trainers to call ahead when they were sending a player to us.

Periodically, someone learned of some magic vitamin or mineral supplement. We were very careful to check the formula and permitted their use as long as they didn't violate any league rules or laws regarding medications. We explained to everyone that by seeing and evaluating an injury as soon as possible after it happens, we could minimize swelling and bleeding and establish a diagnosis to get the player on a successful path to recovery with greater speed and accuracy. That, of course, always occurs at a game since we and a waiting ambulance crew are always there. During practice, it's a far different story. That's why the emergency protocols are so important.

The *Sports Illustrated* reporter asked if we gave any shots or medications to help. I told him how giving vitamin B12 injections became popular after veteran New York Yankee Gil McDougald confided to the press how he credited his longevity in the American League and ability to recover from sprains and strains rapidly to receiving B12. It was common knowledge that all healthy athletes had all the B12 in their diet that they needed and, if given more they would eliminate it in their urine if they didn't need it and thus do no harm to a healthy athlete.

The reporter and I talked for a couple of hours. He had planned to interview six to eight team physicians while developing his story. Within a few weeks, *Sports Illustrated* came out with a cover picture of a table full of pills and medications. Some interviewees had a lot more to say on the subject than I did.

For years, sports teams have been aware and concerned about the use of drugs in sports. As the medical care and fitness management of professional sports teams has improved, the same has occurred in hockey. There always have been nutritionists and dietitians who have, with good reason, made suggestions to teams for use of dietary supplements and health foods that have been known to assist athletes in attaining a competitive edge. Most of these were in the vitamin, mineral, and health-food category.

When Ned Harkness was coach of the Wings, he introduced to the team former Canadian trainer and prominent fitness expert Lloyd Percival, founder of the Fitness Institute of Toronto and a fitness consultant for St. Michael's College School in that city. He had a strong background and interest in vitamins and encouraged the Wings players to take large amounts of these supplements.

I remember Bryan "Bugsy" Watson remarking that he was taking 17 pills each day on the recommendation of Percival, none of them prescription medications. During training camp, the Wings have always been advised of the appropriate foods to eat and warned about what to avoid in order to improve their performance.

The International Olympic Committee has had a very stringent drug-testing program to prevent the use of performance-enhancing drugs (PED). Since the 1980s when NHL players have been permitted to compete in the Olympic Games, they have become very conscious of the need to avoid any medications that contain any of the excluded substances. Many medications, including over-the-counter meds used to treat the common cold, asthma, skin conditions, bumps and bruises, and myriad other conditions sometimes contain these substances.

As team physicians, we are given an inch-thick book naming the commonly used OTC medications, their contents, and whether they may include prohibited substances. Since many players are from other countries, it's difficult to advise them, especially if they have medications from their homelands. Therefore, to be on the safe side, I advised any candidate being considered for his country's Olympic team to avoid taking any medications for at least a six-month period prior to being tested.

It's noteworthy that on November 12, 2005, a potential USA Olympic hockey candidate, Columbus Blue Jackets defenseman Bryan Berard, had a urine sample taken that was found to contain one of the banned steroids— 19-norandrosterone—that is taken by athletes to gain muscle and lose weight. The following January, he accepted a two-year suspension from international competition, publicly apologized, and agreed to help the U.S. Anti-Doping Agency's (USADA) education program while serving his suspension.

Since the test was not part of NHL testing, he wasn't subjected to league discipline. Subsequent to the announcement, he did undergo two NHL/NHLPA's administered tests and both were negative. Berard admitted it was a mistake and promised it wouldn't happen again.

Drafted by Ottawa, Berard was the No. 1 overall pick in the 1995 amateur draft and is well known for his remarkable comeback from an eye injury caused by a high stick in March 2000 that left his vision blurred in that eye. He originally accepted a $6.5 million career-ending insurance settlement, but when his doctors agreed to let him return to play, he returned the money and resumed his career in the NHL.

The announcement sent a shockwave among the players around the league, especially since the chief of the World Anti-Doping Association, Dick Pound, said publicly that he estimated a third of the NHL's players used performance-enhancing substances. In a rebuttal, Wings forward Brendan Shanahan said he didn't know of anyone he ever played with taking those substances, and he condemned the suggestion that doping is widespread in the NHL. He contended that Pound's statements were irresponsible and ridiculous. The NHL noted that of the approximately 100 players tested as part of the USADA's out-of-competition testing, Berard's test was the only positive one.

Doctors have been using these drugs for years to treat various diseases, often of the muscle-wasting variety. Soon gene injections that have been shown to enhance performance in laboratory animals will be available. Inevitably, this will open a whole new chapter in the use of performance-enhancing drugs and medications. It is incumbent on us to be aware of those medications and determine if they can enhance a player's performance and whether they are banned.

In December 2007, after the announcement by former U.S. Senator John Mitchell about the widespread use of performance-enhancing drugs in baseball, NHL Deputy Commissioner Bill Daly told the Canadian press that he didn't think the NHL ever had the same problem. "Hockey players have been tested for many years in international play. It is simply not part of their culture," Daly said. "And we have tested NHL players up to three times a year since January 2006 and obviously have not had many issues other than one failed test."

That one, Minnesota Wild defenseman Sean Hill, received a 20-game suspension in the spring of 2007 while playing for the New York Islanders. The Wild said Hill used a doctor-prescribed testosterone booster approved by the NHL, but he tested positive for the banned anabolic steroid Boldenone.

To date, the NHL has been vigilant and fairly successful in its campaign against performance-enhancing drugs but continued surveillance must be maintained as the science gets more challenging.

CHAPTER 7

Self Defense

**WHEN EQUIPMENT SHOULD BE YOUR BEST ALLY—
AND WHEN IT SHOULDN'T.**

"All goaltenders should go to heaven," the late Red Wings goaltending great Roger Crozier used to say, "since we already know what hell is."

Truth be told, almost anyone who has played the game seriously has experienced a little bit of hell. Hockey is a painful game for even the most protected players. It can be even worse on opponents, however, when a player is too well protected and turns his equipment into a weapon.

Protective equipment, from goaltender masks and visors to body pads, boots, and skates, are essential to a player's well-being. But getting too attached to something, like the ancient shoulder pads worn by now-retired NHL stars Chris Chelios and Jeremy Roenick, can endanger the combatant's safety. It's important for coaches, management, parents, and the players themselves to understand and appreciate every piece of equipment and why it's being worn.

Masking the Problem

In the six-team era, none of the goaltenders wore masks. Repairing goaltenders' lacerations was a very common practice. With few exceptions, goalies had multiple lacerations. Some even sustained career-ending eye injuries, as did Baz Bastien—during practice with a minor league team. In addition, each team only carried one goaltender. If an injury occurred the home team's practice goaltender, or in the Wings' case the assistant trainer, was required to go in to replace him.

Shortly before the Bastein injury happened, Montreal's goaltender, the great Jacques Plante, introduced and used a face mask in a game after sustaining a serious facial laceration against the New York Rangers on a shot by Hall of Famer Andy Bathgate during the first period of a game at Madison Square Garden on November 1, 1959. Andy's Plymouth Whalers grandson said the elder Bathgate explained it this way: "Jacques poke-checked me earlier in the game when I went head first into the boards, and it knocked me out. I came back in and tried to hit him on the cheek with a shot, but he turned and the puck hit him good. It took 10 minutes to stitch him up, and he came back with this ugly mask I guess he practiced with. It was the first time we had ever seen a goalie with one. He therefore changed the game for goaltenders forever."

Shortly after that event Sawchuk admitted to one of our consulting internists (who was examining him to see if he was suffering from some obscure medical problem related to his subnormal play) that he was afraid of getting hit in the face. About the same time, our trainer, Lefty Wilson, learned from his good friend, NFL Detroit Lions trainer Millard Kelly, how to fashion protective pads from fiberglass that were formfitting and could be used as an addition to the hockey player's protective padding. After the Plante face-mask introduction, Lefty developed the technique by making a plaster mold of Terry's face and then fashioning a formfitting fiberglass mask from the plaster mold.

The mask in question was merely a fiberglass facial cover that gave some protection from facial lacerations but did nothing to help the player avoid the severe bruising that always occurred when a goaltender was struck in the face. It did, however, give the goalie a sense of comfort that there was at least some protection.

During the famous Summit Series in 1972—Canada's greatest against the best in the Soviet Union—Russian goaltender Vladislav Tretiak wore a wire-cage facial shield.

In the late 1970s, Dave Dryden was dissatisfied with the molded mask, especially after Philadelphia's Vezina Trophy winner Bernie Parent took a career-ending stick in the eye through his molded mask. He cut the face out of the mask, replacing it with a metal cage like the one he had seen used by Tretiak. Shortly afterward, the molded masks were ruled unsafe and banned by the Canadian Standards Association. By the early 1980s, the fiberglass facial cover was abandoned in favor of a helmet, wire-cage mask and an attached throat shield. Painted masks soon became an art-form, and they gradually matured into the modern-day mask used today by most goalies and painted to their specifications.

Today, goaltenders' face masks have been scientifically developed, and they're comfortable to wear. More importantly, they are universally accepted as mandatory equipment—like seat belts in our cars.

There are a few exceptions. Chris Osgood's helmet supporting the cage was sponge rubber during his first stint with Detroit. On his return to the club, he wore one that looked like the old one but gave him complete facial and helmet protection. The reason: he had suffered a concussion, and he didn't want to sustain another one.

Most masks now have a shield that affords protection of the goal-tender's neck and windpipe. That was such a genuine concern to us that we always had endotracheal tubes, appropriate laryngoscopes, and tracheostomy equipment in our medical room in the event that an injury to the trachea or larynx occurred during a game. During my time with the Wings, we had a fair number of such injuries, but none required tracheostomy. Most blows to that area, either from a puck or stick, created rather severe laryngospasm, which, although very frightening to the player, usually only lasts about 15–20 seconds (though it seems like an eternity to the one who suffers the injury and can't get his breath).

A Perfect Head Case

Helmets—head gear for players—have been in existence for many years, usually associated with a player who had sustained a head injury and the team doctor had mandated wearing it as requirement for being permitted to play. When I first joined the team, we had a defenseman, Warren Godfrey, who had come to Detroit in a trade from Boston. He had a concussion previously and was required to wear a small circular padded head protector, which was more like a "beanie" than a protective helmet. A few years later, a player named Charlie Burns came to us after being drafted from the Memorial Cup champion Whitby Dunlaps. Charlie had a surgically relieved subdural hematoma and a metal plate in his skull covering the opening. His helmet was more substantial but still not up to the standards of the present era.

Upon the death of the Minnesota North-Stars forward Bill Masterton from a head injury on January 15, 1968, several players began wearing helmets during regularly scheduled games—the most notable was Chicago Blackhawks Hall of Famer Stan Mikita.

In the 1970s, helmets began to appear, likely due to the mandatory requirement in the NCAA that all college players wear approved headgear. In 1979, it became a prerequisite that all players entering the NHL wear helmets, but existing players were allowed the choice of whether to wear one. Hockey writer Stan Fischler wrote an article at the time for his column "On The Contrary," in which he decried the use of protective headgear, saying it was ill-advised and against all good common sense. I believe he felt that the players would lose their identity to fans when wearing a helmet.

Fischler's remedy was for the league to crack down on the high-sticking, and he may have had an argument. But Gordie Howe always said he felt he lost the ability to sense another player was near him when wearing a helmet and therefore was unable to protect himself.

However, for those who grew up playing with a helmet in amateur or college hockey, this wasn't a factor. As the European players appeared in greater numbers, wearing helmets developed abroad, and the transition was further bolstered. Now all players wear them. However—and this cannot be overstated—too many wear them incorrectly, which means they do not get the protection they need and deserve. If the chinstrap is not tightened, it is not considered to be protective. Players frequently leave it loose to allow quick removal if they become involved in a fight. Another controversy involves the padding within the helmet. Often ¼-inch padding rather than the required ⅝-inch padding is preferred by the player—sometimes for comfort, sometimes for weight. The thinner padding does not afford sufficient protection.

The Eyes Have It

Presently, the NHL does not require facial protection, but that day can't come soon enough. Face shields and visors came into existence principally as protection from eye injury. However, as facial lacerations became more severe, more players chose to protect themselves by wearing them. Initially it was a macho thing, the player was considered afraid or not tough enough. This attitude is gradually changing as more and more players are choosing to wear them. Also, a number of elite European players wear them, as do almost everyone who has suffered a severe eye or facial injury.

Meanwhile, the talk about toughness and character as they relate to the use of facial protection has died down—and with good reason. This is especially true since the unusual accidental injury to Steve Yzerman during the 2004 Stanley Cup playoffs. He was struck full-force by a slap shot that caromed off the stick of Red Wings defenseman Mathieu Schneider. Had the puck struck him a quarter-inch higher, it could have been a career-ending eye injury.

One of the greatest disabilities is loss of vision, and having been personally involved with the unpleasant experience of caring for four players with lacerated or ruptured globes or serious eye injuries, I support any rule that protects the eye from injury. The players from the pre-headgear era always used to pride themselves on keeping their shots low to avoid striking the eye or head.

The NHL Team Physicians Society is on record supporting a mandatory rule requiring the use of visors, but the NHLPA believes wearing one is a matter of personal preference and it is unwilling to support rule. All North American players from junior or college programs are accustomed to wearing eye protection, but 60–70 percent of players take them off when they turn pro, usually wanting to send a message about their toughness to both management and opposing players. CBC-TV *Coaches Corner* analyst Don Cherry frequently ridicules the use of a visor.

I remember his criticism of Wings Grind Liner Kirk Maltby for wearing a visor and not removing his helmet when challenged by an opposing player. Cherry didn't know that Kirk had suffered an eye injury, causing iritis, while playing in Edmonton, and was cautioned by the attending ophthalmologist there to always wear eye protection because of the danger of further damage. Borje Salming, the tough durable Maple Leafs defenseman from Sweden, donned one after we repaired the serious deep linear facial laceration that extended from his forehead down close to his eye and further lower to the edge of his mouth. Usually, any player suffering facial bone fractures will wear one to protect the repair and avoid further damage—as Steve Yzerman did.

In college hockey, full-face protection has been required since the mid-1960s. When the Great Lakes Invitational Hockey Tournament began at Olympia Stadium, Michigan Tech became the host team. During a game in one of the early years, a player from Boston University was crossed-checked across his unprotected face, causing a bilateral compound fracture of the mandible (jaw) within two minutes of the end of the game. That incident was followed by a facial injury in the mid-1970s to a Tech player, the son of a Minneapolis dentist.

The player sustained an eye injury; the globe of his eye was ruptured and an anterior chamber hemorrhage occurred as well as dislocation of his lens. He was sent immediately to the nearby Henry Ford Hospital, where an ophthalmologist, on duty 24 hours a day, was able to save his eye. But a traumatic cataract occurred. The next year full-face protection was required in all United States college hockey games. I'm sure those injuries were major factors in instituting that requirement.

Protecting the Yappers

Bill Gadsby always said you weren't a real hockey player unless you had lost a few teeth.

Indeed, the dentists serving the Original Six in Gadsby's day all had to be exceptionally skilled in molding dentures that were both true fitting, comfortable, and natural appearing. The results of those battling players—very few of whom wore mouth guards—could often be seen when watching between-period or postgame television interviews, when the loss of their teeth was often apparent.

So it is normal to presume the major reason for wearing a mouth guard is to protect a player's teeth. That's why most players wear them. But in reality, next to helmets, mouth guards are very important in preventing serious concussions, particularly those that occur from blows to the jaw. During my tenure with the Red Wings, we had an exceptional dentist, Chet Regula, who fit and equipped each player with a mouth guard at the beginning of the season. During my years with the club, only a third of the team wore one on a regular basis. In the playoffs of 2000, former Wing Keith Primeau, while playing for the Philadelphia Flyers, took a shoulder butt on his jaw from a New Jersey defenseman, causing a concussion that kept him out of competition for most of the series. Since he was one of our former players, I asked Dr. Regula if Keith wore a mouth guard. Chet said he was never able to convince Keith to use it while he was here.

Mouth guards take some time getting used to and must be fitted properly. But more and more players are wearing them, particularly those from the college teams who have grown accustomed to using them. With concussions continuing to be a major area of medical concern, using mouth guards is an important contribution to hockey safety and concussion reduction.

It's important to note, however, that mouth guards must be personally fitted and fixed properly inside the mouth. The jaw tends to slide when hit, interfering with the normal alignment of the temporal-mandibular joint and our body's natural defense against shock.

Boots and Blades

Significant improvement has occurred in the skates used by our players, most noteworthy in the late 1960s when a Montreal player came into our arena with a change in the skate blade. Instead of being a straight blade attached in front and with two supporting posts, the player attached a clip that extended from the back end of the skate blade up to the heel of the boot. Injuries occurred from being struck from the unprotected end of the skate causing a laceration or serious contusion. This corrected that problem. Next, the metal support from the boot was replaced with lightweight but very durable plastic.

About the same time, there were revolutionary changes being made in ski boots, giving them extraordinary support and durability. Since many of the ski-boot manufacturers were making the skate boots, this was incorporated in the hockey skate boot, as well. Now all sorts of cosmetic design and supporting straps have been added to improve and help identify the skate in unmistakable manner.

Special protective pads over the skate and ankle were tried by defensemen, who commonly are required to block shots. But they found them awkward and cumbersome, so they were seldom worn except when fashioned by the equipment manager to protect a healing ankle or foot injury. Our equipment manager, Paul Boyer, is very skilled in creating this type of protection.

While we often talk about space-age technology helping to protect our athletes, some war-time technology also comes into play. The wars in the Middle East and law-enforcement demands have encouraged the development of Kevlar, the material used in bullet-proof vests and often by factory workers to protect their arms. That technology is now available to hockey players—in their socks and stockings. They aren't completely cut-proof, but they offer reasonable protection for most lacerations that happen from the scrums in front of the net, where most of those troublesome lower-leg lacerations occur.

The Body Guards

Pads protecting the shoulders, hips, thighs, knees, legs, forearms, elbows, and more have all undergone tremendous change. The most significant is that they formerly were padded with cotton. That worked well from a padding standpoint, but because of the tremendous sweating by players during a game, the pads became very heavy and increased the fatigue factor. Synthetic materials have replaced cotton. Shoulder pads were originally made of leather that also soaked up the perspiration, increasing the weight the players carried as the game progressed.

Now pads are shaped better, lighter, less bulky, and more comfortable, improving protection, dispersing heat, and allowing cooling to take place more efficiently. That, at least, is the objective. However, like an army tank they are made of very lightweight firm plastic material that has no give to it, so it does protect the player using it, but—and this is important—it is often used as a weapon by the person wearing it, and it can cause damaging or disabling injury to an opposing player.

I am strongly in favor of player protection, but I draw the line—and the league should as well—when a player deploys protective equipment in his offensive arsenal. Especially certain elbow and shoulder pads. Using the elbow to intimidate opposing players has gone on as long as I can remember in hockey.

Again, the hockey trainers are trying to develop soft external padding on elbow pads to reduce injury and increase the safety of the game. The hard external covering surface of many elbow pads frequently caused serious damage when used as a weapon. I believe they should be outlawed or at least externally padded.

Some equipment padding uses absorbing foam developed by NASA. The player's gloves, which used to extend halfway up the forearm and were somewhat restrictive, are now shortened to the wrist, more manageable, and more comfortable. The downside is that there are far more forearm and wrist injuries from slashing due to the diminished protection.

Comfort Sweets

It is interesting to note the number of elite players who play with the same equipment, readjusting their pads, helmets, skates every year in a way that allows them to be comfortable, protected, and often ensuring not to break their "good luck" tradition developed by using them. This was true of most players but some more than others.

Brett Hull spent more time having the Wings' equipment specialists altering and adjusting equipment than anyone I ever knew. But the important thing was that those adjustments made him a more effective scorer.

Jeremy Roenick said he wore the same lightweight shoulder pads throughout his entire NHL career because they allowed him the flexibility and maneuverability he felt helped him to accomplish more in hockey.

Goaltender Chris Osgood used to worry me during his early days because he wore a helmet made of sponge rubber that he had worn since junior hockey. He suffered a concussion one day, so we tried to get him to change it. He was resistant to it then but eventually had a change of heart. When he returned to us later in his career, he had a similar red helmet, but the new one was hardened plastic like all the other goaltenders wear.

Terry Sawchuk, according to Eddie Giacomin, often replaced his lightweight shoulder pads with a layer or two of soft mattress-pad-like felt padding that allowed him greater flexibility. Whatever works, we on the medical side of these issues like to say—so long as it really does help and doesn't endanger the player wearing it or his opponent.

CHAPTER 8

Behind the Curtain

THE DRESSING ROOM AND TRAINING FACILITIES.
The dressing room of any professional sports team is a special entity unto itself. It is the location where the player's personality and character develop. The established players on an NHL club look to the rookies to grow and mature to aid the team in their quest for the Holy Grail, the Stanley Cup. In reality it is the place where each player attains the authenticity of being a high-quality professional. It is the midway point between real life and the fierce, competitive battles on the ice, where they strive with their teammates to outsmart, out-maneuver, out-hit, out-intimidate, and out-psych their opponents. It is never easy, no matter how some teams make it look.

Physical training, usually under the direction of the trainer or conditioning expert, as well as the very important rehabilitation of mind and body, take place here. Players must be prepared for the inevitable meetings with coaches, striving to educate and convince them to make the team's system work, avoid mistakes, balance their family lives, and handle the media and the many requests for public appearances during which they represent the team, the league, the game, and themselves. It is where they learn, they grow, they give or take advice, as needed. This is their comfort zone. Little wonder athletes like to call the dressing room their sanctuary.

The typical dressing room of the 1950s can still be seen as it existed in the Original Six era. The Montreal Canadiens dressing room is displayed at the Hockey Hall of Fame in Toronto. Their room was better than most, but the rooms of all six teams were very modest—basically benches above which were hooks for their street clothes. After sharpening, CCM Tack skates were hung suspended from the bench edge. Players were positioned in orderly fashion by their jersey number, except the goaltender, who usually wore No. 1. Because of the size of the equipment, he required a little more room so he had his own special space. After 1967 when carrying two goaltenders was mandated, the two sat in close proximity usually at one end of the bench.

In Detroit's Olympia Stadium, as in the other Original Six arenas, the dressing rooms merely accommodated the players, their equipment, uniforms, one or two massage tables, a diathermy machine at one end of the room, and lavatory and showers at the other end. As was common in most professional sports of the day, many players smoked or chewed tobacco, so stand-up ashtrays and spittoons were strategically placed around the room. The trainer's area, and that's all it was, was simply a space at the far end of the main dressing room.

NHL training facilities were far behind other major professional sports. There was no standard exercise program or equipment to stimulate interest in conditioning. Standard treatment of the day for acute injuries was heat rather than ice, but that was changing by the early 1950s. Heat was reserved for chronic injuries. Players seldom drank much water because of the fear that it would make them nauseated and cause them to throw up and possibly aspirate. The pregame meal was always a big steak eaten prior to the afternoon nap. Players used to brag about knowing the best steak places in whatever city they were playing.

As physicians, we always worried about their nutrition. There was a superstition about the pregame meal—players were concerned that they would lack the strength to get through an intense game without the adequate nourishment provided by their big midday meal. Now, of course, players eat a light meal of easily digestible pasta. Players utilize a fair amount of liquid before and during a game and at intermission to avoid muscle spasms, cramping, and impaired performance due to dehydration.

Gordie Howe relaxes in the Wings' dressing room before his final game in March 1971. (Photo courtesy of Jim Mackey)

This is especially important when the games are played in warm climates and the playoffs in late spring in any NHL arena when temperatures rise.

The liquid is usually an elemental composition of those substances lost by the body during strenuous physical exercise. It is well-known that since the body is 70 percent fluid, excess fluid loss quickly results in diminished athletic response. Once this proof was given by physiologic experts, Gatorade became widely used. As Europeans gradually began to appear in professional hockey, some of them imported similar products that they were used to drinking in their own countries.

When the league expanded, new owners who were aware of the lack of emphasis on formal conditioning, raised concern regarding what was happening in college athletics and in other professional sports. They made sure it was part of the regimem employed by each club. Some broadened their coaching staffs, and some hired fitness experts to work with each player to improve his strength, agility, reaction time, and general physical health. The NHL trainers today have degrees in physical education combined with training and real expertise in the development of individual fitness programs.

Personal health, physical fitness, discouraging alcohol and tobacco, and awareness of the many additives frequently in complex vitamin and mineral compounds are important parts of their year-round nutritional and fitness plans. This enables them to stay in shape, improve conditioning and strength, and employ the many subtle fitness techniques that are available to make an athlete a better player.

The Olympic Games showed the world how the year-around programs in Europe—with government-directed specialists supervising them are frequently rewarded with medal-winning performances. Before league expansion, hockey was a much lower-salaried professional sport than baseball, football or basketball. Most players had summer jobs because they needed them to pay the bills. These were frequently unskilled labor positions that required brawn. That was how many of them maintained their strength and stayed in shape. Still, most players and management depended on training camp to work themselves back into shape. This explains why training camp at that time was about twice as long as it is today and usually included many more exhibition games in very distant locations, often where the club had some vested interest.

As television developed—and particularly cable networks—teams had the ability to pay salaries to sustain the players throughout the year. The NHLPA required teams to change their training-camp protocol, insisting on very specific rules and timing of team physicals, exhibition games, and length of camp. Players were given detailed training regimens to follow during the off-season and were expected to come to camp in top shape. Today many of the NHL players even hire private trainers to give them that extra edge, like defenseman Chris Chelios did faithfully, enabling him to extend his career far beyond that of the typical player. More recently, Wings forward Jiri Hudler spent the summer of 2011 with his Montreal trainer, and it made a tremendous difference in his performance the following season.

Taking care of professional athletes means sending players back into action as quickly as possible, which means avoiding having them return to the ice before they are ready while at the same time having them fully prepared to return to play at a high level. That means that while they are rehabilitating the injured area, every effort is made to keep the uninjured parts of the body in top condition.

Without exception, hockey players are tough. Some professional athletes baby themselves, but injured hockey players seem interested only in how quickly they can return to action. Most of the time, players are anxious to return quickly to help the team and do whatever is necessary to impress management before the next round of contract negotiations.

The team physician must weigh the eagerness of the player and the demands of management as well as the physician's own enthusiasm as a fan for the success of the team against the primary obligation, which is the health and welfare of the player—and his risk of re-injury.

The dressing room and training room facilities have undergone some of the greatest changes and advancements since the six-team era. Trainers came from the college ranks. Some trained in rehabilitation during WWII, some from European training facilities, and most had paramedical or nursing backgrounds. The assistant trainer was often a retired or converted goaltender who was interested in staying active in the sport in a training capacity.

In the 1960s, most of the advanced-fitness, muscle-building, and weight-training programs came out of European and college programs. The college-trained athletes, their coaches, and athletic therapists brought those programs into professional hockey. The owners quickly realized that to be competitive they had to provide their athletes with those facilities and they needed knowledgeable people to run them. Through the efforts of principally the orthopedic specialists, the specialty of sports medicine developed. Several other medical groups and specialty organizations were developing sub groups interested in sports medicine—primary care physicians, internal medicine, rheumatology, pediatricians, etc.

Prior to that time, physicians from a variety of disciplines who had a special interest in sports were the ones who became involved in treating athletes, learning how to help them excel and how to manage their injuries more efficiently. Soon the physiologists, internists, nutritionists, and other specialists added the contributions of their specialties to the athletic medicine programs, and the results were self-evident.

The objective of the training staff is to provide the best atmosphere for the athlete to obtain the highest level of fitness, endurance, and strength possible. They also recognize, evaluate, and treat as soon as possible any injury that occurs. Now almost every team has specialized help in the form of exercise specialists, nutritionists, power-skating technicians, and even sports psychologists.

Those specialists' entire education involves the care of athletes as opposed to general physical therapists who, in addition to the treatment of athletes, receive training in rehabilitating stroke, burn, and disabled persons such as amputees, closed-head, and spinal-injury patients. The Wings current trainer, Piet Van Zant, was the trainer for our former American League team, the Adirondack Wings, in Glens Falls, New York. His assistant, Russ Baumann, is an equally talented athletic trainer.

Much of what they do is not well known outside the training room but deeply appreciated by the players, coaching staff, and management. The trainers advise and assist players in choosing the most practical, protective, and state-of-the-art equipment available to them and to ensure it fits properly. Trainers educate players on fitness and design conditioning programs that will benefit them in their performance and injury prevention. Injuries are something every team has to deal with, and when they happen, trainers immediately initiate treatment.

The most often used and reliable medical modality is the ice bag and the pressure (Ace bandage) wrap, which are used extensively both on the bench and in the medical room. They also oversee a rehabilitation program prescribed to aid in the athlete's recovery in consultation with and supervision of the attending physicians. The training personnel are experts in molding protective padding, fitting, and applying sprints or braces used to protect players when they return to play and/or prevent further injury.

Our trainers are prepared to control minor lacerations common in our game. Should it not be easily controllable, the player is taken into the medical room and the laceration is immediately repaired by team physicians. If the trauma is to the mouth and a dental injury occurs, our expert dental staff is always in attendance and equipped to manage most hockey-associated injuries—or at least temporarily control the pain and sharp edges caused by the injury.

Head and neck injuries are of particular concern and therefore are cared for in a special protocol. In addition to the standard neurological evaluation, they undergo a neuropsychological exam. Each player has a baseline pre-participation neuropsychological exam when they first come to the Red Wings prior to any play. This is usually done during the preseason. Following a head injury, an exam is done in 24 hours and again at 72 hours, and the results are compared to his original pre-participation exam. Memory, both short and long-term, reaction time, and pain in the head are all part of the evaluation. Players are not allowed to return to play until all evaluations are normal and the player himself is comfortable to return.

The NHL Team Physicians Society has been doing a study of these injuries in the NHL, how they occur, what protective equipment is worn, and as much detail as possible is obtained to attempt to minimize and prevent these injuries from occurring. In the case of neck injuries, the manner in which players are transported off the ice is particularly important, and all training rooms are equipped with a backboard and medical personnel trained in the technique of stabilizing the player's neck and body to minimize or avoid spinal-cord injury.

All NHL arenas have a standby ambulance and paramedical personnel in attendance at every game ready to take any injured player to the teams' appointed hospital should the need arise. Each club is required to have a physician in attendance. In fact, usually a team of physicians are there—an orthopedist, dentist, and generalist or surgeon prepared to cover any injury or medical problem afflicting the visiting as well as the home team.

All the rinks have in place AED's (automatic external defibrillators), which is part of their medical equipment and carried when the team travels. The importance of this was emphasized when Jiri Fischer's heart stopped on the bench during a game in the fall of 2005 against Nashville. The AED saved his life, successfully resuscitating him along with external chest massage and mouth-to-mouth respiration.

Clearly sports medicine has come a long way since the days of the Original Six when trainers were not required to have special training in the field. During my medical training in Detroit in the mid-1950s, every hospital was beginning the formal development of its own rehab facilities, many of which employed individuals trained in Europe or South Africa. The university athletic programs quickly became prominent in improving athletic medical skills, and those with the strongest programs were able to develop the most competitive teams. Otherwise, most acute injuries were handled by primary-care physicians or their orthopedic consultants.

Professional Hockey Athletic Trainers Society (PHATS) and Society of Professional Hockey Equipment Managers (SPHEM)

Initially, trainers began organizing themselves into regional groups that involved specific sports, athletic conferences, and regions. In 1950, 101 athletic trainers representing the various groups met in Kansas City, Missouri, and officially founded the National Athletic Trainers Association (NATA). Its principal objective was to establish professional standards for the athletic trainer.

The PHATS officially came into existence with the expansion of the NHL. In the early years with only six teams, there were six principal trainers. Their job descriptions included many more roles than just taking care of and rehabilitating injuries. They were also responsible for care and transportation of the players' uniforms and equipment. In that era, trainers were not required to have a qualified background in sports medicine.

During those years, each team's doctor had a very close relationship with the trainers of the other teams since all of the clubs came into every building seven times each season. They would often call us when they arrived, usually the day before a scheduled game, to see one of their players, arrange X-rays, or treat some sudden illness. We would always stop in their room well before warm-up in case there was something they needed. It's the same now, except that close relationship doesn't exist for the most part because the opposing teams come into our building far less frequently. The trainers and equipment managers are quite close. They meet regularly to discuss questions specifically related to hockey as members of NATA. Although their role has become a full-time year-round job, some also work as part-time paramedics during the off-season.

Trainers have always held a special place in the makeup of the team family. They were often Damon Runyon–type characters who were beloved by the men they treated. The close relationship that is present between coach, trainer, and team doctor is very unique. The GM and coach are molding the players into a cohesive unit of highly skilled exceptional athletes, while the trainer and equipment managers are supporting all of their physical, emotional, and personal needs and challenges. The team doctor supports and augments that mission.

Of equal importance and stature to PHATS is the SPHEM. They formed their own organization, and the Red Wings' Paul Boyer and his predecessor, Mark Brennan, have been exceptional and creative members of that group.

The PHATS and SPHEM in conjunction with the NHL Team Physicians Society have been instrumental in urging equipment changes, upgrades, and improvements for years. This has been one of the key changes, and they present their suggestions to the leagues, the physician's society, and the players' association annually. One of the major stumbling blocks has been the players themselves, who sometimes get a little too comfortable with old equipment that offers little protection.

SPECIAL PEOPLE IN THE TRAINER'S ROOM.
Carl Mattson

As a resident in general surgery in 1954 at Detroit Osteopathic Hospital, I had the opportunity to help with the physicals and treatment of the Wings who were under the care of Drs. J. Donald Sheets and John Fetzer, from one of the surgical services. I became acquainted with Carl at that time. He was a very pleasant but serious guy respected by all of the players. He also respected them, gave them good care within the limits of our knowledge of sports medicine of the day, and was an integral part of the team operation—sometimes too integral.

One night, things came to a head when Carl was critical of the team's sub-par performance in a game played at Maple Leaf Gardens in Toronto. On the bus to the train station, he berated Ted Lindsay, singling him out as the one principally responsible for the team's poor play. He continued his tirade in the train's smoking car on the way back to Detroit, whereupon Ted got up and ripped Mattson for yelling criticisms at the players from behind the bench. Deeply embarrassed and dejected by the argument between the two very frustrated individuals, Carl handed in his resignation to Jack Adams as soon as they arrived at Olympia Stadium. He apparently suggested that Jack thought more of Lefty Wilson (who was the assistant trainer at the time) than he did of him.

Ross "Lefty" Wilson

Wilson was one of the true characters of the game. Always the same, he had an irrepressible smile and a mischievous gleam in his eye. We worked very closely together for 25 years. He was lovable, friendly, and a great person to be part of the medical operation. We talked almost every day about the medical condition of the players and the things we had to do to improve the efficiency of the training room and medical care operation.

I admired Lefty from the day I officially started working with the club in 1957. Lefty was originally from, Port Dalhousie, Ontario, a small, blue-collar, ship-building town on the edge of St. Catharines, where later one of Bruce Norris' ocean-going cargo ships was built. Because we were only allowed to carry one goaltender, he would dress in his goalie garb each practice day and cover the net at the opposite end of the ice from the team's NHL goaltender. Like many goaltenders he was an excellent baseball player and a good athlete in his own right. Before WWII, Lefty had been offered a contract with the Boston Red Sox organization, which offered him a minor league infielder's contract because of his quick glove playing for their Savannah, Georgia, and Roanoke, Virginia, farm teams.

His goaltender catching glove was a baseball fielder's glove with a thumb and four fingers rather than the traditional extended first-baseman's mitt. Lefty had a natural, quick wit, a strong loud voice, and was as spontaneous with the one-liners as Brett Hull was years later. Jack Adams first saw Lefty playing goal for the Canadian Navy amateur team in the Windsor Arena in an exhibition scrimmage against the Wings during World War II. In spite of being badly outclassed, Jack was impressed by his resiliency, determination, and competitiveness, as were the Wings' scouts, and Adams invited him to training camp. That didn't work out because he had a bad camp, but Jack liked his spirit and willingness to complete.

Keeping in mind that the Wings needed a goaltender at the other end of the ice during practice, Jack offered Lefty a backup assistant trainer position and sent him to Omaha for experience. From there, Lefty was sent to the AHL club in Indianapolis until 1950 when he was offered an opportunity to come to Detroit as our assistant trainer and spare practice goaltender.

The Original Six buildings were constructed in such a way that sound carried. Because of his strong voice and shrill whistle, everyone could hear Lefty when the Wings were in an opponent's arena. He would raise the ire of the fans with his incessant heckling of their stars and the referees, especially when they made a questionable call against the Wings. This was particularly true in Toronto, not far from Lefty's hometown. The Leafs' owner, Conn Smythe, became so enraged with Lefty's shouting that he complained to NHL commissioner Clarence Campbell.

The Leafs president took exception to Lefty's persistent annoying chatter. Smythe hollered at Lefty that it was against the rules of the NHL for a trainer to cause such a disturbance. The Wings were on a three-game road trip. Before they were back in Detroit, Adams had received a telegram from Clarence Campbell requiring him to bring Lefty to his office in Montreal by noon. Adams took Coach Jimmy Skinner along with him, as well, but in spite of their impassioned argument, Campbell suspended Lefty for three weeks and fined him $1,000. That quieted him down briefly, but he retained his fiery nature throughout his career.

Another time, I happened to be traveling with the team on a weekend road trip to Toronto and then Boston, where we had flown to directly from the Saturday *Hockey Night in Canada* game broadcast by the famed Foster Hewitt. Boston had a relatively weak team at that time, and in spite of our being down 3–0 in the first period, we came back and beat the Bruins, 5–3. Lefty got on referee Eddie Powers, heckling him unmercifully during the first period. Finally, Powers came over to our bench and ordered Coach Sid

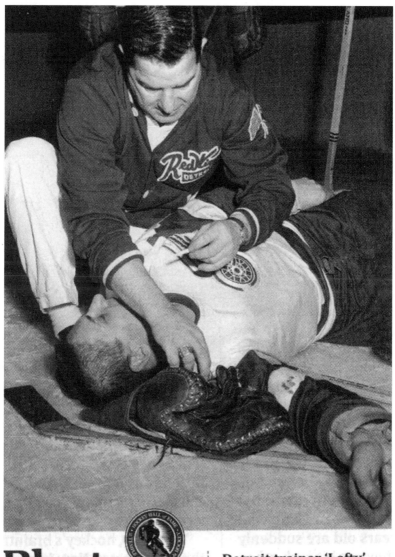

Blast **Past**
from the
from The Hockey Hall *of* Fame

Detroit trainer 'Lefty' Wilson tries to rouse Red Wings goalie Terry Sawchuk with smelling salts.

Legendary Wings trainer Lefty Wilson tends to Terry Sawchuk, who had just sustained a concussion in a game in 1957. (Photo courtesy of Hall of Fame Photo)

Abel to remove him saying, "He's out of here." So Lefty was ordered off the bench and stayed in the dressing room for the rest of the game. Lefty is the only trainer I'm aware of who was suspended and fined by league president Clarence Campbell for his boisterous, fiery nature behind the bench and ejected from a another game.

I loved Lefty, and enjoyed our daily dialogue. We would have pre-season teaching sessions, not only for Lefty, but our assistant trainer and the trainers from our farm teams about emergency medical care as it related to hockey injuries.

To show how much he meant to the players, when GM Alex Delvecchio was chosen to receive the NHL's Lester Patrick Award in 1974, Alex requested that Lefty be permitted to present it to him at the special banquet in New York City. The trophy is presented to the individual who made the greatest contribution to hockey in the United States.

Those of us behind the scenes were all like family. Lefty's wife, Lillian, a delightful lady, was a big part of the club's social scene. They frequently entertained the single players in their home, and some made it their home away from home. There was always a big celebration there on St. Patrick's Day. Their basement family room had wonderful hockey trophies, pictures, hockey sticks, and mementoes from past hockey greats. Especially endearing to Lefty was the plush, red carpet on the floor of the family room emblazoned with the No. 9. It was the carpet rolled out at Olympia Stadium the night Gordie retired, which Gordie had given to him.

We always brought Lefty to our Osteopathic profession's yearly Michigan State Athletic Medicine Seminars. He would attend the teaching sessions, and he and the trainers from the other professional teams would demonstrate taping techniques and the use of protective padding and braces to the doctors. One year, Millard Kelley, the Detroit Lions trainer, was at our meeting, demonstrating the making and fitting of fiberglass pads to protect an injured bruise or part. Millard showed the technique to Lefty, who immediately used it in hockey.

The author's family ready to skate at the Wings' Christmas party in 1975 after a visit from "Lefty Claus." (Photo courtesy of RW Photos)

At that time Wings goalkeeper Terry Sawchuk was having a great problem with fear of getting hit in the face every time he played. That was the scourge of every NHL goaltender of the day, so Lefty offered to make a protective face mask for him. It was really only a fiberglass shield. It protected him from being cut, but it could not protect him from the terrible bruising that always went with it. Nevertheless, it had a great psychological uplifting effect, giving Terry renewed confidence and affording him several more years in the NHL that would not have happened without the face mask.

Making the fiberglass mask, that was actually a form-fitting shield, was an art in itself. It required making a plaster of paris mold of the player's face. Then a fiberglass shield was formed over the plaster impression. Eye and nose-vent openings were cut and smoothed to rid the mask of rough edges. Completing the operation was the application of enough padding to make it comfortable on the player's face. Once Lefty fitted a fiberglass shield on Terry, every amateur goaltender in metropolitan Detroit and Western Ontario areas wanted one. He made several each week.

Soon his customers were coming long distances so they had to make an appointment with him. Most put their own design on them. Others began producing personal fiberglass masks, as well. When Boston goaltender Gerry Cheevers had one made, he drew replicas of all the facial scars he had suffered prior to getting his mask, which made fans appreciate how often goalies were lacerated before a mask of any type was available to them.

The Red Wings annual team Christmas party was always a memorable event during which Lefty played a major role. He donned a Santa Claus outfit and seemingly descended from the sky with a huge bag full of gifts. In reality, he would ride down from the balcony area of Olympia Stadium on the flatbed platform used to transport beer and food to the balcony refreshment areas. Because there was no protective siding on the platform and it was lowered from a pulley attached to the stadium ceiling, it was a somewhat scary ride for Lefty, but the players' children loved the exciting sight of Santa Claus descending from the sky. He accomplished it yearly without incident. Lefty's bag was loaded with presents, a gift from the club—individualized and age-appropriate for each child.

Lefty continued to serve the Wings throughout the Norris ownership but was replaced when the Ilitch family purchased the team. Newly hired GM Jimmy Devellano brought in Nick Polano as coach. Polano brought trainer Jim Pengelly, who had a strong background as a certified trainer. The Wings found a spot in the organization for Lefty, but he was like a fish out of water and soon left to undertake other sports pursuits.

CHAPTER 9

Mr. Hockey

UP CLOSE AND PERSONAL WITH GORDIE HOWE.
Every generation produces one or two great athletes who could excel in any of a dozen sports. In hockey, no one exhibited the kind of extraordinary athletic skills like No. 9, Mr. Hockey, Gordie Howe. The NHL has produced many outstanding and versatile athletes over the three generations in which Howe dominated the sport, including Maurice "Rocket" Richard, Bobby Hull, Bobby Orr, Frank Mahovlich, and Wayne Gretzky. But none had all the game's essential skills all rolled into one tremendous specimen like Howe.

In the opinion of most, Gordie Howe was the epitome of the complete hockey player—a great natural athlete, slope shouldered and raw-boned. He was listed as a right-hand shot, but in truth he could flick an uncanny wrist shot at the net with either hand. He was ambidextrous. When the slap shot was being developed, he didn't use it because he found that he could get off his shot with a short snap of his wrists twice as fast, and with far greater accuracy, whereas the shooter was never sure with the slap shot whether it was going to hit the net. He possessed skill, exceptional strength, superb coordination, toughness, skating ability, hockey intelligence, stick handling, endurance, and most important, that little bit (or more) of meanness so vital to gaining respect from fellow players who gave him room on the ice to make those magnificent plays.

Most teams assigned two players to cover him. The great Al Arbour, who is the proud owner of eight Stanley Cup rings—four as a player and four as a coach—is often asked who was the greatest hockey player he ever saw or played with from the 1950s, when he played, through the 1980s when he was coaching those great New York Islanders teams. Without hesitation, he responded, "Gordie Howe."

Since Al got his start in the NHL with Detroit in 1953, he saw Gordie in his strongest, youngest years. Al recalls playing in a game in which Gordie scored two goals, each in a distinctly different manner. After the game, Al asked Gordie how he did each of those scoring maneuvers. Howe shrugged those big shoulders and said, "I don't really know. The puck was there, the opponents were there, and I just did what was necessary to get around them and fire the puck." Al said he didn't remember Howe doing anything special other than making just the right moves that were natural to him—so innately natural he couldn't remember exactly what he did.

Quiet, reserved, and shy away from the rink, Howe was a different man on the ice. Opponents felt he skated on the fringe of the rule book—and he knew how to bend the rules. Any player who happened to embarrass Gordie with a move on the ice or by stealing the puck from him would ultimately pay. He rarely let on that someone got to him, but during the next brush-up the offender could expect five stitches—skating away wondering how he got an elbow in the jaw—but knowing there was a lesson in there about not embarrassing the Big Guy. Gordie Howe had tremendous pride.

The former Montreal Canadiens' bruising defenseman John Ferguson, one of the toughest men in NHL history and a constant shadow when Howe skated against the Habs, boasted that Gordie never scored on him. He conceded quickly, though, that Gordie "got a few while I was in the penalty box." Fergie also remembers the night Gordie stuck the tip of the stickblade in Fergie's mouth and hooked his tongue, tearing it for nine stitches. Because of his fierce competitive play, Ferguson frequently ended up on our surgical treating table. And probably because I was the one who often did the surgical repairs in Detroit, we became good friends in later years during his visits to the Red Wings Alumni Room at Joe Louis Arena. He lived across the Detroit River in Windsor, Ontario.

Fergie wasn't the only one with such stories. There were so many anecdotes like that about Howe from players describing his uncanny hockey skills to his not-so-pleasant demeanor the way he played the game, that it is impossible to recall them all. He was able to skate so effortlessly that he looked as if he wasn't hustling. And Gordie's "repayments" were often the epitome of subtleness. He never stopped to fling an elbow in anger, but would incorporate it, barely noticeable to even the referees or fans. But his target always seemed to get the message.

One of the most perfect examples of Gordie's inescapable memory of past embarrassing and painful events was told by Blackhawks Hall of Famer Stan Mikita, who was never hesitant to catch an opponent with a unexpected cheap shot—especially early in his career. Stan recalled his initial encounter with the great Gordie Howe in his first or second year in the league in the late 1950s. He caught Gordie with a pretty good hit and as the Big Guy was falling to the ice, he gave him a shot with his stick, cutting him on the way down. Gordie had to leave the game for stitches. Gordie's former Detroit linemate, Ted Lindsay, had been traded and was playing for Chicago. Between periods, Ted told Mikita that on occasion Howe could be "a little vindictive."

Howe had been in the league for about a dozen years by then, and the press was beginning to wonder when he was going to retire. Which is why Mikita shrugged his shoulders and said, "Nah, he's an old man. He's not going to worry about a snot-nosed kid like me." So they went back out and Mikita kept his head up because Lindsay had him thinking. Nothing happened. After the game, Mikita went up to Lindsay and said, "See? I told ya the old man doesn't care." Lindsay again told him to watch out. The next game Mikita was very aware every time Howe was out there, same with the next game, and the next game, and the next game. Still nothing. Then Mikita relaxed.

To this day Mikita doesn't know when or how he got hit. Farm-team goaltender Denis DeJordy was in the building on emergency recall from the AHL Buffalo Bisons and not playing, but he saw the whole thing and later described it to Mikita.

Mikita was offside on a delayed call and was looping back out of the zone after the puck had been shot out of Detroit's end. He was watching the puck as he was circling. When he woke up, he was flat out on the ice and he barely crawled to the bench. DeJordy said Howe circled the other way and as they approached each other, Howe slipped off one glove and popped Mikita right on the button. Howe put his glove back on and kept skating; no official saw it. Nobody knew what happened. DeJordy apparently was one of the only people in the building who did. Mikita missed the rest of the period. When he went back out for his first face-off, Howe was on the ice. Mikita skated over and said, "Well, I guess we're even." Howe smiled and said, "Don't know, Stanley. I'm not sure yet." Mikita said he died a thousand deaths and skated on egg shells for the next three or four games against Detroit until Howe eventually skated over before one game and said, "Okay, now we're even. Now if you get a chance to hit me, by all means do so. But if you ever cheapshot me again like you did, I'll end your career." Mikita believed him and said they had many battles for the puck over their careers after that, but he never gave Howe a cheap shot again.

Gordie had a memory like an elephant. Anyone who tried to get a piece of him usually lived to regret it. He often said he didn't get even; he just got their number. He would quietly skate by the perpetrator and whisper, "I owe you one." Sometime later—in the same game or in a later game or even in the next year, likely using a very subtle tactic not noticed by the referee, he would repay the offender in a way that typically resulted in requiring my surgical talents. Howe's elbows, instead of being waist high, would come up shoulder high, and the victim would often end up flat on the ice not knowing what hit him.

And then Gordie might skate by his adversary and whisper, "Now we're even."

Teammates remember how honorable Howe was regarding the physical side of his game. "Gordie rarely got mad. If you get him a little irritated he might give you a little elbow, but if you get him upset he might give you a little wood," longtime teammate Alex Delvecchio confirmed, adding

94

the perfect description of the way Howe played the game, "He was a dirty hockey player in a clean sort of way."

He also had a big heart off the ice. He was very kind and patient to his fans, and he would stay and sign autographs after a game long after everyone else had left.

Like most of the rest of the single players, Gordie lived at "Ma" Shaw's, a boarding house one block from Olympia Stadium. She catered principally to newly arrived rookies who made the team and unmarried players. The comradeship they developed contributed to the great respect and loyalty that existed on the team. Living there were Marty Pavelich, Metro Prystai, Glen Skov, Alex Delvecchio, and Lefty Wilson. Ma Shaw would even go out for a beer with them after a game. Through her, Jack Adams had one more way of keeping a hidden eye on his players.

The team regularly had a game on Saturday night, was often featured on *Hockey Night in Canada*, and then traveled usually by train back to Detroit, arriving Sunday afternoon or later if delayed by weather. The Wings would often arrive just in time for the regular Sunday night game, which began a half-hour earlier than the weekday games. Monday was often an off day with little or no practice. That evening the guys would have dinner together without wives, coaches, or team officials. If a teammate wasn't doing his job, a couple of senior players would take him aside and point out where he was not performing and letting the team down, frequently helping him get out of his slump.

When Gordie first signed with the Wings, Jack Adams promised him an official NHL Red Wings jacket that only bona fide players were allowed to wear—a badge of honor indicating they had made it in the NHL. But Gordie never got his. The next year, when it came time to sign his contract, Adams handed it to him, but Gordie just passed it right back to Jack unsigned. The flustered GM asked him what was the matter. Gordie said, "You don't keep your word." Adams said, "What are you talking about?" Gordie reminded him about his promise regarding the jacket. Adams quickly called the supplier and sent Gordie there. Since it was a year later, Gordie told me he picked the best jacket they made, the one trimmed with leather. He was proud to wear this visible evidence that proved he had made it.

How Gordie selected his famous No. 9 is another interesting story. As an NHL rookie in 1946, he wore No. 17. At that time most of the traveling between cities in the six-team league was by train. Eventually, Howe approached trainer Carl Mattson and asked how he could get a bottom berth; he didn't like sleeping in the top bunk. "They're assigned by numbers, single digits get the lower berths," Mattson explained. No. 9 became available when Roy Conacher moved on to the Chicago Blackhawks after the 1946–47 season. Howe claimed it, and no Red Wing will ever wear it again because the retired No. 9 hangs from the rafters of Joe Louis Arena.

As a rookie, Gordie scored his first goal on an assist from team captain Sid Abel. He credits Sid for giving him a lot of sound advice that he followed throughout his career. Among the most valuable, "When you jump over the boards, it takes two seconds to know who is for you or against you," and, "Don't drop your stick until the other fellow does. You will be wearing stitches if you do."

While Gordie tended to dish out more than he received, he still endured his share of battle scars. The first game of the 1950 Stanley Cup semifinals was at the Olympia against Toronto. Gordie suffered the worst injury of his career. He was charging Maple Leaf Captain "Teeter" Kennedy, who saw Gordie at the last second and spun out of the way. But as he did, Kennedy caught Gordie with his stick and took him into the boards. Gordie sustained several injuries, the most serious of which were a concussion and subdural hematoma, as well as an abraded cornea and facial-bone fractures.

The Wings won the series, but it took them overtime in Game 7—on a goal scored by defenseman Leo "Radar" Reise. Interestingly, Radar scored very few goals in his career, but two of them were Stanley Cup playoff game-winners. Gordie recovered nicely to continue his remarkable career but endured residual headaches and a noticeable nervous tic that lasted several years.

Gordie's medical history also included, in medical terms, a bilateral knee injury, skull fracture, bilateral inguinal hernia, bilateral olecranon (elbow) bursitis, broken ribs, ureteral calculus, corneal abrasion, dislocated fingers, aseptic necrosis of wrist bone, "Kienbock's Dx," 300-plus facial sutures, broken toes, arthritic knees and wrists, dislocated shoulder, and periodic back spasms.

Among his most uncomfortable injuries was a costochrondral separation due to being checked into the boards in front of the opponents' bench during an exhibition game in London, Ontario, in the late 1950s. The closure on the door to the bench was not snapped closed tightly, so it flew open as Howe hit it, the open end of the boards catching his anterior ribs and the cartilaginous attachment, causing a disabling injury that took three weeks of healing before he was comfortable.

By the time I became involved with the medical care of the team, Gordie was a recognized star, having been in the league 10 years. Since the average career expectancy of major league hockey players at the time was 4½ years, the press was already asking when he was going to retire. He took those comments in stride, shrugged his big shoulders, and just kept compiling record after record.

Our family's relationship with the Howes goes back to my initial contact with the club as the new member of the Sheets, Fetzer, Kosley surgical group. My wife, Genevieve, and Gordie's wife, Colleen, became close friends shortly after we settled in our apartment after our honeymoon. Genevieve and I were married on November 30, 1957, in Liverpool, New York. We drove following our wedding reception to Lake Placid in the Adirondack Mountains, and we were listening to the Army-Navy football game on our car radio.

From left to right: Genevieve and Jack Finley, Colleen and Gordie Howe, and Edna and Bill Gadsby in 1963. (Photo courtesy of the Finleys)

At that time, it was the traditional terminating game of the college football season, always played the Saturday after Thanksgiving in Philadelphia at Franklin Field at the University of Pennsylvania. Genevieve was chatting about the reception and our plans for the future when I interrupted her, "Stop talking, I need to hear this." She thought, "Who is this person I'm married to?" To my surprise, during the halftime report of the nationally broadcast football game, the sportscaster announced that Jimmy Skinner, the coach of the Wings, had stepped down, and Sid Abel had replaced him.

Jimmy had been hospitalized a couple of times during the previous season with severe migraine headaches apparently brought on by the tension of coaching. The condition persisted in spite of medication, so stepping down from the rigors of coaching was not completely unexpected and likely the best option for him.

Genevieve had never seen a hockey game before she came to Detroit. When we were with Gordie and Colleen one night, and because she had watched several bench-clearing brawls—not uncommon during games in the 1950s—she asked him why everyone threw their sticks and gloves on the ice whenever there was a melee. "I don't know about anyone else,"

Gordie told her, "but I'm always looking for a higher-quality stick and a better pair of gloves."

Shortly afterward, Genevieve found herself walking into the corridor after a game with Jack and Helen Adams. Following up on what Gordie had said about the equipment debris on the ice after a donnybrook, she asked Jack why they didn't give the players better equipment. "What do you mean?" Jack asked. Genevieve related what Gordie had told her. Jack merely smiled and walked away, covering his face to stifle his laughter. Gordie also told Genevieve that if a team scored a short-handed goal it counted two. The next game we scored one. Genevieve became very upset when only one point went up on the scoreboard. Eventually, she began to understand Gordie's wonderful sense of humor.

Colleen was taking night-school courses at Highland Park Community College across the street from our apartment and near Detroit Osteopathic Hospital. Gordie would often come to the apartment to wait for her, or if he was late she would wait there for him. We got to know them both very well and often went to dinner together. Our favorite place was a wonderful seafood restaurant called the Clam Shop. The four of us loved their specialty, baked lobster with a delicious peanut-butter bread-crumb dressing. When the entrée came, Gordie would have great fun cracking the lobster shells with his bare hands even when the shells were harder than usual.

A true crafter, Colleen was always making unusual items for friends. We still have Christmas ornaments of photos picturing our children together that were an example of the many unusual things she had constructed. Fortunately, her Aunt Elsie and Uncle Hughie were available daily to help her at home with the kids, which gave her the freedom to do many of those projects. She kept a running scrapbook of newspaper and magazine articles written about her famous husband. She was especially involved in helping Gordie perfect his signature—in perfect penmanship—that he signs literally hundreds of times each week throughout his retirement.

In addition, she was the driving force behind answering his fan mail, principally sending a signed picture postcard of Gordie as a memento for them. One of the local sports photographers, Charlie McCarthy, made a business of making photographs on what were then penny post cards, typically of the athletes in their home uniform. In Gordie's case, he would sign it and Colleen would send it back to the fan who sent him the letter, thereby showing his appreciation and respect for his fans. Her closest friend, Edna Gadsby, always said, "Colleen was more like a hostess than a hockey player's wife."

When we first met, Gordie and Colleen lived in a very humble home on Stoepel Avenue just off Grand River, a couple of miles from Olympia Stadium. Our wives were doing some household project together, so while they were busy Gordie and I went out in the backyard to play catch. He threw the ball to me so hard I could barely see it. I loved baseball in those days, having grown up playing on a local city park team called the Giants. I could easily handle most of the balls thrown at me. By the end of the afternoon, my hand was swollen and sore, which was tough for a surgeon, but I wouldn't let on to Gordie that I couldn't take it.

He was such a good ballplayer that he would go to Tiger Stadium with his close friend, Detroit Tigers great Al Kaline, and take batting practice. Although he was right-hand dominant, Gordie was a natural switch hitter and could hit equally well from both sides of the plate. In conversations with Gordie, he often wondered if he should have tried to make it in baseball, where he might have had a chance for a longer professional career. Obviously he made the right choice.

Many will remember Eddie Feigner, the famous fast-pitch softball pitcher of that era. He and his four-man team were called "The King and his Court." Eddie had the reputation for being the greatest softball pitcher in the U.S. His court was the rest of his team—a catcher, first baseman, third baseman, and one outfielder. His team was featured in *Life* magazine and many other publications at the time.

Feigner was known for his trademark crew cut, bulging right arm, and a fastball once clocked at 104 mph. He was pitching in an exhibition softball game at Tiger stadium against a team of celebrities. Howe hit more than one home run against him, which was quite rare even when playing baseball professionals. In a television exhibition in 1964, Feigner struck out, in order, Willie Mays, Willie McCovey, Maury Wills, Harmon Killebrew, Roberto Clemente, and Brooks Robinson. Gordie Howe? A different story.

Gordie's summers were spent in Saskatchewan. He would talk about Waskesiu Lake in Prince Albert National Park, where he would spend a great deal of time. Most of the players in the league at that time had summer jobs; their salaries were very low compared to professional baseball and football, and the off-season period was much longer—from late March to September.

During the summers before he was married, Gordie worked as an assistant golf pro at the Waskesiu Golf Club. His job consisted of raking the sand in the bunkers, changing the water in the ball washers, and putting new holes on the greens every other day. Goaltender Johnny Bower languished in minor league hockey for many years early in his career in Cleveland before becoming one of the dominant NHL netminders for the Maple Leafs. Johnny was from nearby Prince Albert, formerly worked at the golf club, and had a hamburger restaurant in town where he featured "Bower's Big Boys"—giant hamburgers that were a hit with the teenagers.

Gordie would begin at 7:30 AM. Since it was a private club, Johnny would meet him on the second hole, and they would play a round using Bower's clubs. Gordie said he did everything he had to for work, and he and Johnny would get in a round of golf at the same time. One member complained, but Gordie's boss said his predecessor took all morning and half of the afternoon to do the job that Howe did in four hours, so they didn't bother him after that, and he and Johnny played a lot of golf.

Genevieve and I would tell Gordie and Colleen about our hometown and Skaneateles Lake, one of the spring-fed Finger Lakes in upstate

New York whose water was as clear and cold as the Waskesiu. Gordie and Colleen joined us there one weekend in July, giving us a chance to introduce them to our parents and explore the area with them. We waterskied on Skaneateles, played golf at the Onondaga Country Club, and even had an interview with veteran sports editor of the *Syracuse Post Standard* Bill Reddy, whose writing I had admired through my formative years.

Since that was not hockey country, Gordie wasn't constantly troubled for autographs. However, we were having dinner in the famous Krebs Restaurant in Skaneateles when a man from an adjacent table came over and said that his wife thought he was Gordie Howe and would he sign an autograph for her. Gordie smiled, said he wasn't that person but would sign it anyway. He signed it "Gordon How." When she saw the signature, she immediately got up, came right over to our table, confronted him, made him admit he was really the hockey star, and asked him sign it right. We all got a big chuckle over that.

Two years later, Genevieve was expecting our first child. Colleen wanted to have a surprise baby shower for her. We had no family in or near Detroit, so most of our friends were professional colleagues from the hockey club or from our church, Blessed Sacrament Cathedral. Colleen asked me for a list of about 24 of our friends she then invited to their home in Lathrup Village.

Since it was a surprise shower, we had worked out a strategy. Gordie and I would play golf while the ladies would spend the afternoon doing some craft projects. After we returned from playing golf, the four of us would have dinner together that evening. The guests were all asked to be there a half hour before we arrived. Gordie drove everyone's car to a nearby schoolyard so there was no evidence of anyone there. The Howes had a tri-level home and all the guests were in the lower level, so even as we entered you couldn't tell there was a party going on. Helen Sheets, my mentor's wife, worked with Colleen to make it a special event. The entire affair was a great success and a complete surprise to Genevieve. It gave us a great start with all the customary baby necessities.

Thanksgiving Day in Detroit was always a big day for sports fans, especially in the 1950s and '60s. Detroit's annual Thanksgiving parade, hosted by Hudson's Department Store, was held at 10:00 AM. The Lions had their annual football game (in those days, usually against Green Bay) at 12:30 PM at Briggs Stadium, and in the evening there was always a Red Wings hockey game at Olympia Stadium. It was Gordie and Colleen Howe's style to invite all the single players to have Thanksgiving dinner in their home before their afternoon nap. The games were always sold out and highly contested, completing a full day of sports and holiday activities.

With only six teams and so few hockey jobs available, nearly everyone who played possessed a degree of toughness, and was his own enforcer in order to survive in the league. A very few were called what Gordie described as "honest players" who didn't fight but merely played the game. Every part of Gordie's body was made for the game. He was a perfect blend of grace and grit. The sharpness of his elbows was so well-known that when he was a guest at a Toronto banquet, he was presented with a pair of oversized elbow pads, more like pillows, that his host suggested he wear when playing against the Maple Leafs.

Whenever he went in the corners, he possessed a repertoire of secretive stick and elbow pokes to win the battles for the puck. Howe never looked for a fight, but he never backed down whenever anyone challenged him. When it came to survival, Gordie Howe would get Biblical on his opponents, always professing that, "It's better to give than to receive."

One night, Toronto defenseman Bob Baun was the recipient of Gordie's wrath. It came during a home-and-home series—a Saturday night game in Toronto and Sunday evening contest at Olympia Stadium in Detroit. Baun caught and hurt Gordie a couple of times. The next night in Detroit, Bob had a breakaway. Gordie caught up with him so he couldn't shoot on net. Baun went behind the net, planning to throw the puck out front. Gordie went with him and caught him behind the net with his big elbows forcing the Leaf defenseman's head against the glass, opening an 8" (23-stitch) laceration across the top of his scalp from forehead hairline to the back of his head. Since the scalp bleeds briskly, there was blood all over the ice. The wound erupted like a volcano as Gordie skated away innocently.

Baun, meantime, looked like a scalping victim. When he was brought into the medical room for repairs, he said to me, "I don't why he had to do that." I suggested that it was likely a payback for a shot or two he had given Gordie the night before. Later I asked Gordie about it, and he kiddingly said, "Yes, it was seven years ago, but I wanted to keep the ledger clean."

Gordie was one of the most formidable fighters of his time. I don't remember him ever being the instigator, but because of his style of play, he often received opponents' ire. His most famous fight was in the head-quarters of championship boxing, New York's Madison Square Garden, in February 1959. The Wings were playing against the Rangers, and their heavyweight was "Leaping Lou" Fontinato. Utility forward Eddie Shack was playing for them and always had the assignment of shadowing Gordie.

While trying to be a general nuisance and distraction, Shack was the brunt of many slashes, elbows, and the usual techniques Gordie used to discourage those assigned to check him. Fontinato was on the other side of the ice when he saw the generally mild-mannered but former St. Michael's boxing champion Red Kelly nail Eddie behind the net in a minor altercation. Gordie was leaning on the net, admiring the Kelly-Shack tussle and was starting to move into it when he realized Lou had dropped his stick and gloves and was coming full speed across the ice. Some games before, Lou had high-sticked Gordie, cutting his lip. He then taunted Gordie by skating past the Wings bench saying, "What's the matter with your nose and lip?" Gordie returned the favor by cutting Lou's ear a short time later and skated by him saying, "What's wrong with your ear?"

That night in New York, Gordie remembered the incident and had his antenna up for the inevitable confrontation. He told me that he saw Lou coming out of the corner of his eye, so he planted his right skate in the ice. Lou took a swing at him. Gordie ducked out of the way so the blow missed him completely. Then he grabbed Louie by the neck and caught him with a haymaker that moved his nose to the right side of his face, and the fight was on. The officials let them go. Actually, referee Red Storey said he held Louie back, but Lou is yelling, "Let me go, I want him." Storey cautioned him, "No, you don't." "Yes, I do," Fontinato pleaded. So the referee let him go.

Wings trainer Lefty Wilson had a ringside seat and said every blow— pop, pop, pop—could be heard all over the Garden arena. The fight lasted more than a minute. Lou went to the hospital, and Gordie nursed a dislocated little finger, from the vice-like grip he had on Lou's jersey, and a black eye. Everyone agreed that it was the hockey fight of the century. The next week, *Life* magazine, the most significant weekly magazine of the day, had a centerfold of opposing full-page photos and three additional pages of copy dedicated to the story. Gordie, pictured in the Wings dressing room bare-chested, sloping shoulders and muscles bulging, was hailed as the victor on the left, and Lou on the right, in the hospital, encased in bandages like a mummy, described as the vanquished.

Later, Lefty told me that Gordie had suffered a costochondral separation (separated rib cartilage, likely a recurrence of a preseason injury in London, Ontario) the previous game and he had taped his rib cage to control his soreness, which makes the fight even more remarkable. One unnamed victim of Gordie's called him the perfect hockey player: soft-spoken, mild-mannered, and thoughtful, but also the most vicious, meanest, and cruelest person in hockey.

Even when he moved to the WHA as an elder hockey statesman, his ill-tempered on-ice demeanor continued. Son Mark tells the story of the three Howes—Gordie with Mark and Marty—playing for the Houston Aeros against the Edmonton Oilers. One of the Oilers' tough guys was on top of Marty, manhandling him. Gordie skated over and told him to get off his son. The tough guy foolishly said, "Get out of here, old man." Gordie promptly got on top of the villain, grabbed him by the forehead, pulled his head back, stuck a finger into each nostril, not-too-gently lifted him off Marty, practically tearing his nose off his face. The message was delivered to the WHA, and Gordie Howe was rarely challenged after that.

Although he was tough on his opponents he was always very aware of and kind to his teammates. The season before I started, teammates told a story about Gordie, on the last regular game of the 1956–57 season, inquiring between periods if there was anyone just short of making any scoring bonuses. Billy Dea spoke up, saying he had 14 goals and needed 15 for his bonus. Gordie told him to get in front of the net and keep his stick on the ice. Gordie then proceeded to feed him until he scored, and Dea was able to collect his bonus of a few hundred dollars.

In spite of his temperament on the ice, Gordie was actually a shy, humble individual. The atmosphere that generated the most uneasiness around the club and the league was the effort to begin a players' association or, more correctly, a union that would represent all players against league management. The principal players behind it were Montreal's Doug Harvey and Detroit's Ted Lindsay. To make an association like that work, it needed the support of all the major superstars in the league because everyone knew that owners and management would trade any one, which included those in the group they considered malcontents. This was particularly true in a league that consisted of approximately 110 players.

While there was reasonably strong support by the players, Gordie just wanted to play hockey and was unwilling to take a chance of losing that opportunity. He had always exhibited an attitude of trust and deference to authority or to anyone senior to himself. That posture, I believe, kept him from giving his support to that group, which in effect sealed the death of that effort. Ted Lindsay was quickly traded to Chicago, where he played for three seasons before retiring in 1960. Ted was offered the opportunity by Sid Abel to make a comeback with the Wings in 1964. When asked by management if he thought Ted could help the team, Gordie said he was sure he could, knowing his feisty nature and the competitiveness he brought to the game. Ted returned, and he was credited with helping linemate Bruce MacGregor enjoy his best and most productive years in hockey.

Like many hockey players Gordie was a marvelous golfer, enjoying exceptional eye-hand coordination. He could drive the ball a country mile and often played in celebrity golf tournaments. He would stand and address the ball in a half crouch and swing like he was hitting a baseball. One time, one of my surgical colleagues, Dr. Paul Trimmer, invited us to play Oakland Hills Country Club, the Wednesday following the 1961 U.S. Open tournament won by Gene Littler the previous Sunday.

The course was probably a little easier that day because the large gallery had trampled down the rough, but otherwise the pin positions on the course were still the same as the last day of the tournament. Paul's playing partner did not enjoy very good golf etiquette, often walking or talking while Gordie was putting. In spite of those distractions, Gordie shot a par 72, shooting six pars, six birdies, and six bogies, one of the best rounds of his life—on a championship course.

Due to his superstar status, Gordie was often called upon for interviews and personal appearances. One time he was being interviewed by author and former ABC sportscaster Dave Diles at a recreational vehicle and outdoor activity show. He spotted Genevieve and me as we walked into the partitioned area where a question-and-answer, audience-participation session was taking place. A lady asked Gordie who he felt had the hardest shot in the NHL.

Montreal's "Boom Boom" Geoffrion had developed the slap shot, as had Bobby Hull, both of whom were in their heydays. So everyone expected Gordie to select one of them. Instead, seizing the opportunity to kid me, he answered, "I don't know about the entire league but, in Detroit it's the guy who just walked in, in the back of the room, Dr. John Finley." And all I'd done was give Gordie several antibiotic injections.

Physically, Gordie had the most perfect athletic physique of any player I have ever known or taken care of. He was very much like cartoonist Al Capp's Lil Abner with his sloping shoulders and muscular arms, forearms, and thighs. This was before the sports medicine specialty had developed. There was no regulated fitness program that the players followed in the summer. Instead, they depended on the elongated preseason training camp to get into shape. Gordie did many things naturally and unconsciously that kept him in shape.

The late referee Art Skov told me that the summer after one of his early seasons in professional hockey, Gordie worked construction jobs for his father, who was the foreman on the job in his hometown in Saskatchewan. His father, Ab (Alfred), said Gordie was the best construction worker he ever had. Ab put Gordie and his brother, Vern, on the cement mixer. Gordie could pick up a 90-pound cement bag with either hand. The tightly filled bags were tough to grasp and lift. Gordie would pick them up by the middle, one under each arm, and empty them into the mixer. Vern gave up after two days, but Gordie stayed on it all summer. Obviously, that activity helped develop his great shoulder and arm muscles.

Another time, during a playoff series against Montreal, Gordie and I were sitting on the bus early one morning on our way to Laval Airport for our trip back to Detroit. We saw a group of schoolchildren waiting for their bus. He said it reminded him of how, when waiting for the school bus in Saskatoon, he used to play tricks on his brothers and sisters. The Howes lived seven miles from the school. While they were waiting for their school bus, he would pass the time by shooting the puck against the side of their house. Once they all were on the bus and it left, he would quickly grab his things and run the seven miles to the school. When the bus arrived, he would be there, shooting the puck against the side of the school building, asking them, "What took you so long?" I believe he knew that heavy labor and running was his natural fitness program and would enhance his hockey career.

While Gordie was big and strong, he wasn't indestructible. One Friday afternoon in early March near the end of the regular season, I had just come out of surgery when I received a call from Colleen saying that Gordie had developed severe back pain. It had been coming on gradually since practice that morning, but by mid-afternoon he was worse. Since Gordie was such a stoic individual, when she called we were immediately concerned. It was not unusual for muscular hockey players to develop severe back spasms. As

In the Wings dressing room (left to right): Dr. Finley, five-year-old Mark Howe, who later became an NHL All-Star, a member of the U.S. Olympic hockey team, and a Hall of Fame defenseman, and Mark's dad, Gordie Howe. (Photo courtesy of RW Photo Gallery)

osteopathic physicians, we often had an opportunity to use our training in manipulative medicine to effectively treat them. I asked her to bring him down to D.O.H. immediately so we could begin treatment right away.

When they arrived, she told me he was in so much pain that they almost stopped at one of the hospitals they passed on the way to get some relief. The Wings had a matinee game against New York the next afternoon at Olympia Stadium, and the Wings and Rangers were competing for the fourth and final Stanley Cup playoff position. Losing Gordie would make that battle much more difficult. We immediately medicated him to control his pain and did the usual evaluating lab and X-ray work. When we found microscopic blood in his urine, the diagnosis that he was passing a ureteral calculus (kidney stone) was easily made. Lucky for Gordie and the Wings, he passed the stone during the night.

We wanted to keep him hospitalized, but by morning he was pain-free, signed himself out of the hospital, and went to the arena. We recommended he not play and advised Coach Abel. He said he would dress Howe but only play him in an emergency. But not only did he play the entire game, he scored the winning goal for Detroit late in the third period.

During the years that the Howe children and our family were growing up, we lived in adjacent suburban communities. We flooded a 30' x 50' skating rink in our backyard. Gordie would occasionally stop by and give hockey instruction to our son, Michael, then 5 years old and starting to play Squirt hockey. Wearing his buckle overshoes, the Big Guy would go on the ice and pass the puck back and forth to Mike and his friends. I remember hearing him tell Mike, "If anyone bumps you too hard, just rap the back of his calf with your stick blade, just above the top of the boot, to teach him respect."

Mike and the Howes' youngest son, Murray, both played on the same team for a few years. Several other players' sons played briefly on the club, as well. While playing a game in Port Colborne along the Welland Canal, near Fort Erie, Ontario. Everyone except Murray was waiting on the bus to return to the Welland Hotel. Murray was still at the arena signing autographs as Gordie's son. He was a bright youngster with an infectious smile, just trying to mimic his father and satisfying Gordie's fans. They also attended Gordie's hockey school in Port Huron together. Mike billeted with Ted Lindsay's sister whose home was only a few blocks from the McMorran Arena.

Colleen and daughter Cathy would often accompany the kids' team with the rest of the parents. The hockey parents were very close in those days, traveling with their teams, attending the games, and having parties together during and after the season.

As the boys grew older, Colleen helped organize the first junior

The Finley's backyard skating rink in 1965. From left to right: daughters Mary, Maureen, and Bridgit (holding on to the chair), and son Michael. (Photo courtesy of the Finleys)

hockey team—the Detroit Junior Red Wings—playing out of Olympia Stadium. They were a Junior B level team and members of the Ontario Amateur Hockey Association that included teams in Windsor, Dresden, Wallaceburg, Amherstburg, and Chatham. One of Bill Dineen's sons, Kevin, played for a year or two in the Detroit junior program and stayed with the Howes.

Unlike the average hockey wife of that era, Colleen was very much involved and she always felt that the Wings ownership never gave Gordie the respect or the salary he deserved. That attitude was commonplace throughout the NHL. Management considered Colleen an interfering wife. There would always be innuendos from the owner and his staff at Olympia about her aggressive nature. Her constant complaint was that her husband was not receiving fair treatment.

Under Jack Adams, Gordie would represent the Wings at father-son banquets and service clubs as a shy, self-conscious person. He would save the very small honorarium he received until the holidays and give it to his mother at Christmas to buy something special for herself. She, however, always took that money and bought things for his sisters rather than herself. After a couple of years, he would present it to her during the summer, so he could make sure she got something for herself. Later, Colleen took charge of the arrangements for his personal appearances, saw that he was appropriately compensated, and in effect assumed the role of Gordie's agent. She secured an endorsement contract for Gordie with Eaton's of Canada for $10,000, which was considered a milestone signing for him.

Also, having learned what other players were making, Colleen went to work getting Gordie the salary he deserved. It was widely assumed he was the highest-paid Red Wing, but when told by Bob Baun, who had by then become a Red Wing, that he was not, Gordie found it easy to let Colleen step in and negotiate for him. When management was forced into giving Gordie the salary he deserved and signed him for $100,000, Bruce Norris said publicly that he hoped the new deal "would make Colleen happy." Gordie resented those words, responding, "Colleen isn't on the ice, I am."

Gordie chose to retire at the end of the 1970–71 season after 25 years with the Wings. At the time only "Dit" Clapper of the Boston Bruins had a hockey career that lasted that long. Gordie had been promised a position with the Wings as an adviser and a sort of goodwill ambassador. But his next two years were the epitome of frustration. He would go to practice, but his techniques and those of the coaches differed, so he abandoned trying to help out there. After Ned Harkness arrived, when Johnny Wilson was coach, Gordie was requested (he interpreted it as being forbidden) not to attend practice or enter the dressing room to avoid his detracting from the instructions of the coach and management. In other words, Gordie Howe

Above, Gordie Howe chats with his son, Murray (in hockey school jersey), and Mike Finley (2) on the bench when the youngsters attended the Gordie Howe Hockey School in 1970 in Port Huron. Inset, the boys all grown up in 1989. From left to right: Gordie, Dr. Michael Finley, Dr. Murray Howe, and the author. (Photo courtesy of the Finleys)

had a job, but no job description. With no specific duties, he likened it to what he called, "The mushroom treatment. They would keep you in the dark and then once in a while come in and throw a little manure on you."

Meantime, his sons continued to practice their hockey skills in summer, shooting on net in the driveway of their Lathrup Village home for hours. Gordie and Colleen were very fortunate to have a dependable young man, Dave Agius, available to take the boys to their hockey obligations. Dave later joined Little Caesars as an administrative assistant to Marian Ilitch.

Soon the Howe boys were playing on Junior A teams in Canada, learning from outstanding competition. Mark, then 17 and Marty, 18, were playing on an advanced junior team, the Toronto Marlboros. Mark had been selected to the 1972 USA Olympic team. Both were considered excellent potential for the NHL Draft. The rules at the time opposed drafting under-aged players. However, the WHA had no such regulation. In fact, the upstart league appeared to enjoy stealing signature players (Bobby Hull, Dave Keon, Frank Mahovlich, Vaclav Nedomansky, and others, as well as top prospect junior players (Wayne Gretzky, Mark Howe) before they became available under NHL rules. Doug Harvey was an assistant coach and scout for the WHA's Houston Aeros.

He contacted Gordie to let him know that Houston was going to pick Mark as their No. 1 draft choice. When the NHL and Wings got wind of Houston's plans, Gordie was immediately contacted by NHL President Clarence Campbell to try to dissuade him from permitting Mark to be drafted by the WHA team at such a young age. Campbell urged Gordie to have loyalty toward the league that had made him famous. Bruce Norris tried to make amends by creating a bona fide position for him in the front office, but Gordie, having been personally hurt by his retirement treatment and the unkind way Colleen was treated, chose to allow the boys to make their own decisions.

I was surprised because during all the years we were close friends, Gordie always stressed to me how important it was to get a higher education and complete it. Their youngest son, Murray, went into medicine and became a radiologist, practicing in Toledo. Marty was chosen 12th by Houston in the same draft. The Howes always had a close relationship with Houston coach Bill Dineen from his playing days in Detroit in the mid-1950s to later days when one of Bill's sons played junior hockey in Detroit. After the draft Gordie was talking with Bill about the boys playing in Houston, and—half serious and half kidding—asked Bill what he thought of the prospect of having three Howes in Houston's lineup. It was a surprise to Bill since he was aware of the pain and stiffness in Gordie's wrist. Gordie had suffered for some time with a very painful recurrent traumatic wrist injury that the eminent University of Michigan orthopedic and sports medicine surgeon, Robert Wayne Bailey, M.D., had surgically operated on and provided some relief. Gordie also had issues with his knees that would prevent any other retired player from returning to play.

However, having secretly considered playing with his sons for years, the opportunity was too good to pass up. As it did for Red Berenson and many others, the WHA gave new life to Gordie, particularly after the depressing atmosphere he had been subjected to in Detroit. This gave the WHA a marvelous public relations subject to attract fans as well as press, radio, and TV interest. When asked about the most important game of his phenomenal career, Gordie quickly acknowledged that the first game he shared the ice with his sons was the best and proudest moment of all.

The rest is history. Mark went on to enjoy a stellar career in the WHA and later in the NHL with Hartford, Philadelphia, and the Red Wings. Marty was sent down to Springfield, Hartford's AHL affiliate, where he broke his wrist. Gordie always regretted that the Hartford management never permitted Marty to play one game with him in the NHL.

In his later years, Gordie became a recurring problem for opposing coaches—psyching up their players to treat Gordie as an equal rather than a living legend—especially since they had grown up worshipping him as the exceptional hockey player he had always been. It's interesting to note that Gordie won the scoring title at age 35. In four seasons he had 100 or more penalty minutes. At age 51, the Big Guy played in all 80 games and scored 15 goals. I smile when I think that when players retire from the NHL, they seem to do so for one of three reasons: they are too banged up to continue playing the game; their skills have eroded to the point that they can't keep up with the level of competition of the other players in the league; or they lose their passion for the game.

Not so for Gordie Howe.

Genevieve's Memories of Colleen and Gordie

When I think of this remarkable couple, I always smile as I am fortunate enough to have many happy memories of the personal rather than public side of their lives. I met Colleen in 1957, when Helen Adams, the wife of the Red Wings' general manager, sent me a beautiful hand-lettered invitation to a luncheon at the Women's City Club in downtown Detroit to "Meet the New Coach's Wife, Gloria Abel." This was especially exciting because I had just arrived following our honeymoon, and other than my husband, I knew no one.

We all wore suits, hats, and gloves in those days, and as I slid into my chair the stunning blonde next to me grinned ear to ear. We were both wearing the same suit—she in blue, I in brown, and we each had made it from the same Vogue pattern. To this day, I remember how comfortable Colleen Howe made me feel. She graciously introduced me to all the wives, and it was a great beginning to a treasured friendship. She knew I was the new wife of one of the team physicians and never flinched when I asked her, "What does your husband do?" She just smiled and said, "Oh, he plays hockey." Even after all these years, Gordie occasionally will kid me by asking, "What does your husband do?"

Colleen was so creative and a very accomplished dressmaker. We would make girls' dresses for the annual Ruth Alden dress drive, and she taught me how to do the very difficult English hand-smocking details. We made hats and craft projects together and went to arts-and-crafts shows. Every year we would exchange a Christmas creation. To this day, I hang ornaments we made from photos of our children, sparkling tuna cans, and a lot of tinsel-trimmed treasures as ours is a Memory Tree with mostly hand-made decorations.

The only time I ever remember Gordie saying anything about our projects was when he opened the garage in Lathrup Village with his remote door opener and he was furious. The whole garage was covered with a mist of gold paint. Aerosol cans were the rage, and we had dozens of wreaths made from macaroni glistening all over. Because it was cold, we had decided this was an inside project.

As years passed, we saw each other socially more than on a one-on-one basis. Our six children kept us busy, and we had moved farther apart as our housing needs expanded with our family. The hockey wives did not have their own private room in which to gather as they do today, so we settled for hugs in the hallway after the games. We did go annually to the youth hostels ski movie on Thanksgiving Eve at the Ford Auditorium and tried to get to our favorite Clam Shop restaurant for baked lobster as often as possible. One year they joined us at my parents' home in the Finger Lakes region of upstate New York. They loved Skaneateles Lake, and we had a great time. Gordie, Jack, my father-in-law, and one of his best friends played golf at the Onondaga Country Club in Syracuse, and Gordie said how nice it was to play uninterrupted and unknown.

The Howes were a fabulous couple, devoted, talented, great parents and role models. Our lives and our family were richer for having known them, and we were honored to have them for dear friends

—GKF

CHAPTER 10

Old Scarface

"TERRIBLE TED" HAD A FACE ONLY A HOCKEY MOM COULD LOVE.
Ted Lindsay was a true friend through the years, particularly after his sad and unfair dismissal from the Detroit hockey club. Ted sponsored me and our family as members of the Birmingham Athletic Club. He was a sincerely warm individual, a medical patient through all the years, and he was our hospital system graduation speaker, telling our graduates of the need to fight hard—as he did—to be successful in all our areas of their medical endeavors.

I have many fond memories of the grace, respect, and special effort he took with all those close to him, especially his wives. His first wife, Pat, the mother of their three children, was always treated with dignity, respect, and admiration deserving of a player's wife. His second wife, Linda, had two sons who were given the type of guidance they needed through those difficult teenage years. Ted was a compassionate and considerate husband. I always marveled at how devoted and care-giving Ted was through the years of her devastating illness. When his present wife, Joanne, came along, she gave our beloved "Terrible Ted" the remarkable love and attention that a man of his stature and responsibility deserved. She's been more than a companion and loving wife; she's been his soul mate.

As a player, our friend was incomparable. No other hockey player I know of had a career like Ted Lindsay. The youngest of 13 children, the son of an NHL goaltender, Ted was of relatively short (5'9") stature, but he possessed the love and enthusiasm for the game that only NHL players can appreciate. He was fanatically tough and was considered one of the most

Dr. Finley and Ted Lindsay (right) in 1997. (Photo courtesy of the Finleys)

rugged men to have ever played in the NHL. He was often described as similar in sentiment and demeanor to a pit bull but with the talent and ability that completes the picture of a player who consistently gave the fans an unexpected thrill each time he stepped on the ice. Neither he nor opposing players or coaches knew what subtle, sometimes not-so-subtle maneuver he was going to do next. His ability to react to unexpected situations was legendary. He appeared to have little regard for protecting his own body.

Ted often told me that when he knew there was going to be a confrontation, the best way to handle it was to get in the first blow, taking advantage of the surprise and distraction it created to give him the puissance to be on equal terms with anyone. His behavior and style confounded nearly everyone he had to answer to, especially Red Wings GM Jack Adams and NHL President Clarence Campbell. He exuded an aura of self-confidence, arrogance, and disrespect that tested their patience and their ability to manage or control him.

Ted grew up in Kirkland Lake, Ontario, a gold-mining town just a few miles west of the Quebec border. Consequently, he was fluent in both English and French. According to Ted, when Canada was part of the British Empire, the Empire's largest gold mine was in Kirkland Lake. It finally closed after being mined out in the early 1970s. He described it as a wonderful place to grow up. Athletics were a big part of their lives, especially winter sports. The town boasted two outdoor ice rinks, one for pleasure skating and the other for hockey. There was always a game going on. If 20 people showed up, there were 10 on each side; if 10 were there, the teams were five apiece.

There is a great story about how Ted became Wings' property. He played junior hockey for St. Michael's College School in Toronto. It was always presumed that he would automatically take the next step and become a member of the Maple Leafs. In those days, the Original Six teams had what was called a negotiation list where they could list the 25 juniors (18-year-olds) they had the privilege of signing, and no other club could offer those juniors a contract. Ted was playing for St. Mike's in Hamilton and sustained a laceration of the back of his leg. The beloved chief scout of the Wings, Carson Cooper, who was part of the original Detroit team purchased from Vancouver, came by and told Ted he would like to put his name on the Red Wings' negotiation list.

About a week later, someone from Toronto did, too, but with Ted out, the Leafs put the wrong name in and they missed getting Ted. This was in the early 1940s. Frank Selke was general manager in Toronto at the time since Conn Smythe was in Europe with the Canadian armed forces. When Smythe came back, Selke had moved on to Montreal and Ted was a Red Wing.

Ted first came to training camp near the end of World War II. Most of the senior players still had wartime jobs. Because equipment was scarce, when the first group finished playing the next group up had to put on much of the same cold, wet, cotton-and-leather equipment that likely weighed 10 pounds or more than it did when fresh and dry. Although offered a pro contract, Ted still had a year of junior eligibility left, so he went back to St. Mike's, knowing it would guarantee him a great deal of playing time rather than warming the end of the bench and not playing in Detroit. Adams wanted Ted, so he promised him he would get a regular shift, signed him for two years, which was uncommon in those days, and even gave him a signing bonus.

In his rookie year, everything came together for Ted. He found his scoring touch with linemates who could compliment his ability. He scored 17 goals his first year. By this time, the war was over and Conn Smythe was back. To Smythe's surprise, when the Leafs went to sign Ted, he had already been picked up by Detroit and the Toronto club realized it had put the wrong name in, losing the opportunity to get him. Ted is forever grateful since he was with the Wings when they became an exceptional team—and Ted was a major part of that remarkable club.

In the following years, every time Ted scored a particularly picturesque goal while playing in Maple Leaf Gardens, he would point with his gloved hand in an acknowledgement to where Smythe was sitting in the stands. Since Smythe was a person easy to dislike, it made his actions that much more fun for Ted. Also it added fuel to the fire of hatred between Smythe and Adams. Both men loved tough talented players. But Jack Adams got there first. Years later, Smythe returned the favor by stealing widely heralded Frank Mahovlich from the Wings after Frank's father had given Wings scout Johnny Mitchell assurances that his son would sign with Detroit. St. Mike's was Toronto's sponsored junior club. With the encouragement of St. Mike's athletic director, Father Ted Flanagan, the opportunity to be in a Catholic school environment sold the Mahovliches, a devout Catholic family, on the Maple Leafs' affiliate.

For much of his career as a Red Wing, one of Ted's primary responsibilities as a left winger was to check Montreal right winger Maurice "The Rocket" Richard. One evening, with his usual ruggedness, Lindsay pestered Richard all night, and it ended in a short encounter that was considered a draw. Although not considered a great fighter, Lindsay carefully selected his moments, usually when both the opponents and the fans were ready. His most significant fight was against the Boston Bruins' celebrated tough guy,

Bill Ezinicki. In the 1950s, Boston was well known as an extremely rugged team. Every game at the Boston Garden frequently led to a donnybrook.

Both Lindsay and Ezinicki were near the top of the league in penalty minutes. Each had opposed one another during their junior hockey years, and both men had long, vivid memories. Their bitter rivalry continued into the NHL. Finally, on January 25, 1951, in Olympia Stadium in Detroit, they went through a series of elbow checks and unrelenting cheap shots that led to the fight of the year. Ezinicki speared Lindsay in the face, and Ted responded by carving Ezinicki vertically from hairline to eyebrow, and the bloody fight was on. As they started to skate away, Bill saw Ted with his back to him and tried to catch him by surprise. Ted realized Bill was coming, spun around, and nailed him flush on the jaw. Bill was knocked out before he reached the ice.

Unaware, Ted jumped on him, continuing the battle until he realized Eznicki was unconscious. Both men were given major penalties and thrown out of the game. After he showered, Ted came out of the Red Wings' dressing room and looked in the medical room, where the doctors were repairing Eznicki. Ted quickly realized it was the wrong thing to do. Bill saw him and said, "I'll get you, you SOB." The battles continued for some time after that, but they had to be much more subtle since they were marked men as far as the referees were concerned. Both players were fined $300 for that incident, a tidy sum in those days.

While I was a resident in surgery at D.O.H., during a game at Olympia, Ted crosschecked Boston Bruin Jerry Toppazini across the face, fracturing Topper's nose and facial bones. He was immediately brought to the hospital where facial plastic surgeons Lloyd Seyfried, D.O., and his wife, Helen, did a miraculous repair on him. Topper was hospitalized about 10 days. During that time, everyone at the hospital became his fan because he would make rounds on all the pediatric patients there, helping to encourage the youngsters to get well. Even though he had big bulky dressings over his face, the kids all felt he was a big lovable guy and looked forward to his visit each day.

Our games in Toronto were always particularly hard-fought. In 1956, before Game 3 of the Stanley Cup semifinal match against the Maple Leafs, one of the Toronto newspapers received an anonymous phone call. The caller stated he would shoot Lindsay or Howe if either one stepped on the ice. In the dressing room, someone suggested that Cummy Burton wear alternately No. 7 and No. 9 in case the caller was serious. (Burton, coincidentally, was the nephew of Red Wings great Larry Aurie, the last player to wear the No. 6 for Detroit.) Everyone in the room thought it was a good idea except Cummy. Both Ted and Gordie played and combined for three goals, and the Wings won the game 5–4.

To show his cockiness, Ted flaunted their victory and insulted the caller by tucking the blade of his stick under his arm and pointing the shaft at the crowd like a rifle, creating the appearance of systematically circumferentially shooting at the crowd. That was typical of his irreverence toward the Toronto fans. After the game, Gordie said, "If someone set off a firecracker, they would have dug foxholes in the ice." It was one of the great moments in the lore of the Red Wings. A statue of the incident was created and donated by Ted as a memento at one of his Autism Foundation golf outings.

Ted, Gordie, and Sid Abel made up one of the most impressive lines in hockey—the "Production Line," of the late 1940s and early '50s. They were not only highly talented but were also very creative. They used to practice for hours, timing a play in which Gordie on right wing would shoot the puck in against the left corner boards as Ted was taking off from left wing blue line, then with Teddy retrieving the puck as it rebounded off the boards, fire an explosive wrist shot on net against an ill-prepared goaltender. Sid would drive to the front of the net to finish the play by scooping up any rebound and firing it into the net. The three of them ended up 1–2–3 in scoring in the NHL in 1949–50, an unheard of and never-since-repeated event.

For such a battler on the ice, Ted was a perfect gentleman off it. His interest in developing a players' association caused serious friction with management and resulted in his shocking trade to Chicago in 1957 along with Glenn Hall. Ted returned to the Wings for the 1964–65 season and, as has always been one of his signature traits, served as a mentor to Bruce MacGregor, who played almost 11 seasons with the Wings, two seasons in the WHA, and more than three with the New York Rangers before returning home to serve the NHL in the front office of the Edmonton Oilers.

Ted's father, Bert Lindsay, was an NHL goaltender who played for the Montreal Wanderers in 1917–18 and for Toronto the following year. I was told a story that Ted had not heard by Montreal General surgeon Dr. Rae Brown, who was well known for his extensive expertise in sports hernia repairs. His father was a contemporary of Ted's father. Both worked in the mines in Kirkland Lake. During their noon break from the mines, as the story goes, Ted's father would take shots from other hockey-playing miners, who would shoot chunks of coal at him. Simulating the style of a goalkeeper, Ted's dad would deflect them with a coal shovel. He played his last game in the NHL six years before Ted was born.

Ted was constantly in trouble with the league office because of events on the ice that resulted in fines and suspensions. He spent a lot of time in Red Wings coach and GM Jack Adams' dog house, too. "Terrible Ted" took on the hockey establishment in the 1950s. Although Adams admired Ted's playing toughness and skill, he privately suspected him of being disloyal because of his involvement in attempting to establish an NHL players' union, which the owners and management vigorously opposed. That's why Ted was traded to Chicago.

Although Ted and I had a casual relationship from his more-frequent-than-average visits to the hospital for emergency X-rays and repairs, I got to know him well when he returned to Detroit in 1964 and have served ever since as his personal physician. Since his retirement, Ted has unselfishly aided a great many charities and volunteer groups to raise money for their individual causes. He also established the Ted Lindsay Foundation, and one of its principal goals is finding the cause, treatment, and cure of autism. It is my honor to serve on its board.

Ted was a feisty, hard-nosed hockey player with just enough meanness to make him known throughout the league as one to be aware of when he was on the ice, someone who fought tooth-and-nail for everything he attained in the game. To him, being tough was going in the corners without phoning ahead to see who's there—as Lindsay was described in Glenn Liebman's book of hockey one-liners. And when discussing the many stitches he took, Marty Pavelich, Ted's former business partner, always said, "You cut him for five, he would cut you for 10." How? The hockey stick, Lindsay always said, is "a great equalizer."

He wasn't shy about using his stick as a weapon and, looking at his face, it's easy to see the evidence that his opponents used their sticks as a weapon on him. He had his share of injuries, including a broken shoulder, a broken instep, a broken hand, and several hundred stitches in his face. Ted was interviewed on a video played on the scoreboard before a game at Joe Louis Arena when the Wings celebrated my 40th year with the team, and with a broad smile on his face he explained how he was responsible for much of my surgical success. "I donated my body," he said.

In 2003, Detroiter Michael Ray, a filmmaker of mostly family documentaries, made a film called *The Road to Hockeytown*, in which he used archival footage from the 1940s and '50s as well as interviews from NHL Hall of Fame greats Jean Beliveau, Andy Bathgate, Ted Kennedy, and referee Red Storey to help tell Ted's story. At the time he retired, Ted held the record for the most goals scored by a left-winger and the most penalty minutes by anyone who ever played in the NHL.

On the personal side, I have a great admiration for his love and respect for his family. When Ted was nominated and elected to the NHL Hockey Hall of Fame in 1966, he refused to attend the Hall of Fame dinner, which was a stag affair. He stated that he appreciated the honor, but unless his wife and family, who had been so supportive during his career, were allowed to be there and to share his honor, he would not be there, either. The next year the entire affair was changed. The Hall of Fame committee quickly acquiesced, allowing female guests to attend.

During the 2008 Stanley Cup Finals in Detroit, the NHL continued a custom it had begun a few years before in Montreal, hosting a dinner for the living legends of the Wings Stanley Cup champions from the 1950s. The evening between the first and second games in the finals featured a dinner that Ted, Gordie Howe, Marty Pavelich, Red Kelly, Marcel Pronovost, and Alex Delvecchio attended. Iron-man Johnny Wilson was also due to be there, but he was suffering from a reaction from chemotherapy, and his doctor kept him in the hospital.

Each player was presented with an 18" Stanley Cup replica by NHL Commissioner Gary Bettman, who told the more than 200 people in the audience that it was Ted who is credited with the tradition of the winning team's captain hoisting the Cup over his head and skating around the arena for all the fans to enjoy. It happens after the winning team's captain is presented with the Cup from the president or commissioner of the NHL and skates around the rink with the Cup raised high overhead. Actually, Ted said, he didn't really hoist it up over his head, but rather picked it up and carried it around the arena to give the fans a chance to see it up-close through the protective wire fencing. Ted felt it wasn't the owners who were paying his salary, it was the fans, and they deserved the honor of seeing the Stanley Cup.

Making it even more poignant, the arenas of the late 1940s and early 1950s didn't have protective glass surrounding the ice and allowed the players and fans the opportunity to communicate directly through the wire-mesh fencing. Ted was captain from 1953–55, the seasons that the tradition began. The Cup presentation tradition prior to that time was made at center ice with the trophy sitting on a table there, and the only parade was the players carrying it into the dressing room, where they filled it with champagne and drank from it.

The recognition of all of Ted's contributions was culminated both during and after his 17 years in the NHL by the renaming of the Lester B. Pearson Award. Ted, along with Doug Harvey and others, sowed the early seeds of the NHLPA. During the many years following his retirement,

The Ted Lindsay Award shows the undying respect that the NHL Players Association has for all the efforts Ted has made on behalf of the players throughout his career. Shown here in 2010, the author stands alongside the trophy that goes to the best player each year—by vote of his peers. (Photo courtesy of the Ted Lindsay Foundation)

Ted took great pride in his hockey career, and as Detroiters he and Marty Pavelich built their own company, serving the automobile industry in a city both came to love. Ted continues to serve as a manufacturers' rep of Gil-Mar Manufacturing of Canton. He is also ever-present with his daily workouts and visible prominence throughout the region.

In addition to his many contributions to local and national organizations, Ted has put both his name and exhaustive effort into the Ted Lindsay Foundation for Autism. Autism is a complex neurodevelopment disorder characterized in children principally by impaired social interaction. With family members and his good friend, physical therapist John Czarnecki, Lindsay hosts a major annual golf outing and other fundraising efforts for the benefit of autism research.

CHAPTER 11

"Everything but Guts"

THE JACK ADAMS ERA AND THE ROOTS OF "HOCKEYTOWN."
The most interesting person I knew in the Original Six era was Mr. Jack Adams. An icon who enjoyed a persona that lived up to his name and position, he always wore a bow tie and usually a fedora. Jack had the appearance of a real hockey person, having spent all his life around the game. His early years were spent in Fort William, Ontario, now called Thunder Bay, playing on local teams, some on outdoor ice surfaces during a period when the teams were seven-man rosters that included a positional player called a rover. (Many years later, some experts said defenseman Bobby Orr's style of play approximated that of a rover.) Mr. Adams was a very complex person, dedicated to loyalty, duty, and compassion, all for the game of professional hockey and for the owners who kept the game going during the difficult years through the Great Depression followed by World War II.

Jack had a very interesting style in the way he ran things. The dressing room was Spartan—open benches and hooks for the players to hang their clothes and to drape their wet uniforms and long underwear to dry after a game. Above the doorway exiting to the corridor, which led to the ice area was a 3' x 4' sign in giant letters that said, "WE SUPPLY EVERYTHING BUT GUTS," reinforcing the toughness he demanded of his players. From there, the players crossed a common arena corridor the spectators used down a narrow aisle between the stands to the player's bench and the ice surface. The protection above the boards was heavy chicken-wire fencing.

Jack Adams' original 1914 YMCA team picture from Fort Williams, Ontario. Adams is sitting all the way to the left in the front row.
(Photo courtesy of Jack Adams)

Behind the players' benches, there was no protection from the fans sitting there, nor any partition to escape their wrath and jeers.

The three rows behind the Red Wings' bench were all Jack's seats filled with people friendly to the team and not likely to be hostile. They typically included the team doctor, his wife, and guests; the team dentist, wife, and guests; former 1930s Wings goaltender John Ross Roach, and his wife; president of the Ontario Amateur Hockey Association Lloyd Pollock and his wife; Dick Smith, the head of the stadium ushers; and Coach Jimmy Skinner's family and other personal friends, including the captain of the police detail.

Gordie Howe (9) in a discussion with Coach Sid Abel on November 10, 1963, the night Howe scored his record-breaking goal. The scene reveals the control GM Jack Adams exerted on his team with the way he dispersed his tickets behind the Detroit bench. Directly behind the players are Joe Falls (left, in glasses), then a sports columnist with the Detroit Free Press, and Dick Smith, who was in charge of Olympia ushers. Between them in the row behind is my wife, Genevieve, with Dorothy Fetzer and Dr. J. Donald Sheets, and to his left, Dr. John Fetzer. The author is to Fetzer's left. Behind is Pete Marudas and Wings assistant trainer Danny Olesevich. Behind Genevieve are Gloria Abel's brother, Pete Tomei, and his son. (Photo courtesy of the Detroit News)

Jack and his wife, Helen, sat in the box just above those three rows with their guests for the game, often a celebrity of the time including various TV stars, heavyweight boxing champion Ingemar Johansson, and Detroit baseball stars John McHale, Billy Pierce, and many others. Stadium manager Nick Londes and his family and guests frequently used that box. In later years, as management changed, Olympia Stadium manager and Red Wings vice president Lincoln Cavalieri and his wife, Margaret, and their guests sat there. While Jack was GM, Helen Adams was there with a beautiful corsage given to her by Highland Park florist Walter Schulster. He had the shrillest whistle and raspiest voice and often would berate the referees if they made a decision unfriendly to Detroit. Helen was always a lady, never revealing her feelings toward the game regardless of how it was going.

At that time, all of the Original Six clubs sponsored junior amateur teams in order to develop players for their major NHL team. Our junior teams were in Hamilton, Ontario, coached by former Red Wings defenseman Eddie Bush, and in Edmonton, Alberta, by Bud Poile, a forward with the Wings in the late 1940s, plus minor professional teams in Omaha and Indianapolis, where the Norris' owned the arenas. Most of these cities were reached by the train networks that ran all night. Jack Adams added to his intimidation over the players he controlled by having train tickets sticking out of the breast pocket. If a player played poorly one evening, he was presented with a ticket on the midnight train to Indiana or Nebraska. Not even being able to go home to pack his clothes since he was expected to show up for practice in the minor league facility the next day and play in their game that evening. That reputation was well known and guaranteed that Adams got the best performance out of each player every game.

Jack and Helen had no children, so hockey was their entire life, and the players were their family. He would often come in and lecture to the team between periods and vent his frustration. If players did not play in the style that was prevalent at that time, Jack would come in after a game and make them practice until they did. Sometimes after a poor game, he would wait until the crowd left and assembled the team on the ice for a full practice. At the time, we had a young right winger, Billy McNeill, who had come up through the Edmonton Oil Kings. Billy, in Jack's opinion, would wander all over the ice, very much like the players of today, rather than staying on his wing to closely guard his check, the opposing winger. One day at practice, Jack placed a line of sticks the entire length of the right side of the ice and made Billy practice that day for hours without crossing over those sticks.

Training camp each year was held in Sault Ste Marie, Michigan. Many of the players in camp had little or no chance to make the club or even sign on with one of the farm teams. Jack was always interested in looking over the raw youngsters and keeping the best of them. He always gave those in camp a chance to play alongside bona-fide NHL players so when they went home they would tell everyone how great the Wings were and how well they were treated.

Camp ended with a showcasing road trip west, going through many small towns in Canada. Part of the purpose was to drop off a player or two from the training-camp roster to stay in that community and play in their typically remote venue all winter. Many of the players were under stress, worrying about getting dropped off. Most of their contracts were by handshake rather than the printed, guaranteed variety, since the players felt privileged to have an opportunity to play the game they loved on a major level. One story the players told about was how Howie Young ran out of money on one of those trips and went up and knocked on Jack's door, asking for an advance in order to have a beer with the guys in a local bar. Incredibly, Howie got it, and nothing further was said about it.

Meeting the Press

Jack was a favorite with the media, always outspoken, always controversial. His No. 1 objective was to promote the team and contribute to the progressive advancement of the game in the U.S. He was an expert at managing the press. The hockey writers always knew they were going to get a good story from Jack and loved to listen to him talk about the sport. Since many of them knew very little about what he used to call "an alien Canadian game." In addition to courting the press, he always took time to sell the game to luncheon and dinner groups. In fact, he would have a summer press trip through Michigan sponsored by one of the club's major advertisers, taking along a couple of the more prominent players on the tour to get more exposure for the team since most of the games were carried throughout the state on radio. During the playoffs, he would take the press and anyone from staff, team doctors included, to a prominent restaurant in the playoff city. In Boston it was Locke-Ober and in Chicago it was a popular State Street restaurant next to the Chicago Theater where Jack had once seen Al Capone. The stories flowed fast and furious during those dinners.

One of Jack's favorite stories was about "the year the Wings went to prison." It all started when he was on his regular summer promotional public relations tour. The Strohs Brewing Company sponsored the trip, and Ted Lindsay was the featured player that year. One of the planned stops was at the maximum-security prison in Marquette in the Upper Peninsula of Michigan. While there, the team was approached by two murderers of the infamous Purple Gang—who also happened to be Red Wings fans. They suggested to Jack that he bring up the team for a scrimmage game. Knowing they had neither a rink nor a team, Adams quickly agreed.

But to his surprise, the warden also agreed. They had no idea where they would find the money to build a rink and field a team. The warden took the first step by hiring a member of that year's NCAA champion University of Michigan hockey team to build a rink. A regulation-sized rink with boards was built, and a team was chosen from selected inmates with equipment donated by the Wings from their recently disbanded Omaha Knights farm team. The cost of the trip to Marquette was funded by the semipro Marquette team, the Sentinels, on the condition that if the Wings agreed to play them after the prison game, the Sentinels would fund the cost, which they did. The Wings quickly made the score 18–0, then they split up and played half Wings and half Marquette prison inmates.

The inmate's goaltender (who I believe was serving a sentence for murder) threatened to kill anyone who scored on him. Well, Gordie Howe had a surprise for him. Howe hammered a nail through the end of the blade of his stick in such a way that nobody could see it. He then stick handled around the rink as though the puck was magnetized to his stick. When he got in front of the net, he deked the goaltender and flipped the puck off the nail on his stick and into the net over the exasperated goalie. Howe, of course, lived to tell that story—but not with the gusto Adams did.

Interestingly, while playing at the prison, one of the inmates in the audience called out to Marty Pavelich, whom the player recognized as a former mailman from his hometown in nearby Sault St. Marie, Ontario. After the game, each Detroit player received a handmade wallet with the Red Wings logo on it. The first time I visited Gordie at his home, I admired his many trophies and awards. One was a handmade sailboat with a red sail and a white Red Wings insignia on it. Gordie said one of the inmates made it and gave it to him. The trophy awarded at the end of the game was the "Honey Bucket Trophy," a container the convicts used as a toilet. It was their version of the NHL's Stanley Cup, which was won by the Wings a few months after their trip to prison. All in all it was quite a day—and quite a story.

Another story came from Johnny Wilson, told at an Alumni meeting during the 2004 playoffs. Some of the alums were critical of the goaltenders who they thought had allowed a few goals they shouldn't.

"You should all remember what Jack said about that," Johnny reminded them. "The trouble always begins up front with the forwards not forechecking and then the defensemen not doing their jobs. So don't blame the goaltenders."

The End of an Era

The following year, 1961–62, the Wings finished fifth in the six-team league and out of the playoffs. Owner Bruce Norris came to Detroit and summarily "retired" Jack Adams. It came as a complete surprise to everyone, but dissatisfaction with the trades made, players drafted and lack of progress being made by the team prompted Norris to make the change.

Adams was 66 years old and had been in hockey 44 years, 35 with the Wings. Jack had been cautioned by his close friend, neighbor, and personal physician, Dr. Charles Karibo, that he should retire for health reasons, the event wasn't entirely unexpected. He had worked well with "Pops" Norris and Marguerite, who was given the ownership reins of the team after James Norris died in 1953, but the chemistry between Jack and Bruce Norris, once he assumed control, was never very smooth.

Coach Sid Abel and former coach Jimmy Skinner were summoned to the office. Bruce came out and asked Sid if he would like to be general manager and he asked Jimmy to take charge of all amateur and farm teams. Sid was surprised, but he accepted. Jack was disappointed since he had always assumed he would be allowed to pick his replacement, and he had been quietly grooming Bud Poile, the former Red Wing and manager-coach of the Wings' junior team, the Edmonton Oil Kings. It was obvious that Bruce was going to take a more active role in the management of the club. He had a phone installed near the end of the bench close to where we sat—where trainer Lefty Wilson used to stand on an elevated step so he could call down his observations from his box, figuring he had a better view of the action on the ice from up high, than Sid did from ice level.

Often Norris would call down from his skybox and tell Lefty to alert the coach that so-and-so was not playing well and to use someone else instead. That caused no limit of conflict, and when Bill Gadsby was coach, having to answer the phone frequently during the 1968–69 season, he had it pulled out. That may be why, after winning the first two games of the following season, Gadsby was fired, to the surprise of nearly everyone.

Because of the suddenness of the firing of Jack Adams, the local hockey press corps honored Jack by arranging a special testimonial dinner on October 6, 1962, at the Pick Fort Shelby hotel that was attended by the entire press corps as well as most of his many friends in hockey and around Michigan. Detroit Mayor Jerome Cavanagh and Dearborn Mayor Orville Hubbard declared it Jack Adams Day in their cities, and more than 400 attended the banquet.

A new award for the outstanding hockey player in the Detroit Recreation League was named after Jack Adams. Former owner of the Cleveland Barons, millionaire Al Sutphin, and King Clancy from the Maple Leafs were the principal speakers. Clancy had known Jack as a player and spoke of his intense desire to win and his toughness, saying that if Adams didn't get you with his body, he'd get you with his stick. Sutphin had great fun putting him on with many stories of his long relationship with Jack, suggesting that Jack always sent him players long after they were over the hill—and made him pay twice their worth.

A month or so later, the NHL held a banquet in Jack's honor at Detroit's prestigious Sheraton-Cadillac Hotel with NHL President Clarence Campbell and 14 members of the NHL Hall of Fame in attendance. Jack was presented with a gold pass to all NHL arenas and a gold replica of the Stanley Cup engraved with the many records he had attained. When he spoke, he laughingly said he would have the last word in an NHL event.

A year later, the NHL made Jack president of the Central Professional Hockey League, which replaced the former Eastern Hockey League. He had the able assistance of Matt Dennis, a close friend and longtime hockey reporter for the *Windsor Star* newspaper. Underwritten by the NHL, the league served as a training ground to develop young hockey players for the NHL. Their playoff championship trophy was named after Jack.

I had the distinct pleasure of attending both of those dinners. They were like a Who's Who of sports, political, and national notables. It was amazing to see how many people respected Jack and the game of hockey. Attendees included many who had held grudges and hated one another during their many battles on the ice and in the hockey boardrooms, but they came to pay homage to Jack Adams for all he had accomplished during his long career. Especially notable were the comments of his arch-enemy, Conn Smythe, with whom he had bitterly fought and competed during his entire NHL experience. Smythe said Jack Adams made Detroit "a great hockey town" when it was more than a slick marketing campaign.

CHAPTER 12

Eclipse Behind the Bench

**TWO DECADES OF "DARKNESS"—
AND THE MEN RESPONSIBLE FOR IT.**

Coaching in any sport at the professional level is one of the most sought-after vocations available and the most difficult to master. Those who are successful have developed the talent of getting the best out of their gifted players. Hockey coaches solve problems, cover up weaknesses, juggle the lines to generate more scoring, and refine the power play so it is sharper.

Like the old cliché goes, "Coaches are hired to be fired." Many have tried it several times with various teams. Putting the proper people on the ice at the right time and getting the match-ups desired is an incredibly tricky business. These days, with players on the ice an average of 45 seconds per shift, it takes a special skill to get them off in a timely manner—and getting the right players back on. The ability to get your best checking line against the opposition provides a coach the best chance of a successful outcome. Recognizing who is going well on a particular night—and more importantly who is not—and being ready to make the changes necessary to cope with the circumstances of the game, separates the very good coaches from the average coaches.

There have been 27 coaches in Detroit Red Wings history. I've worked with 24 of them. Having spent years sitting behind and very close to the bench, listening to the coaches' strategy and to a lesser degree their conversations with the team has given me a unique insight into their approaches to making it successful. Those with incredible recall and the ability to remember innate details about a player, the specifics about a game, their own players, as well as the opposition's are typically the most successful. The best coaches are those who spend a great deal of time planning a practice, making it relevant and interesting, and who work harder than the players not just during practice but before and after.

When a team is not playing up to its expected potential, it is often easier to move the coach than those players causing the problem, hoping another coach with a different style and personality can effect a transformation. In reality, experts generally say, you have to have the horses to make the team successful. As a consequence, we see multiple coaching changes every season. Management and scouting staffs recommend and supply the players, but coaches are responsible for developing and molding them into a cohesive unit, responding to the constant injury problems, overcoming illness, family, and social challenges to keep the team focused.

Jack Adams' playoff style was to take the players away to an often unknown location or at least out of town, usually Toledo (in the Original Six days), busing them back and forth for practices and the games. Even for home games the players were eating, sleeping, and talking hockey all day away from the distractions of their families and non-hockey responsibilities. Their free time involved strategy sessions, bowling, or attending movies.

The team physicians have the rare privilege to understand the intense atmospheres and pressures these special individuals go through. It was my custom to visit the opponents' dressing room before every game, usually after their team went out for warm-up. We would acknowledge their presence and make sure they didn't have any special needs or health problems requiring immediate attention. While in their dressing room, we often overheard comments, concerns, or criticisms that were affecting the team's play—and all that we heard, of course, remained completely private.

Coaching styles differ, and the smartest coaches vary their techniques from player to player. Coaches who make it fun for players, I believe, have the most success. Those coaches whose tactic is to pressure the puck, not allowing any room for the opposing players, are most preferred, especially by those offensive players in great shape.

I'm reminded of the reaction of the great Rocket Richard after assuming the position as Quebec Nordiques coach. It took only two games to convince him that he was, in his words, "not cut out to be a coach." On the other hand, most men who have served in the role of coach in the NHL count that experience among the major achievements of their lives.

But no one said it was easy. Especially the series of men—14 in all—employed by five general managers from 1970–85, a period in which the Wings qualified for the postseason just three times. And no one personified this period, this era of darkness, more than Ned Harkness.

Harkness and his Cornell University hockey team won the NCAA Championship in the 1969–70 season, so who better to run one of the NHL's premier franchises? Or so Bruce Norris thought. Inspired by the growth of interest in college hockey and the remarkable improvements in athletic training throughout the collegiate level, Norris believed Harkness was the perfect candidate to reinvigorate the backsliding Wings. Harkness came to Detroit, bringing with him his college-training method that helped him post a 163–27–2 record and two national titles in seven seasons at Cornell.

Here was a coach far ahead of his time, as far as the NHL was concerned. Ned's first major change was to enlarge the dressing room and develop a dedicated fitness training room, which was state of the art at that time.

Additionally, he brought in Lloyd Percival, director of the Fitness Institute in suburban Toronto, to assist in the training program. Lloyd was deeply involved in using all types of high-energy, health-food supplements and vitamins. Athletic training programs, although strongly developed in colleges, were rare in professional sports, especially in hockey, which lagged way behind the other sports at that time. I believe our program was the first of its kind in the NHL.

After Ned's arrival, our players were given fitness training programs to follow during the summer. Some of our players were taking more than 20 vitamin and mineral supplements a day, feeling they enhanced their endurance and strength. These did not include steroids; this was well before the widespread use of such supplements became popular in the NFL. We were very careful to be sure that neither steroids nor excluded products were being used by our players.

Ned's background also included boxing and lacrosse. He took his national champion lacrosse team to the 1948 London Olympics. Prior to Cornell, he was coach of the Rensselaer Polytechnic Institute (Troy, New York) from 1950–63, which had an outstanding record of 187–90–7 in hockey, and it won the NCAA title. Among his prominent hockey players was goaltender Ken Dryden, who when finished at Cornell quickly started winning Stanley Cups with the Montreal Canadiens.

Another player was a forward and one of Ned's tri-captains. John Hughes is the father of the 2002 woman's figure skating Olympic gold medalist Sarah Hughes, who won in Salt Lake City. John Hughes graduated from Cornell's law school in 1974 and started his own firm in New York in 1976. He remained good friends with Harkness until Ned's death in 2008 at age 89. Ned's general manager, Jim Bishop, also came from a lacrosse background, but their ideas came before the NHL owners were ready to accept them. Bruce Norris had played hockey at Yale, so he was aware of the progress those schools were making in athletic training and fitness programs.

But managing elite NHL players was far different from controlling college scholarship student-athletes. Problems began the first day of training camp. Ned objected to their style of clothes, their hair cuts, and he criticized the veterans who smoked cigars and cursed. He battled everyone during whistle-blowing practices and the games. Initially the general manager when Harkness arrived, Sid Abel stepped aside after three tumultuous months of controversy. In the meantime, the fighting with the players and the press, whose headline "Darkness with Harkness" became something of a mantra among the media and fans, some of whom began wearing paper bags over their heads at games. The final straw was the Wings' disastrous and painful 13–0 defeat in Maple Leaf Gardens in front of the nationwide *Hockey Night in Canada* television audience.

In the first period of that game, Ned was charged with his seventh bench penalty in less than three months as coach. During the ensuing power play, Toronto scored its third goal, and the score was 6–0 by the end of the second period. Unfortunately, Harkness, who worked wonders with collegiate athletes, wasn't able to adapt himself to the tough, hard-nosed NHL workhorses. Ned's prejudice quickly created unrest among the more socially progressive (and long-haired) individuals like Pete Stemkowski and Garry Unger, who were eventually traded after failed attempts by Harkness to get them to conform to his team standards.

Ned's experience as a coach was short-lived because of his inability to adjust his style from collegians to professional NHL players who left him looking down the players' bench yelling, "Can't anyone here play this game for me?" He couldn't get them to respond, and after 38 games Wings owner Bruce Norris realized he had an emergency situation on his hands. The dignity of the Detroit Red Wings had been shattered with their 10th loss in 13 games, entrenching them deeply in the sixth-place basement of their division. Abel, wishing to fire Harkness, asked Wings council John Ziegler if he was authorized to do so.

Failing to get a clear opinion from Ziegler, and with Ned telling the press that Norris said he was the victim of the Wings not doing their homework for the past 10 years, Sid flew to Chicago to confront Bruce face-to-face, asking him for the authority to fire Harkness. "No!" Norris said, convinced he had chosen the right course for his team. Sid returned to Detroit and promptly resigned, saying he had never seen a more disorganized, dysfunctional team whose coach could not even change lines effectively. Obviously, this was reflected on everybody within the franchise from the owner on down, and the behind-the-scenes calamity initiated the most disastrous period in Red Wings history.

While Harkness was an extraordinary college hockey recruiter, his abrasive style badly hurt our club—setting it back decades—and by doing so, he damaged the NHL, too. One of its premier franchises was being decimated by two NHL outsiders, hockey professionals who tried to create a new competitive model based on their collegiate success. Norris envisioned his Wings becoming a model franchise in the expanded league and defusing the competition of the currently developing World Hockey Association. He also felt European hockey was becoming stronger, with each country competing to become the European champion and eventually playing the North American champion for the Stanley Cup.

Another quirk in Ned's customary manner was to use small coins to plan and demonstrate a play. While it might have worked well with coins, it did not prove applicable to the arena ice surface. Moving "Big Gordie" to defense also failed to accomplish the result he desired.

Recognizing Harkness' lack of NHL ability, the players revolted, holding a private meeting in a hotel room in Buffalo before a game. The fledgling NHLPA had just begun, so the players called their president, Alan "The Eagle" Eagleson, from his home in Toronto to mediate the situation. The result differed from anything anyone expected. The Eagle's primary objective was to keep the revolt out of the papers. Abel was gone, and in a move that shocked the team, Harkness was moved upstairs as general manager. He in turn brought back Doug Barkley, who was coaching our farm team, and four swinging-door trades created a roster full of players who didn't know each other and were struggling to play together.

Trades seemed to occur every two weeks. The first sent Frank Mahovlich to Montreal for Mickey Redmond, Guy Charron, and Bill Collins. Two weeks later, NHLPA player rep Bruce MacGregor and Larry Brown went to the New York Rangers for Arnie Brown, Mike Robitaille, and Tom Miller. A week after that, the player Ned called untouchable, Garry Unger, was traded with Wayne Connelly to St. Louis for Red Berenson and Tim Ecclestone; and "The Stork," Dale Rolfe, went to the Rangers for Jim Krulicki, who played 14 games for us before disappearing.

Nothing Harkness did led to any kind of sustained success on the ice for the Red Wings. When he stepped down as Wings coach, the reins were assumed by Barkley. Doug was a very talented defenseman for the

Wings from 1962–63 and 1965–66 when he suffered a career-ending eye injury. A Red Wings hero, Doug's arrival on the scene helped stem some of the bad press. In spite of all the hype he couldn't turn around the team.

Doug lasted only 11 games the next season, so on Halloween he said the team wasn't responding for him, and Johnny Wilson was brought in from our Tidewater minor league affiliate in Norfolk, Virginia. Johnny was a good choice in the Harkness atmosphere, since he had experience as a college coach at Princeton and in the NHL at Los Angeles prior to his time with the Tidewater Wings. However, during his first game, he was handed a note by trainer Lefty Wilson from Ned Harkness not to play Brian Conacher. He was so mad that he threw the note under the bench and played Brian as much as he could. After the game he told Harkness and Jim Bishop that if they ever did that again, they could find a new coach.

Despite what appeared to be a nifty turnaround after Johnny Wilson's arrival, the team slumped in the final third of the season and he was fired. But Johnny was defiant in his press conference, expressing his frustrations at trying to work with Harkness and saying they were firing the wrong guy.

Norris finally got the message after the 1973–74 season. Though he told the media he resigned due to media pressure, Harkness was fired by Norris, ending a turbulent four-year career that set the franchise back at least a decade. Harkness returned to college hockey at Union College in Amsterdam, New York. He then spent several exciting years in Lake Placid, New York, working with the New York Olympic Regional Authority, which hosted the 1980 Olympic Winter Games and, most importantly, the Miracle on Ice game when the American amateurs upset the famed Soviet National Club en route to a gold medal.

Harkness was inducted into the U.S. Hockey Hall of Fame in 1994 and the National Lacrosse Hall of Fame in 2001.

A Memorable Postscript

During the summer of 1975, while vacationing in upstate New York, Genevieve and I were invited to Ned's vacation summer home on the St.

Lawrence at Thousand Islands. It was located on a private island with eight other homes. The island even had its own post office and could only be reached by boat.

Ned greeted us at the local harbor in Clayton in his beautiful antique wooden Boston Whaler. He took us to the impressive boathouse in front of their home. In addition to its inner slip area to stow the boats, there was a deck sunning area at land level with a flat-roofed observation deck above. The summer retreat house was a beautiful 1920s Victorian. Ned purchased it from one of the descendants of the Du Pont family of Wilmington, Delaware, and it was completely furnished with everything, including wicker furniture and the finest monogrammed linens to suit every purpose.

The other homes were far enough away so it was fairly private yet close enough so neighbors could help each other if the need arose. Ned's daughter, who had worked in Olympia Stadium's administrative office, joined us for dinner, traveling by boat to the mainland and by car to the restaurant. Erma, Ned's wife, took great pride in showing us their beautiful summer place, and it truly was a memorable experience for us.

CHAPTER 13

Home Ice

For generations of Detroiters, it was the Olympia.
Affectionately called the Old Red Barn because of its red brick exterior, Olympia Stadium was built in 1927 at a cost of $2.25 million. It was home not only to the Red Wings but to all kinds of events—prize fights, circuses, political rallies, horse and auto shows, rodeos, figure skating reviews, and virtually every imaginable sporting event, including track and field and gymnastics. A lighted marquee over the main entrance, similar to the typical motion picture theaters of that era, served as the building's signboard, announcing current or forthcoming events.

Like many of the Original Six buildings, Olympia Stadium was basically built for boxing. And like the others, it was not conducive to a healthy environment. At the Chicago Stadium, players had to climb 23 stairs from the floor below to the ice surface. At Madison Square Garden in New York, the rink was several feet shorter than the other NHL arenas. And at the Boston Garden, the dressing room had no windows and the entire building was connected to the railroad station with its strong coal-dust aroma permeating the arena.

Louie Marudas was the building boxing and wrestling expert in charge of arranging and scheduling those events at Olympia. A young Joe Louis staged many of his early fights there, beginning in 1934. Jake LaMotta became World Middleweight champion in 1949 and fought 18 times in Detroit, mostly at Olympia Stadium. Sugar Ray Robinson fought there in the 1940s. The Beatles and Rolling Stones played before thousands of screaming fans, as did Elton John and Elvis Presley. The famous Austrian Lipizzaner Cavalry Troupe also performed there. When the National Basketball Association's Zollner Pistons transferred from Fort Wayne, Indiana, to Detroit and became the Detroit Pistons, they played their earliest games at Olympia on a special floor laid directly on the ice surface and then taken up for hockey.

But hockey and the Detroit Red Wings ruled at Olympia Stadium.

During the days of the Original Six, great rivalries developed—strong love-hate relationships among teams and their fans. Most of the old buildings had their share of obstructed-vision seats due to the supporting iron columns. Youngsters would run up the 100-plus steps to the balcony for coveted standing-room spots as soon as the building opened. The area around the organ was a favorite because it offered essentially unobstructed views.

A Bulova time-clock scoreboard was positioned high above center ice, controlled by the game timekeeper next to the penalty box. It could be lowered to ice level for light bulb replacement and repairs. When glass boards were first installed, they wouldn't just crack like today, but rather the glass would crumble and shatter into thousands of minute glass splinters, showering and cutting fans in the first row. Since we also doubled as arena physicians, we had the responsibility of taking care of the fans and would spend an inordinate amount of time during the game removing splinters from their skin and clothing.

The building opened for hockey on November 22, 1927, with the Detroit Cougars, a team composed of the personnel from the Victoria, British Columbia Cougars of the disbanded Western Hockey League. They brought their western Canadian nickname with them. Ticket prices when the building opened in 1927 ranged from 50¢ to $2.

The noise from cheering fans was incredible. The mezzanine and balcony were positioned so close to the ice that fans could almost reach out and touch the players. Before glass was installed, they felt as though they were actually on the ice. Olympia's balcony stairway was very sharply

A 1976 photo of Olympia Stadium, home of the Red Wings from 1927 through 1979. (Photo courtesy of Robert Wimmer)

angled, making some of those fans feel like they could fall right out of the upper gallery onto the main floor.

The building had among the smallest seating capacities in the NHL—14,000 when it opened in 1927. In 1965, more seats were added, expanding the capacity to 16,00. Renovations included a long escalator to allow people headed for the balcony to get there quicker. A more up-to-date Olympia Room was also built, allowing its Olympia Club members easier access.

Olympia was the only building in the NHL where players had to walk 20' across the lower level corridor, through the crowd from the locker room, and past the audience seating-area access tunnel to get to the ice surface. Unlike today, when canopies protect the players from the crowd until they reach the ice, fans would be standing beside the players as they walked to the ice, separated only by a thin wooden guardrail and minimal security. Devotees cheered and yelled for the Wings and booed the opposition. Both teams could feel the excitement. Olympia enthusiasts were hockey people, and opponents knew they were in for an exciting game with all the noise fans made.

The atmosphere was electric, and it became part of the league's lore in that era. Off the corridor near the front of the building was the ticket office. The Stadium Bar was on the corner of McGraw and Grand River, where fans could go before the doors to the arena opened. Close by in the main corridor, was the Red Wings' area that had pictures, sticks, jerseys, and a short history of each individual. Nearby was a large showcase with a model of one of the Norris-owned freighters named the Red Wing.

Pregame warm-ups were short, not a 20-minute ordeal. Because there were only six teams, every fan knew all the players on the opposition roster. When the Wings made the playoffs and advanced to the Stanley Cup Finals, interest in the team rose to a fever pitch. Once in 1978, after Billy Lochead scored a dramatic goal eliminating the Atlanta Flames in the first round (then a best-of-three series) of the postseason, fans were lined up around the building the night before to purchase tickets that went on sale the next morning.

It was early spring and freezing cold, so management opened the building to allow the fans to wait inside. Some people were drinking, and about 1:00 AM somebody hotwired the Zamboni and drove it through the Olympia's wide street-level corridors. Also, people were running out on the ice and chaotically through the corridors. By morning, though, things quieted down and everyone got their tickets, and the Zamboni made it home to keep doing its job on that amazing ice surface. Olympia Stadium had great, fast ice and most players loved to skate there.

The dressing rooms were very barren. Our room consisted of benches lining the walls with hooks above where the players were seated to hang their street clothes during games or uniforms after games or practices. The uniforms and equipment contained a large amount of cotton. By the end of practices or after games, they had to be hung out to dry. When traveling to another city after a night game, the wet uniforms and equipment would be packed, taken to the arena in the next city, dried there by the trainer and equipment person as soon as they arrived and before they went to their hotel for the night.

There was a small, separated area at the end of the dressing room where the trainer used a massage table where ice and diathermy was employed. The coach and general manager and any visiting scouts also used that area to prepare their strategy for the game. At the other end of the room was the shower room and adjacent lavatory. When a player was sick or excessively nervous, his heaving was easily heard throughout the entire room. While goaltender Glenn Hall was a Red Wing, from 1952–53 to 1956–57, he would typically return from the warm-up, go into the lavatory and dry heave—an unpleasant sound that could be heard throughout the entire relatively silent dressing room. The louder and more severe it was, the more players would look at one another and say, "We're going to have a good game tonight."

Between periods, the trainers and dressing-room staff would serve tea and honey in small paper cups as their liquid nourishment. The Lipton Tea Company was so impressed with players drinking tea that they took a photo in the dressing room and featured it in a full-page ad on the inside back cover of *Life* magazine. Contrary to the well-documented attitude of today, where it's frequently advised that drinking appropriate quantities of fluid is the best way to ward off muscle cramps, the prevailing attitude then was to limit liquid intake. It was considered a cause of a player becoming nauseated and being in danger of aspirating.

The dressing room, always guarded by a big, strong and responsible usher, exited onto the general hallway, so after the games a long line of fans would wait for autographs from that door to the nearest exit about 40' away. Most of the Wings were very patient and would stay there as long as necessary to sign for everyone.

To all those who worked there, Olympia Stadium was known simply as "the building." There was great comradeship, loyalty, mutual respect, and a family-like atmosphere among the employees from the box office to maintenance to concessions. Ushers wore military-style, easily identifiable uniforms including brimmed red caps with Olympia embroidered in gold above the brim.

Many families worked there—the Opalewskis for one, father Bill, an usher from the time the building opened, followed by two sons in maintenance and a daughter in concessions; Charley Escoe was prominent in the ticket office, with son Eddie persuing the same professions and becoming agent for the ticket sellers union; Louie Marudas was the boxing promoter while his brother, Pete, worked in the ticket office. Those in charge at various times were Dan Distal and later Ellen Munley, whose husband, Mike, also was there. Dan served as manager of the Junior Red Wings before he left to join middleweight boxing champion Chuck Davies' insurance group. Another ticket-office expert during the great Stanley Cup days of the late 1940s and early '50s, Lou Cromwell, became head of J.L. Hudson's ticket service.

The employees took great pride in making the building as attractive and presentable as possible. During the playoffs, many different embellishments were added, including bunting around the front of the balcony and mezzanine. This was true of the other arenas of the Original Six, as well. Current Joe Louis Arena building operations manager Al Sobotka began working there and learning the ropes of ice making and care in the variations of changing outdoor temperature during the hockey season.

The majority of the building staff would be laid-off in the summer and not reinstated until training camp in early September. A fair number of building employees worked at one of the horse-racing tracks during the summer. Frenchy Fouchet drove the tractor that refreshed the track between races at the Detroit Race Course and drove the Zamboni to resurface the ice at the Olympia. Even the press had a similar routine. The hockey writers during the winter were typically the golf writers during late spring and summer. I always found it difficult to understand how they could follow and write about our exciting game all winter and then leave to cover golf.

It was the Stanley Cup versus the Masters. Several of those reporters rose to prominence in golf. Marshall Dann, hockey and golf reporter for the *Detroit Free Press*, was such a knowledgeable golf writer that he became the secretary of the prestigious Western Golf Association. Jack Berry, who covered hockey in Detroit, was a golf writer for the *Free Press* and later the *News*. Jack was elected president of the Golf Writers Association of America in 1984 and received the American Professional Golf Association's Lifetime Achievement Award in 2007 at Augusta. Prominent golf writer for the *Detroit News*, Vartan Kupelian, did insightful columns on hockey until his retirement a few years ago.

Some of hockey's most memorable moments were recorded at Olympia Stadium, including one of the most famous photos of all time— "The Production Line" of Ted Lindsay, Sid Abel, and Gordie Howe, taken by James E. "Scotty" Kilpatrick, who became nationally famous for his photo of Walter Reuther and the union leaders on the bridge from the parking lot with the giant Ford Rouge Plant in the background. He was the most famous of the newspaper photographers of the Original Six era. Exceedingly talented, Kilpatrick spoke with a Scottish brogue and was loved by all who had contact with him. He began his career at the *Detroit News* in 1930 and did everything—amassing a portfolio of treasured photos involving business and industry icons, political figures, and sports heroes. His images of the Production Line and the business-labor "Battle of the Overpass" were two of his gems.

Olympia Stadium is also where the tradition of tossing an octopus on the ice during the Stanley Cup playoffs—one of the more weird and wonderful customs in sports—was born.

Olympia Stadium outlived its usefulness as one of America's great sports cathedrals, and the Wings moved to Joe Louis Arena in December 1979. It was eventually razed in 1986 to make room for a National Guard armory—but not before memorabilia seekers ravaged the building. Its seats, boards, and even its Zamboni doors are scattered in homes and sports bars throughout the Detroit area.

CHAPTER 14

He Shoots, He Misses!

MY BRUSH WITH DEATH OUTSIDE OLYMPIA STADIUM.
On a bitter, cold winter night in Detroit, the city was beginning to pick itself up by its bootstraps after the violent, devastating riot that ripped it apart in the summer of 1967, destroying many of its businesses in the area surrounding Olympia Stadium.

The city was changing rapidly, but on that January 4, 1970, it was hockey as usual at the Big Red Barn, with the Red Wings facing the class of the NHL at the time. The Chicago Blackhawks were making a serious run at their first Stanley Cup title since 1961. They were in first place, led by Hall of Fame greats including Bobby Hull, the first player to break the 50-goal barrier, Pat Stapleton, and Stan Mikita. This was a very good hockey club whose roster was complemented by players stocked by GM Tommy Ivan and Coach Billy Reay, some selected in the newly formed amateur draft and others from the established interleague draft, which was used to claim an amazing young goaltender, Tony Esposito, from the Montreal Canadiens. Esposito, Cliff Koroll, and Keith Magnuson were collegiate additions in those days of intense Canadian junior programs.

We had not beaten the Blackhawks in Detroit in three years, so every game was epic and considered the ultimate challenge; in fact, the Wings had not even made the playoffs in the three seasons since 1965–66, but the disparity did not reflect the intensity of the series.

The Wings had great goaltending from Roy Edwards and two spectacular lines. The first line had Gordie Howe, Alex Delvecchio, and Frank

Mahovlich, while Garry Unger, Pete Stemkowski, and Wayne Connelly comprised the second line. Gary Bergman and Carl Brewer anchored the defense. Just prior to that, the Wings had made one of the most gigantic trades in NHL history in 1968 when Detroit and Toronto traded their big lines of Norm Ullman, Floyd Smith, and Paul Henderson for "Big M" Mahovlich, Stemkowski, Unger, and defenseman Carl Brewer. The trade reaped rewards for both clubs. Sid Abel always said, "You can't trade a row-boat for an ocean liner," so he traded ocean liner for ocean liner.

Our 11-year-old son was playing in the Silver Stick tournament in Forest, Ontario, and since he was not able to join us, we took another couple to the game. Larry Cain, president of the Michigan Amateur Hockey Association and one of the original members of the Detroit Red Wings Alumni Association, often set up a beautiful display of cold-cuts and appetizers for the guests in an early "alumni room" (that formerly housed the Olympia Club) on the mezzanine floor over the main-floor ticket office. Genevieve and our guests went there before the pregame warm-up.

It was our custom to arrive an hour before game time, so the team physician would be available for the players before warm-up, check any recovering injuries, and evaluate any new problems. Next, I would go to the visitors' room while their players were warming up, in case any care was needed there. Experienced and very talented Chicago trainer Skip Thayer was there, enjoying life with one of the greatest Blackhawks teams ever to take the ice. The building was still in the festive atmosphere following the Christmas holidays, and we were anticipating playing against Chicago's best. The crowd in the building was anxious and tense, everyone expecting an enthusiastic game with the Wings so determined to beat Chicago—and beat them we did. The ice was perfect, Sid Abel had our team ready for war, and everyone was healthy. The game was hard-fought, and the atmosphere was as electric as it could be only in those old-style barns with everyone so close to center ice.

At the end of the game, even though everyone had played hard, there were very few medical problems. We had a couple of minor lacerations to close that were quickly taken care of, but nothing serious. After I finished taking care of the team, I joined our guests in the Alumni Room upstairs, so it was about an hour after the game before we left. Since it was a very cold night and our car was parked behind the arena where the players and other management parked, I suggested to our friends that I would get the car and come by the front side entrance (the only one still open) and pick them up. The management of the building turned off all but a few of the outside lights as a cost-saving measure, but it was still somewhat light. I left them in the inside hallway by the front side door and started walking back to my car.

About halfway there, I happened to look around. Walking about 30-40' behind me alongside the building were two nicely dressed (coat and tie) African American young men who appeared to have come out of the restaurant/disco/bar across Grand River Avenue. Considering the late hour, and the fact that there was no one else around, I thought it was unwise to continue walking to the parking lot. So I snapped my fingers as though I had forgotten something and turned back toward the entrance. The rest of the entrance doors were all closed, locked, and barred since everyone had left. By the time we were face to face, I realized the taller one of the two had a pistol in his right hand, which he stuck out saying, "Turn around and keep walking."

Probably because my juices were still up from the big win, I answered, "Not a chance." To my surprise, he stuck the gun out further and fired. It looked like a .32-caliber pistol, and it made quite a noise. I kind of pulled my stomach in. The bullet went through my Loden car coat and the brand new suit I was wearing, but I felt no wound. The two perpetrators ran toward the back of the building lot—the players' fenced parking area— which was locked. I smiled, thinking that if I could find a police patrol car and officers we might trap and catch them since the entire area except the entrance gate was closed and locked and the overhead lighting was turned off. Quickly going back to the entrance where our guests were waiting, I warned them to stay inside. Genevieve, having heard the gunshot, asked me if I had just witnessed a holdup and shooting. "Yes, so stay inside," I told her. Then I went back out onto Grand River Avenue, looking for a police car, but the area was deserted so I returned to the arena.

By this time, a few others were around and a police car showed up. I explained to them what happened. Their response: "Boy, were you lucky." And they made their report.

We then went back to my car and left. When I got home, I could see the gunpowder on my car coat. Then I looked at my suit coat and realized it had two through-and-through bullet holes in it, and the inside lining had a 4" linear tear caused by the bullet. The small holes required reweaving of the fabric, and indicated the seriousness of the encounter and how it could have affected our lives. Shortly after we arrived home, our son was dropped off from the Silver Stick tournament, which his team had won. Considering we had six small children 11 years old and under, a more devastating outcome could have changed everything, and we'd never have this story to tell.

After the Detroit riots, it had become necessary to protect the back of the building and adjacent parking lots with 10' wire fencing and a gate that was locked unless an event was taking place. Because we parked with the players and team management in the fenced area right behind the building, it was reassuring to have our car close by.

The next day at the hospital, several colleagues had learned of the shooting, so it was a big part of the conversation. Trainer Lefty Wilson said he was "going on an immediate diet to slim down and be harder to hit." Toronto's Red Kelly, then coaching the Pittsburgh Penguins, also had some interesting remarks about it the next time he came to Olympia Stadium, saying I had the courage of a hockey player.

Almost immediately, Linc Cavalieri and the management of Olympia Stadium improved the lighting around the arena that was useful and minimized the danger of further incidents such as mine. Cavalieri and other Stadium officials had a meeting with Detroit police the following day and indicated that police would be assigned to stay at the stadium until 90 minutes after games.

Detroit Free Press sportswriter Jack Berry, in his "Wing Notes" column, led off with a more aberrant description of the episode. The headline read: "Olympia Area Policing Intensified After Gunmen Menace Club Medic." The story he was told was that the perpetrators moved behind me, saying, "Keep marching," but fortunately a car pulled into the parking lot and its lights distracted the gunmen. He then wrote that I swerved around and my hand hit the gun. "The gunman shot and the bullet tore through the doctor's overcoat and sport-coat but he was not injured and the gunmen fled," the newspaper said. The way I've described the incident is how it happened, but I found the writer's story of the event interesting—especially since he hadn't talked with me about it.

Another fascinating postscript was the response of the players and training staff. They all seemed to have an unexpected opinion of their behind-the-scenes quiet guy, implying they all felt they were tough but they weren't sure they would have reacted in a similar manner. Olympia Stadium Corporation later bought all the houses around the parking lot to improve parking as well as safety around the building. Remarkably, since we took care of the fans attending the game, we rarely needed to treat anyone who had been assaulted either coming into or leaving the building.

Bob Probert remarked in his book how dangerous it seemed to him as a Grade 8 student around Olympia Stadium in the 1970s. He cited an incident in 1976 when a businessman was killed walking to his car after a tennis match, noting the security guards had gone home and turned out the parking lot lights—saying even they didn't want to be around Olympia late at night. Probert further explained that when his father, a Windsor police officer, would take Bob and his brother, Norm, to hockey games there, he would take his little snub-nosed .38 he kept in his belt, showing the border officials his badge and the gun. When they walked to their car after the game, he would have it in his hand, dangling at his side.

I never felt the need to carry a gun—either before or after that rather harrowing experience. It's accurate to say, though, that afterward I was a lot more vigilant about my routines around Olympia Stadium.

CHAPTER 15

Hail (Little) Caesar

THE ILITCH FAMILY BUILDS A WINNER IN DETROIT.

I have the most profound admiration and respect for Mike Ilitch and his family. He and Marian have always been individuals who work tirelessly to make their teams successful, but most of all they care about their players and their families—and especially their fans. And those who know Mike Ilitch best, people like Jimmy Devellano, say he cares just as much about his Midget and Peewee teams and the tens of thousands of youngsters who proudly wear the Little Caesars logo on their hockey sweaters.

Mike Ilitch has always been a very humble person—a blue-collar guy who describes himself as "a fan with a wallet." He not only has been an exceptional owner and leader in the NHL, as well as in Major League Baseball, he and his family have a strong love and passion for the city of Detroit. They have led the way in downtown development and are among the city's strongest supporters.

After 50 years of Red Wings ownership by the Norris family, the torch was passed from Bruce Norris to Mike and Marian Ilitch on June 22, 1982. By accepting the new challenge of team ownership, the Ilitches brought stability and dynamic hometown leadership to an ailing franchise. The franchise was hard-pressed financially and suffering a declining fan base. The Wings had failed to make the playoffs in 14 of the 16 preceding seasons, and their season-ticket base had dropped to just 1,500.

The seven Ilitch children were great hockey fans and very excited to learn their parents had purchased the Detroit Red Wings. They were enamored with owning a professional hockey team until their mother brought them back to earth. "I'll show you how glamorous it is," Marian said, and she immediately put them to work promoting the team. She took them to the ticket office, pointed to the phones and said, "Start calling people and urge them to buy season tickets." The children did their research and obtained information on all the major companies and corporations in Metro Detroit and called management leaders personally. Prospective clients were told about a turnaround plan and a stronger, tougher club. Improvements for the arena were described, and clients were encouraged to get on the bandwagon to help support the team and assist Ilitch with his plans for a powerhouse Detroit team. But that wasn't enough. To bring people back to hockey at the Joe in support of the Red Wings, Mike developed a marketing plan never before envisioned. He gave away a new car at every home game. One lucky hometown fan drove home in a new car after each of the forty home games.

Attendance rose, but the franchise continued to lose money in its first five years before the Wings were able to draft their own superstars and develop their own talent through an elite minor league system. Jimmy Devellano, who was Mike Ilitch's first hire and general manager, played a key role in the rebuilding of the Wings. Lured away from the New York Islanders, Devellano promised he would build a winner in eight years. Helping to secure that promise was the drafting of Steve Yzerman in the 1983 draft. Another key move was the 1986 hiring of Jacques Demers, who led the Wings to the playoffs in his first three seasons as coach and began a payoff tradition that has lasted 25 years.

It took more than eight years to win a Stanley Cup, but in 1997, with Scotty Bowman behind the bench, the Red Wings finally ended a 42-year drought. Since then, the Red Wings have become the team to beat, consistently making the playoffs and bringing home three additional Stanley Cups since 1997. A once-dead hockey town has now become "Hockeytown" where winners emerge year after year. Detroit has become the envy of all cities where hockey is played.

Mike Ilitch is the perfect example of a self-made man. His life and achievements could be called the classic American success story. He was born on Russell Street on Detroit's east side, the son of immigrant parents from Macedonia. His father, who had gone to night school to learn a trade in his adopted new land, was a machine repairman for the Hamtramck Chrysler Plant. Mike's mother was a homemaker who spoke very little English. From a very early age, Mike showed an interest in baseball and played the sport in fields near his home. When he was only 14 years old, he was the lead-off batter for John's Café, playing with men in their twenties. At age 15, he was allowed to work out at Briggs Stadium with stars such as Hank Greenberg. While attending Cooley High School, Mike excelled in track and baseball, but baseball was always his true love. As an All-City champion, Mike was scouted by the Detroit Tigers, who offered him a contract with their minor league system after graduation. However, with the Korean War going on, Mike chose to serve his country and enlisted in the U.S. Marines. Mike continued to play baseball while with the Marines, and the Tigers continued to scout him. Upon his discharge, the Tigers again offered Mike a contract with their minor league affiliates. This time he accepted.

While playing for the Tigers, Mike earned the nickname of "Scooter." The slick-fielding shortstop played for four seasons until persistent knee injuries forced him to hang up his cleats. During his minor league career, as he traveled from town to town, he often envisioned where he might put a little pizza shop. He had developed an interest in pizza while working in the back of Haig's bar on Detroit's west side during the off-season. He liked everything about the product—the smell, the taste, and especially the kneading of the dough. He realized he could make some dough of his own by investing in this popular menu item.

Enter Marian Bayoff, the daughter of Macedonian parents who was also athletically inclined, having played intramural basketball and softball at Fordson High School in Dearborn, Michigan. Fortunately, she was also an avid hockey fan. Mike and Marian met on a blind date arranged by Mike's aunt and Marian's mother. Mike had not attended any of the Macedonian church dances, so Marian had not had an opportunity to meet him beforehand. She was told he was a pretty good ball player, which spiked her interest in the arranged date, so she agreed. Mike was a physically rugged guy and rather short—not at all what she had expected. Her hopes had been set on more of an Al Kaline–type.

Their first date was a movie, and Mike picked her up in a 98 Olds convertible—a car that belonged to a buddy who was playing winter ball in South America. However, when they left the movie, the car was gone. Mike called the police and discovered the car had been repossessed. Apparently, his buddy had not made a payment on the car since leaving town. Embarrassed, Mike arranged for a ride home, but the fire of love had been lit. Mike and Marian were married a few months later.

The newlywed couple lived in the upper flat of his parents' home in Detroit. But now Mike needed a way to provide for his bride. With few skills outside of baseball, Mike took up the door-to-door selling of aluminum awnings and pots and pans. Times were tough, and money was tight. Most of the men that Mike worked with worried about getting doors slammed in their faces—not Mike. He was more concerned with seeing someone he had gone to high school with who might think he was not very successful. Selling was very difficult for Mike. However, with their first baby on the way, he worked exceptionally hard and developed his own special technique. He would line up appointments during the day and make his potential customer calls in the evening.

Just like baseball, the harder he worked, the better his stats. He used an old family accounting system involving three cigar boxes. One box was for the bills. The second box contained the money to pay the bills. Whatever was left over was placed in the third box. Soon Marian opened a savings account and within three years they had saved enough money to open a little pizza shop in Garden City, Michigan, a suburb of Detroit. First, they needed a name for their new business. Mike liked Pizza Treat. Marian was not so sure. She saw in her husband the strength and character of a

Caesar, but this early in his career he had not accomplished a great deal, so he was a "little" Caesar. They compromised and the first pizza stores were called Little Caesars Pizza Treats. Over the years, the Pizza Treat portion was dropped. When the company celebrated its 50th anniversary in 2009, Marian admitted that her husband was now a "big" Caesar.

The menu at that first pizza shop included more than pizza. They also sold chicken and fish dinners and shrimp snacks. Since it was a carryout store, there were no tables or chairs for dining. The need for tableware, waiters, and busboys was eliminated. Mike did the cooking, and Marian handled the counter and the finances. At the May 8, 1959, grand opening, Mike was so excited that he gave the first pizza order away for free. He also gave the first chicken dinner away for free. Marian immediately took over and started collecting the money. They were in business to make a profit!

By 1961, a second Little Caesars opened in Warren, Michigan, followed by a third in Westland, Michigan. In 1962, they started franchising, and the first franchised Little Caesars store opened in Warren. Today, Little Caesars operates on four continents and is the largest international carryout pizza chain in the world.

Marian Gets an Assist

Whoever said that behind every great man is a great woman must have had Marian Ilitch in mind. Not only does she have grace and beauty, but she also has tremendous business acumen and she revels in the family's many successful businesses and civic projects. Her leadership has always been profound, and she is equally modest. Marian lists her wedding day, the birth of her children, and purchasing the Red Wings as the most thrilling days of her life—and Mike's, too. She credits the timing of the Red Wings purchase as the trademark of their successes and the beginning of their solid commitment to the city of Detroit.

On September 13, 2010, Marian was inducted into the Michigan Sports Hall of Fame, joining her husband who had been inducted a few years earlier. She is one of only a handful of women so honored.

The man behind it all, Mike Ilitch, was inducted into the Hockey Hall of Fame in the builder's category in 2003. No one deserved it more. I get a big broad grin on my face every time I think of his tremendous achievements. He is a modest person for all that he has done in the pizza business, as well as his accomplishments in amateur and professional sports. Equally noteworthy is the generosity he has extended to countless individuals in every walk of life throughout metropolitan Detroit and beyond. In his acceptance speech at the Hall in Toronto, he described himself simply as a blue-shirted working man from a working-class family from Detroit.

Business Outside of Hockey and Pizza

Several months after the Ilitches purchased the Red Wings, they also acquired the management company for Joe Louis Arena, Cobo Arena, and Glens Fall Arena in New York. The business has expanded greatly since then and is currently known as Olympia Entertainment. It operates the historic Fox Theatre in downtown Detroit, which the Ilitches purchased in 1987 and restored to its original 1928 splendor. The Fox Theatre reopened in November 1988 and is currently the largest remaining movie palace. Designated a National Historic Landmark, attendance at the Fox is among the highest for a theatre of its size. In addition to the Fox Theatre, Olympia Entertainment manages Hockeytown Café and several other venues in the Detroit area.

In another show of support for the city of Detroit, in 1989, the Ilitches moved their Little Caesars corporate headquarters from the Detroit suburbs into the renovated Fox Office Center adjacent to the Fox Theatre in downtown Detroit. This brave action, taken at a time when businesses were fleeing the city, provided a catalyst for additional investment in the downtown area.

Other businesses currently owned by Mike and/or Marian Ilitch include Blue Line Foodservice Distribution Company, Little Caesars Pizza Kit Fundraising Program, Champion Foods, Uptown Entertainment, Olympia Development of Michigan, and Ilitch Holdings, Inc. Mike

The author and his wife, Genevieve, with Michael Ilitch.
(Photo courtesy of the Finleys)

Ilitch also owns the 2011 Central Division Champion Detroit Tigers, and Marian Ilitch owns MotorCity Casino Hotel. The last two investments alone have changed the Detroit skyline with a new state-of-the-art ballpark and a luxurious 400-room hotel and permanent casino.

In spite of their many successes, Mike and Marian have never lost sight of the less fortunate. In 1985, the Little Caesars Love Kitchen was established. It is a big-rig truck with a full kitchen that travels the United States and Canada, feeding the hungry at soup kitchens or wherever hungry people gather. It also serves victims affected by natural disasters, such as hurricanes and floods. It fed workers following 9/11. Since its inception, it has fed more than 2 million people.

Mike Ilitch also established a Little Caesars Veterans Program in 2006, which offers honorably discharged veterans returning from service and veterans looking for a career change a business opportunity with Little Caesars at reduced investment costs.

And then there is youth hockey! Little Caesars is one of the most recognized and respected organizations in amateur hockey throughout North America and one of the cornerstones of the High Performance Hockey League. Little Caesars has been supporting youth hockey since 1968. It started when Mike's nephew asked if he would sponsor his amateur hockey team. That one team sponsorship has expanded to now include more than 900 teams, and tens of thousands of kids have learned to compete on and off the ice. More than one hundred AAA youngsters have made it to the NHL. Players such as Derian Hatcher and Mike Modano sharpened their skates as Little Caesars AAA youth players and came back home to join the Red Wings. Thousands of Little Caesars youth players have received college scholarships or found success in other professional hockey leagues.

From youth hockey sponsorship that began in 1968 to a 30-year ownership of the NHL Detroit Red Wings, Mike and Marian have demonstrated their love of hockey and proved they know how to win. I am honored to know them and to have been part of that winning spirit in a place called Hockeytown.

Hail "Little" Caesar indeed.

CHAPTER 16

The Captain

THE WONDER YEARS WITH "STEVIE Y."

Once the Ilitches had secured ownership of the declining franchise, their first decision was to hire a general manager. Mike Ilitch took the advice of many of those he trusted, including Hal Middlesworth, longtime senior sportswriter who covered the Tigers, and hockey people he knew. They included David Poile, current general manager of the Nashville Predators NHL hockey team, and Red Berenson, the former St. Louis Blues coach and the NHL's Coach of the Year in 1981, who went on to coach the University of Michigan and turn that program into a national powerhouse.

Mike interviewed and hired the very successful assistant GM and director of scouting of the four-time Stanley Cup–winning New York Islanders, Jimmy Devellano. Also involved in some interview discussions were Marian Ilitch, Mike's wife, and their oldest daughter, attorney Denise, who helped make the GM decision.

But by the time Devellano was on board, the 1982 draft had taken place and the first-year owners were struggling to put forward a competitive hockey team—after making some bold promises about their intentions for the team during a season-ticket sales blitz involving the entire family. The Wings played in the Norris Division in those days, which included five teams, four of which made the playoffs. Sadly, the Wings weren't one of them. And none of the other four teams were even remotely threatened that Detroit would step up and steal their playoff berth.

Devellano knew this, and the first thing he did was to caution every-one, especially the Ilitch family, about how mammoth the task ahead of them was.

"It won't be easy, and it will take a lot of work," Devellano said of building a team through the Entry Draft. In order to do that right, though, he told them he would not keep players beyond their time, nor would he even con-sider obtaining frontline players by trading away draft choices. As an investor, Devellano was shrewd and patient, amassing a fortune through his "buy-and-hold" investment strategy. He would do the same with his hockey club.

The 1983 amateur draft took place at the Montreal Forum on June 8, and unbeknownst to anyone at the time it put the Wings on the path to greatness. Keeping in mind the owners' interest in building a strong fran-chise through the draft and also keeping their sights on the success for Detroit, they thought the ideal player to select was hot-shot Detroit native and exceptional junior, Pat Lafontaine. Minnesota and Hartford had the first two choices. With the same idea Detroit had of taking a local boy, Minnesota took Brian Lawton out of Mt. St. Charles (Minnesota) High School. The North Stars also needed to kick-start ticket sales, and who better to help in that endeavor than the state's top prep player?

With the second pick, the Whalers chose Sylvain Turgeon, a skilled French-Canadian who played junior hockey with Hull in the Quebec Major Junior Hockey League. The Islanders, the club from which Devellano had recently departed, had the third overall pick, and they targeted Lafontaine, the Waterford native who had starred with Verdun in the Quebec League and who was now so highly coveted by Ilitch.

The Wings, to the dismay of Ilitch, who had urged Devellano to make a deal with the Islanders to swap draft picks, wound up with Steve Yzerman from the Peterborough Petes of the Ontario Hockey League. When he showed up at the Wings' table a few minutes later, they met a shy and under-sized young man who looked more suited for his junior prom. Yzerman had just turned 18 a month before. He stood barely 5'11" and might have weighed 170 pounds with a wet towel around his waist.

Scouts knew Steve from his days with his hometown Napean (Ontario) Raiders as a creative playmaker, able to make moves at full speed and battle in the corners against the opposition's big defensemen with grit and heart—the kind of player who would be a wonderful addition to any team. Jimmy D. had several discussions with the Petes' Coach Dick Todd, who played four lines fairly equally, limiting Steve's production because of far less ice time than other first-round picks were afforded.

But clearly Steve Yzerman had plenty of opportunity to display his exceptional talent. With a head fake here and a shoulder fake there, he had opposing goalies at his mercy. And he had shown enough toughness to handle himself if provoked. Still, the thinking among the Wings at the time was that because of his age and size, Yzerman would be allowed to mature with another year of junior hockey and perhaps some time in the minors before he was brought up to play in a league full of much larger, ill-humored men.

Only Denise, the eldest Ilitch daughter, had an inkling that the club had drafted the right player. "He was wearing a beautiful red tie," Denise said, recalling the moment team officials met Steve Yzerman.

The rest, of course, is history. In more ways than one.

The Wings that day did more than draft a superstar and their future captain who would lead them to Stanley Cup glory. They completed one of the more remarkable drafts in the history of the NHL taking players like Lane Lambert, Bob Probert, Petr Klima, Joey Kocur, and Stu Grimson, and giving the franchise a nucleus of talent that would carry them into the Stanley Cup years that Devellano, only a year or so earlier, had promised.

In the Beginning

In 1983, as Yzerman came to training camp, team management expected him to work hard, learn some things, make an impression, and then return to his junior team in Peterborough for further development. The first day in camp, the coaches and leaders running the practice were astounded by his skill level. They kept increasing his role as his performance grew, and he made it all look easy. Early in camp, during a discussion with his coaching staff, Devellano mentioned that despite how good Yzerman was playing in his first NHL camp, he was destined to return to juniors for his final year.

"Oh no, he's not," Coach Nick Polano said. "You can't send him back. He's our best player."

Steve enjoyed everything about the game, not just the scheduled games but the practices, the travel, the camaraderie, and the games' highs and the lows. By the end of the season, he had proven his coach right, scoring 39 goals and finishing second only to Buffalo goaltender Tom Barrasso for the Calder Trophy as Rookie of the Year. Barrasso was selected with the fifth pick, right behind Yzerman.

Yzerman had a clause in his contract for a $50,000 bonus if he won the trophy as the league's top rookie. But owner Mike Ilitch was so impressed—and so grateful for the kind of performance Yzerman delivered—that just before the awards were announced he handed Stevie an envelope, saying, "You're my rookie of the year." Inside was a check—for $50,000. That's the kind of owners the Ilitches were.

The only downside to Steve's early career was the problem he kept having with his tonsils. Inflammation kept recurring all season long. In order to stay close to the rink, he had taken an apartment next door to Joe Louis Arena in the Riverfront Towers. Because of his recurrent tonsillitis, at the end of the first season we arranged for him to undergo a tonsillectomy at age 19. Living by himself, and with everyone gone at season's end, we had him spend the entire week after surgery with us, convalescing in our home—and we came to know a really fine young man.

After missing the playoffs for six straight seasons, things began to change—thanks to Steve and the changes Jimmy D. brought to the team. The Wings made the playoffs in Yzerman's first two seasons—1983–84 and 1984–85. The team had added enforcer Tiger Williams and superstar Darryl Sittler in the 1984–85 season, both of whom were near the end of their careers. Unfortunately, neither was happy in Detroit. The Wings made the playoffs but were decimated by the Chicago Blackhawks by huge scores in three straight games. That triggered a coaching change from tough, rigid Nick Polano (who was moved upstairs as assistant GM) to likeable, engaging, and funny Harry Neale, the former Vancouver coach and general manager. That summer, the Wings made an enormous number of changes, including spiriting Petr Klima out of communist Czechoslovakia.

The Wings also signed five collegiate free agents, among them Adam Oates, from NCAA champion RPI, and three experienced players from NHL teams, defenseman Harold Snepsts (Minnesota), defenseman Mike McEwen (Washington), and right wing "Scorin'" Warren Young (Pittsburgh). All three teams filed tampering charges against the Wings, who were celebrated at training camp that fall in Port Huron with a cover story in *Sports Illustrated*, which featured the Wings' brass in pizza chef outfits.

Colin "Soupy" Campbell was a first-year assistant coach at the time who remembers feeling how certain the Wings were to win the Stanley Cup that year. *It's almost too easy*, he thought to himself. As it turned out, it wasn't so easy. The Wings did so poorly they fired Neale at midseason and brought in Brad Park, the former defenseman whose stellar playing career ended in Detroit. The Wings finished last, by far, in the 21-team league, finishing with a record of 17–57–6 for a meager 40 points.

The team then hired Jacques Demers, whom they stole from Norris Division rival St. Louis after the Blues thought they had an agreement on a contract extension. But in the absence of a contract filed with the league, Demers signed a large deal with Detroit, and the NHL again slapped the Wings and Jimmy D. for tampering.

One of the first things Demers did was to make Yzerman captain of the Red Wings. At age 21, he was the youngest man to serve his team in that role in NHL history. Being made captain was recognition of his leadership. The captain is the spokesman of and for the team and should possess the qualities by example to hold the team together. Both Yzerman and Demers were in agreement about one thing—it would have been a much more difficult role to assume without the presence of some great veterans, such as Snepsts, defenseman Mike O'Connell, and goaltender Glen Hanlon.

During the 1984–85 season, Yzerman became the youngest player to be named to the NHL All-Star Game. The relatively new NHL Team Physicians Society began meeting during the All-Star break, rather than at the end of the season with the trainers, so we were there in Edmonton for our meeting and that game. Stevie was delighted and honored to be there. As a member of the board of the Hartford Whalers, Czech tennis star Ivan Lendl also attended. Yzerman wanted to meet the tennis great he admired, so we asked Gordie Howe, an All-Star Whaler at the time, if he would introduce Steve to Lendl, which he was happy to do. I had been involved as a surgeon in the NHL for almost 30 years at the time, and NHL Team Physicians Society president, L.A. Kings surgeon Steve Lombardo, nominated me, and the Society elected me a member of its executive committee.

As captain of the Wings, Steve never ducked the media. He always tried to say the right thing in public, making Wings ownership very proud. On the other hand, Steve's intelligent play was unappreciated by some, including Team Canada Coach Mike Keenan in 1987 and 1988, who cut him from Team Canada's World Championship team, leaving Yzerman so bitter he had to choose his words very carefully.

In 1995, after Scotty Bowman had served two seasons as Wings coach, word was leaked to the press that trading Yzerman to Ottawa was being considered due to his lack of defensive play. The media and fan reaction, however, was so extreme that Bowman was overruled by owner Mike Ilitch. Although it humbled him, Steve soon became an outstanding two-way player. Scotty later admitted that a trade involving Steve would never have happened, simply because Mike Ilitch knew what a great captain he had.

Yzerman's team-only talks were legendary, as exemplified by his speech to them in the first round of the 2002 playoffs against Vancouver. After losing the first two games in Detroit, we team doctors were on the bus with the players when we were confronted by a car full of young Canuck fans mooning the Wings bus as it was traveling from a Vancouver airport to the team hotel at 2:00 AM. Stevie said to the Wings players that he believed in the ability of everyone in the room to get the job done. After he spoke, the team went out and won four games in a row, the two in Vancouver, one back in Detroit, and the sixth game in Vancouver, beating the Canucks 4–2 in the Conference Quarterfinals en route to winning the Stanley Cup.

Playing Through Pain

For all his unforgettable greatness, Steve Yzerman may be remembered most to those he played with for his incomparable pain tolerance. All hockey players suffer injuries; many suffer major physical damage that forces them into early retirement. Not Yzerman. He fought through more serious injuries than most of the great ones, working harder, practicing longer, and epitomizing everything that is good about the game, playing with passion every night no matter how much it hurt.

Steve endured far more injuries than the average elite player. After overcoming recurring tonsillitis, for which a tonsillectomy was performed, he suffered a broken collarbone in Detroit in a collision with an opposing St. Louis defenseman, Lee Norwood, who was later traded to the Wings.

Some of Yzerman's other aches and pains:

1988: Ruptured posterior cruciate ligament, right knee. On March 1, minutes after scoring his 50th goal against Buffalo, Yzerman was taken down on a breakaway by a Buffalo defenseman while going full speed. It was a clean check, but it occurred just a few feet from the side of the Sabres' goal. He slid knee-first into the left front corner of the net, his lower leg just below his knee striking the post at about a 45-degree angle. Although the net was designed to come off its magnetic moorings if run into by a player, this time it did not because of the angle from which he had collided with the goal. The hit caused a complete rupture of his posterior cruciate ligament.

There was considerable controversy among the specialists who examined him about whether or not to repair it surgically. Immediately following the game, after conferring with team orthopedic specialists, Jimmy Devellano announced that Yzerman would undergo major reconstructive surgery and be lost for 12–18 months. Not so fast, owner Mike Ilitch said. He sent his young captain to Madison, Wisconsin, to see one of the world's foremost orthopedists, James Andrews, M.D., who determined that the result of surgery would be no better than rehabbing without surgery.

Surgery would require Yzerman to be out at least a year. But Dr. Andrews, after arthroscopy, found that the remainder of the knee ligaments were intact. Yzerman and the club decided to forgo surgery and rely on rehab, which he did religiously under the tutelage of physical therapist Jim Pengelly. Barely six weeks later, Yzerman was back on the ice, competing in the playoffs. He even elected to play without the recommended, but somewhat cumbersome, Lenox Hill brace since it really didn't support his knee well enough to overcome the instability of his torn PCL. In spite of what would be a major disability for some players, Yzerman went on to become one of the most prolific scorers in NHL history.

Additional Major Injuries

1993–94: Sidelined 26 games with a serious neck injury.

2001: Both he and teammate Brendan Shanahan suffered foot or ankle fractures at the beginning of the playoffs.

2002: Osteotomy surgery plus application of donor bone to the right knee. As the cartilaginous surface of his knee gradually eroded, Yzerman was sent to Western Ontario University Hospital for a procedure that would realign the knee to take the pressure off the eroded area and place more on the healthy cartilaginous area. He also suffered tendonitis in his shoulders and multiple groin injuries that season.

2004: Struck in face by a deflected slap shot, sustaining multiple facial and teeth fractures in the second round of the playoffs against Calgary. He suffered multiple facial bone fractures and an injury to the base of the orbit of his left eye. He was taken immediately to Henry Ford Hospital where a several-hour facial surgical procedure mended the orbital rim. Thanks to the procedure, Steve did not suffer from diplopia, commonly known as doublevision.

And those are just some of the major injuries. During his 22 seasons with the Detroit Red Wings, Steve sustained, as do many players, many unreported injuries that he considered minor. He dealt with pain almost every game, and even while not 100 percent, he always showed up on the ice. His fans expected him to give his best effort, which he always did. Toward the end of his career, loyal spectators would cringe when they saw him use his stick as a crutch to get up after being checked by an opposing player. The crowd stood up and cheered wildly when he came out and took the next shift.

Before each game, Yzerman always made a point of silently, often privately, relaxing. Once dressed, before warm-up in his playing attire, he would work crossword puzzles, and if stuck for a word he would ask for help from the local team expert, Brett Hull. Being mentally prepared was as important as being physically ready, and that was Steve Yzerman's trademark. As team physicians, we would watch him after each game, how he would be the first man on the stationary bike in the exercise room and work feverishly for a protracted period of time to continue to improve his endurance.

His gritty determination combined with his dedication to the sport he loved was his hallmark throughout his career. His major injuries were most memorable since many were often shown on Jumbotron highlights. He sometimes chose rehabilitation to repair the damage instead of having a surgical procedure, decreasing recovery time and continuing to play. Hundreds of hours of rehab for weeks and months enabled him to build up the supporting muscles. One of his most strenuous exercises was jumping from a standing position to the top of an adjacent table 30" above the floor for an extended period of time. It was that kind of work ethic that helped strengthen his body and allowed him to return to the ice, continuing his stellar performance and remarkable career.

Incredibly, Steve's list of honors and awards are even longer than his litany of injuries:

1989: NHLPA players awarded him the Lester Pearson Award as the NHL's best player in voting by the player's union.

1993: Became the third Red Wing to score 1,000 points, after Gordie Howe and Alex Delvecchio.

1996: Became the 22nd player to reach 500 goals, scoring on Colorado's Patrick Roy.

1996: Passed Alex Delvecchio for second on the Wings all-time scoring list (1,281 points).

1997: Contributed three assists, playing in his 1,000th game, against Calgary.

1997: Celebrated Detroit's first Stanley Cup win in 42 years in a sweep over Philadelphia.

1998: Hoisted the Stanley Cup again the following year against Washington, when he won the Conn Smythe Trophy as the MVP of the playoffs.

1999: Became the 11th player to reach 600 goals, scoring on Edmonton's Tommy Salo.

2000: Won the Selke Trophy as the NHL's best defensive forward.

2002: Won Olympic Gold with Canada. Then hoisted the Stanley Cup with the Wings again, becoming one of three players (joining Ken Morrow of the New York Islanders and teammate Brendan Shanahan) to claim Olympic Gold and the Stanley Cup in the same year.

2003: Won the Masterson Trophy for dedication to hockey and perseverance after returning to the ice following radical knee surgery.

2006: Retired after 22 seasons, 1,514 games played, 692 goals, 1,063 assists, 1,755 total points, and 924 penalty minutes.

2007: His No. 19 jersey was retired in Joe Louis Arena, joining Terry Sawchuk, Gordie Howe, Ted Lindsay, Alex Delvecchio, and Sid Abel.

2009: Elected to the Hockey Hall of Fame

Yzerman led a cast of future Hall of Famers featured on the 2002 Stanley Cup team. From left: goaltender Dominik Hasek, Luc Robitaille, Igor Larionov, Chris Chelios, Yzerman, Nicklas Lidstrom, Sergei Fedorov, Brendan Shanahan, and Brett Hull. (Photo courtesy of the Detroit Red Wings)

More memorable moments:

October 10, 1983: first goal

December 23, 1983: first hat trick

January 4, 1989: 28 game point streak

March 15, 1989: 6-point game

March 17, 1990: natural hat trick

February 24, 1993: scored 1,000th point

January 17, 1996: scored 500th goal

May 5, 1996: 5-point playoff game

May 16, 1996: playoff overtime hero with game-winning goal in the second overtime of Game 7 against St. Louis in the second round

24 team records to Gordie Howe's 10

History will record his many contributions to the sport of hockey. But I prefer to remember Steve Yzerman as a true gentleman, honest and dedicated. He was and remains to this day an outstanding role model for young hockey players.

CHAPTER 17

The "Perfect Human"?

THE ULTIMATE HOCKEY PLAYER—AND AN EVEN BETTER PERSON.
The most talented of all the great Swedish players in the proud and distinguished history of their game is Nicklas Lidstrom. There is no better example of a talented, skilled, unassuming player anywhere who epitomizes the perfect hockey player than Nick Lidstrom, which explains why *Sports Illustrated* dedicated an article on Nick entitled, "Mr. Perfect."

Nick was drafted 53rd overall, the 15th defenseman chosen in that exceptional Detroit draft of 1989. When he came to our training camp in Flint in the fall of 1991, we all expected to be overwhelmed by this big, tough man with a persona of our impression of what the ultimate hockey defenseman should look like. Rather, he appeared like a completely average individual whose build and slightly taller physique did not standout like an Adonis that would get your attention. And he was nice—soft-spoken and very well-spoken, a perfect gentleman in every way.

Once on the ice, however, it was a different story. The change from the big European-style rinks did not bother him a bit. By developing his positional play as advised by Wings assistant coach Dave Lewis, when an attacking forward or bigger player had to be taken out of the play, Lidstrom would gain the advantage by merely easing him into the boards and out of the play without much fanfare. He developed his upper body strength and learned the art of staying in front of opposing forwards.

When Nick began with the Wings, initially under coach and GM Brian Murray and later Scotty Bowman, he was the defensive playing partner of very talented defenseman the late Brad McCrimmon, former captain of the Stanley Cup–winning Calgary Flames in 1989 and a Wings assistant coach from 2008–11, Norris Trophy–winner Paul Coffey, and the immensely gifted offensive defenseman Larry Murphy. He also played on the same defense corps with Mark Howe, Mike Ramsey, and Slava Fetisov. He learned a great deal from each of them.

With McCrimmon, Nick was the offensive defenseman and led the rushes while Brad would stay back. With Paul Coffey, an exceptional skater on his own, Lidstrom would do just the opposite, staying back and playing defense and letting Coffey lead the charge. He and Cof were exceptional passing the puck between one another, especially on the power play. From Larry Murphy, whom Nick describes as one of the smartest defensemen he has ever played with, he learned patience and timing. Larry was particularly adept at hanging on to the puck until the last second and then making the best available play.

Having the chance to study, watch, and add to his game all that these great defensemen did so well, Nick developed into everyone's dream defenseman. Captain Steve Yzerman, who always chose his words carefully, was unabashed in his praise of Lidstrom, calling him, "the best player I've ever played with." And Steve played with some of the best of all time.

Even the great Scotty Bowman was in awe of Nick's exceptional skill. When he first came to Detroit, Bowman—who coached some of the greatest players in NHL history in his tenures with St. Louis, Montreal, Buffalo, Pittsburgh, and Detroit—recognized Nick as one of the most fundamentally skilled defensemen he had ever seen play. "Just watch him," Bowman said to me at practice one day. "He is about as perfect as you can get." Years later, when Nick was in his forties, Scotty mentioned something only a coach would remember. There were two things he didn't recall ever seeing Nick do—fall to the ice and get caught leaving his partner stranded on a two-on-one break.

Scotty felt Nick's flawless fundamentals were largely self-taught, but that didn't stop the coach from moving Nick from the right to the left side, making him even more dangerous from the point on the power play. And he kept Lidstrom on the ice in all the critical moments. More than once, Bowman mentioned to me privately that he felt Nick was almost the perfect player, asking, "Have you ever seen anyone like him?" I will tell you what I told him: "Never."

Scotty's approval gave Nick a great deal of confidence. Lidstrom possessed a tremendous slap shot, scoring 11 goals his rookie season and being selected on the NHL All-Rookie team along with the Wings other great rookie defenseman, Vladimir Konstantinov. Nick placed second behind Vancouver's Pavel Bure in voting for the Calder Trophy, which goes to the league's top rookie every year.

Lidstrom is from Vasteras, Sweden. He was studying to become an electrical engineer and as a teenager drove a truck for the Swedish Army while playing hockey, which he had considered his ultimate goal. Because he had played for three years with Vasteras in the Swedish Elite League, Nick was able to become an integral part of the Wings immediately without spending time in the minor leagues. Also prior to joining the Wings in 1991, he developed insight into what hockey in North America was like by playing for Sweden in the Canada Cup series. Although Sweden lost to Canada 4–0, he played against Canada's top players and gained the confidence that he could play in the NHL.

Consistency is the hallmark of Nick's personality and his game. He is steady, quiet, thoughtful, and unassuming. Because he didn't get rattled, you hardly noticed when he was out there on the ice. This was because of his smart play. He didn't take dangerous chances or make foolish plays. He was always under control, playing with intelligence, taking away the good ice, and containing any opposing player in his area by cutting off advancing players, stripping the puck from them, and avoiding taking penalties.

At 6'1", 190 pounds, Nick wasn't a big hitter, delivering checks that were heard all over the arena. Nor did he try to scare opponents with a fiery look on his face. Rather, he merely got position on them and rode them into the boards or corners. His stick-handling and passing were exceptional, as evidenced by his 1,007 assists in 20 NHL seasons. And that powerful, accurate slap shot helped score 318 regular season and play-off goals.

In February 2006, during the Winter Olympic Games in Torino, Italy, he fired a hard slap shot from the left point just 10 seconds into the third period of the gold medal game that landed just under the crossbar and held up for the rest of the period to give Sweden the gold over Finland. Even though it didn't involve teams from North America and the time-zone differences made it more difficult, that very close relationship we had to European players in the NHL drew a huge local TV audience when replayed for us at a more appropriate hour.

When Larry Wigge, NHL columnist with *The Sporting News*, inter-viewed Nick, he caught the essence of the man and what an exceptional person he is. Nick said, "It's amazing the details you think about when you picture a play in your mind—and how it sort of replays for you in slow motion, when in reality you know the play happened in the blink of an eye." He never expected the goal to be the game-winner.

He described the play by saying he remembered Peter Forsberg win-ning the face-off and drawing the puck back to Mats Sundin. As the play developed, he saw a spot in his mind where he thought Mats might drop the puck to him. Nick was amazed at how open he was, not realizing that Saku Koivu had broken his stick and taken himself out of the play to go to the bench to get another one. Then he remembered while winding up that Peter told him, the Finnish goaltender, his Philadelphia Flyers teammate, covers everything so well down low that if any of the Swedes could get an open shot to drive it high. Nick said he saw that kind of opportunity "and just drilled it."

After the final buzzer, Lidstrom remembered being proud that he and his teammates, who had competed in previous Olympic battles together, were able to overcome all the prior negative feelings toward them heading into the Games. This also furthered the respect he had for his teammates and for those great friends he played street hockey with, who taught him to be so competitive as a youngster growing up. Nick's gloves, worn while taking that winning slap shot, are now on display in the Hockey Hall of Fame. He has placed his winning stick and puck in his own trophy room at home in Sweden.

Later the same year in Riga, Latvia, the "Tre Kronor" experienced what no team had ever done in international play. Lidstrom and his Swedish teammates won the elusive double, winning both the Winter Olympics and the World Championships played as separate tournaments in the same year. Sweden had eight Olympic champions on its world championship team that beat the Czech Republic team, 4–0, five of them were from the Red Wings including Niklas Kronwall, who was selected the most valuable player in the tournament, Henrik Zetterberg, Mikael Samuelsson, and Johan Franzen.

When the Wings, playing against the New Jersey Devils, failed to win the Stanley Cup in 1995, I asked Steve Yzerman during the post-season physicals who he felt was our most important player. Without a moment's hesitation, he answered Nick Lidstrom. Although Nick was a finalist three times previously for the NHL's Norris Trophy, it wasn't until the 2000–01 season that he was finally selected as the top defense-man at the NHL awards ceremony in Toronto. Nick says he remembers it well because prior to the ceremony he and fellow nominee Ray Bourque were talking. Bourque said that 2001 was Nick's year, that he would win the Norris Trophy, which was pretty special after being nominated for the fourth time. Nick went on to win it again in '02, '03, '06, '07, '08, and '11.

After Yzerman retired, leaving huge skates to fill, Nick was named captain and became more visible as he continued to represent the Wings in a classy and very dignified manner.

He retired after the 2011–12 season to return to Sweden to join his family and sons during their teenage years.

CHAPTER 18

Velikolyopnaya Pyatyorka*

IN ANY LANGUAGE, "THE RUSSIAN FIVE" WERE SIMPLY FABULOUS. (*BORROWED FROM A HEADLINE IN THE DETROIT FREE PRESS, IT TRANSLATES LOOSELY AS "THE FAB FIVE")

In the late 1980s, the Iron Curtain was still in place. The 1972 Russia-Canada Series had taken place and through the International Hockey Federation, further efforts were underway to thaw relations between some communist countries like the Soviet Union, the former Czechoslovakia and the West. NHL clubs were starting to consider drafting European players, usually late in the draft since there was no assurance they would ever be able to bring them to North America.

The 1988 Winter Olympic Games in Calgary, Alberta, were dominated by the Soviet team that captured the Gold Medal with the three players on their famed Green Line—Vladimir Krutov, Igor Larionov, and Sergei Makarov up front and Slava Fetisov and Alexei Kasatonov on defense. Krutov, Larionov, and Fetisov finished 1–3 in scoring, in that order, in the tournament.

A year later, the Berlin Wall fell and with it the Cold War ended, opening the doors to freedom for players from the crumbling USSR. Sergei Priakin, Calgary's 12th choice in the 1988 Entry Draft, was allowed to leave Russia for North America without defecting. The Green Line players soon followed—Krutov and Larionov going to Vancouver; Fetisov and Kasatonov to New Jersey; and Sergei Makarov to Calgary.

By 1994, Larionov was playing for San Jose and was the dominant player involved in the shocking defeat of the Wings in the opening round of the playoffs that spring, when the Sharks were the No. 8 seed against the Stanley Cup–favorite and top-seeded Wings. By 1996, Larionov and Fetisov found their way to the Wings. Larionov arrived early in the 1995–96 season in a trade for Ray Sheppard, and Fetisov came at the '95 trade deadline for a third-round draft choice. With previous drafts of Sergei Fedorov and Vladimir Konstantinov in 1989 and Slava Kozlov a year later, the Wings had an unprecedented weapon they would deploy strategically en route to their first Stanley Cup championship in 42 years. They would become known through the hockey-playing world as "The Russian Five."

Detroit's Red Army

Here was a unique group of exceptional individuals, each with a very unusual story of his development through the Soviet system and on to the NHL. I have the utmost admiration for them and for what they were able to accomplish in their remarkable careers. Each man was a very gifted athlete who had worked long hours each day for many years to reach his goals.

In the Red Wings' case, one of the key individuals in scouting, appraising, and encouraging the selection of key unheralded Russian and European players were the Wings European scouts, Hakan Andersson, and, before him, Christer Rockstrom. Often these scouts discovered players very early in their development, long before they become known to the average scout. Andersson was directly responsible for recommending the drafting of Pavel Datsyuk, chosen 171st overall in 1998, as well as a host of other European players selected in the later rounds, several of whom have become important parts of the Wings' roster.

With the fall of the Iron Curtain, it wasn't long before a large number of talented Eastern European hockey players appeared on the NHL scene. The Red Wings led the way. Nick Polano, former coach and confidant of Jimmy Devellano, had many European contacts, and the team developed a European scouting network second to none that allowed the Wings to draft high-quality relatively unknown (at least in North America) players fairly high and with very little fanfare. The NHL Entry Draft of 1989 was the most remarkable example of that, providing the heart of what would become a dynasty that produced the great Stanley Cup teams of the mid and late 1990s and early 2000s.

During the 1989 Entry Draft, former Red Wings communications director Bill Jamieson, who sat at the Wings table with Red Wings scouts and coaches, recalled how excited they all were when they drafted Sergei Fedorov, picked 74th overall in the fourth round. Jimmy Devellano said that if Fedorov had been playing in North America, he would have been drafted first overall, but with the Iron Curtain still in place, there was no assurance they could get him out of the Soviet Union.

Based on Sergei's performance since then, Jimmy D. was right. Sergei went on to win the Hart Trophy (most valuable player) and Lester Pearson Award (the NHL's top player as selected by his peers) in 1994 and the Selke Trophy (best defensive forward) in 1994 and 1996. More importantly, he had his name engraved on the Stanley Cup with the Wings in 1997 and 1998.

But as great as he turned out to be, Fedorov wasn't even the best player drafted by the Wings that year. They also acquired defenseman Nicklas Lidstrom in the third round with the 53rd pick overall, and all he accomplished in a 20-year career was to win the Norris Trophy seven times and prompt debate about who was the league's all-time best defenseman, Lidstrom or Bobby Orr. Even Orr acknowledged that was a reasonable topic of discussion.

The Wings also selected Vladimir Konstantinov, who went on to succeed Fetisov as captain of the famed Soviet Red Army club, with the 221st selection in the 11th round. Konstantinov was a Norris Trophy finalist, too—and a Stanley Cup champion—before his career was tragically cut short in a limo accident just seven days after the Wings won the Cup in 1997.

A year later, the Wings selected a dazzling young forward named Slava Kozlov with their third selection, 45th overall. Devellano raved about him, too, describing Kozlov as the best 14-year-old hockey player he'd ever seen—and he saw Wayne Gretzky play at age 14.

So in the era when the Wings were coached by Scotty Bowman, whose roster included an impressive group of future Hall of Famers from the mid-1990s until he left coaching, five of his best players were from Russia, trained as elite athletes by the Red Army club and used as a single unit in Detroit. They went by various nicknames like "the Detroit Red Army" and "the Wizards of Ov," but to most throughout the hockey world they were simply The Russian Five—and they took the NHL game to another level.

They played the game with such enthusiasm, grace, pride, and control that their talent, to all who watched, was obvious. They performed complex plays, especially retreating from the blue line and reloading if a play at the offensive blue line wasn't there, and they did it with such apparent ease, working as a unit the likes of which had never been seen in the NHL, and controlling the puck in a way that frustrated opponents as they chased it around the rink.

Their stories on how they made it to Detroit and, in the process, changed the game and the league, were uniquely different and equally compelling.

Viacheslav "Slava" Fetisov
Generally considered the Godfather of all Russian hockey players, Slava came to North America late in his hockey life after a brilliant career in the former Soviet Union. He represented the USSR in three Winter Olympic Games, starting with the powerful that lost to Team USA in the Miracle on Ice game at Lake Placid in 1980. He won a silver medal that year followed by two Olympic golds in Sarajevo, Yugoslavia, (1984) and Calgary, Alberta, (1988). Fetisov was among the earliest Russians drafted by the NHL, originally drafted by Montreal in the 12th round in 1978.

Fetisov resisted many attractive overtures from New Jersey Devils GM Lou Lamoriello to come to North America during the early and middle days of his hockey life because he was unwilling to do so without the blessing of the Russian Sports Federation. That opportunity did not come

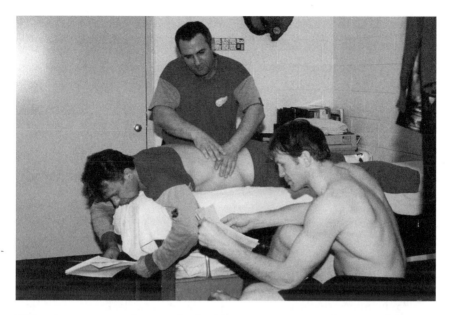

This picture was taken in the locker room prior to the 1997 limo accident during which all three men were injured—masseuse Sergei Mnatsakanov (severely injured), Slave Fetisov (moderately), and Vladimir Konstantinov (severely). (Photo courtesy of Mark Hicks)

along until many of his fellow players had already made the move—generally without the approval of the Soviet government. Fetisov was a fatherly personality. His teammates not only respected his outstanding hockey ability, but even more they were drawn to his kind, friendly, and compassionate manner. When problems arose, they always looked to him to suggest a solution that would be fair and agreeable.

His career took a turn after a confrontation with his coach, Viktor Tikhonov, who ruled his team with a brutally iron fist. All members of the Soviet National Team were ranked members of the Soviet Red Army and therefore enjoyed special privileges that went along with their positions. However, when the dispute with Tikhonov took place, Fetisov was returned to the Army with the rank of major and given a desk job unrelated to hockey. But his teammates, led by Larionov, rebelled just prior to the Calgary Games, demanding the return of their captain. In effect, they refused to play without Fetisov.

In a stunning turn of events, Tikhonov backed down. The Soviets won the gold, and as part of the deal they struck with their leaders, some players received permission to continue their careers in North American with NHL teams. Fetisov and his defense partner, Kasatonov, were soon playing together in New Jersey. Ironically, the two rarely exchanged a word as Devils teammates. Kasatonov sided with Tikhonov in that pre-Olympic dispute with the players.

To this day, even as one of the highest executives in the Russian Sports Federation, Fetisov prides himself on having been an instrumental figure in opening the door to the West, allowing players to get out of the Soviet Union legally without defecting to sign a NHL contract. On April 3, 1995, he joined the Red Wings in a trade deadline deal.

Our first personal contact with Slava, after the usual initial medical examinations, was when Sergei Fedorov brought him to our home to our annual team family spring/Easter party—just players, their wives and children, no coaches, managers, or other club employees. Slava seemed so amazed to see the unusual friendship all the players had for one another and the great respect they all had for him. His only regret was that his wife and daughter couldn't be there; they were still back in New Jersey.

Of all our Russian players, Fetisov may have been the most important—not so much for his remarkable skills as for his ability to create a special element of pride in The Russian Five. Clearly he had more influence on the younger players, especially Sergei Fedorov, than any member of the coaching staff. With merely a few words, and sometimes just a look from Fetisov, Fedorov—who often frustrated his teammates because they never knew when he would "show up"—would lockstep into place with his Russian teammates.

When the Wings won the Cup in 1997, Slava, Vladimir Konstantinov, and team masseuse Sergei Mnatsakanov were riding back from a team golf outing in limousines rented for the occasion when their driver fell asleep and crashed the vehicle head-on into a tree along Woodward Avenue in Birmingham. Konstantinov suffered a severe career-ending closed-head injury, and Mnatsakanov suffered a broken back, spinal cord injury, and contracted left arm that left him paralyzed from the waist down. Slava was the least severely injured, but he still suffered rib and significant body injuries.

Our office looked after Slava when he was released from the hospital and, as an indication of the kind of thoughtful person he was, we were given a signed and autographed painting of The Russian Five with the additional comment, "To best Doctor John Finley from Russian Five, Thank You, All the Best." It was signed by each player, and he brought it to the office just before he, Igor Larionov, and Slava Kozlov made a triumphant return to Russia with the Stanley Cup, parading it around Red Square near the Kremlin and making a rather interesting stop at Lenin's tomb. That picture remains one of our most treasured possessions from my days with the team.

The author with one of his personal treasures, an artist's rendition of the famed Russian Five. (Photo courtesy of Eric Seals, *Detroit Free Press*)

Another remarkable recollection of Slava in the following years was while he was still playing for the Wings. After a game at Joe Louis arena, he returned a telephone call in trainer John Wharton's private, glassed-in office to Russian premier Boris Yeltsin. They talked for 40 minutes. I thought to myself, *How remarkable is that?* When the Wings didn't re-sign Slava in 1998, he returned to New Jersey as an assistant coach under Larry Robinson, living in a Russian community of more than 800 families not far from the rink. While Slava was one of the assistant coaches with the New Jersey Devils in 2002, Russian Premier Vladimir Putin was the guest of President George W. Bush in Washington. Putin invited Slava to come to Washington as one of his Russian guests at a state dinner at the White House.

Putin, a great hockey fan, had developed a friendship with Fetisov. Slava was a national hero in the former Soviet Union, serving as the captain of their national team for more than eight years. Slava excused himself for the day from his assistant coaching duties with the Devils and made the trip to Washington. He had no hint of what was in store for him. He had originally considered possibly becoming an NHL coach.

At that dinner, Putin told Slava he could give him "a bigger team" and offered him the position of Russia's Sports Minister, the head of Rossport. To any Russian sports person, Sports Minister is the country's dream job and as Russia's national sports hero, he was the perfect person for it. Slava quickly accepted, telling Putin he wanted "every kid in his country to have the chance I had."

Rossport was a new federal agency dedicated to the revival of the country's sports infrastructure, which had declined since the fall of the Iron Curtain in 1989.

"We are trying to rebuild the system," Fetisov said. "We are trying to take what was best from the Soviets and the best from what is going on in North America and Europe and build a system for the youth and obtain the funding that it requires." His plans were to have gifted Russian athletes show their ability on the world stage and compete on the highest level rather than just competing at home. The Fetisovs had just built a new home in New Jersey, but after he accepted the position of Russia's Sports Minister, Slava quickly grabbed his suitcase, wife, and daughter, and was on his way home to Moscow.

One of the first of the great young Soviet players to defect to the NHL was Alexander Mogilny, whose career began in Buffalo in 1989. He was a teenaged linemate and close friend of Sergei Fedorov's on the Red Army team. Genevieve and I were introduced to Alex by Slava Fetisov at the All-Star Game breakfast reception in Los Angeles, where they both were on the roster, Slava as an honored elite elder player and Mogilny as a chosen participant.

There is no one in all of hockey whom I have a more respectful opinion of than Slava Fetisov. Considering all the hurdles and problems he was confronted with, he is so remarkable to have risen above them all to earn the admiration and respect of every player on any team for which he has performed—and most of his opponents, too.

Vladimir Konstantinov

Vladdie joined us in 1991, a former member of the Central Red Army team born in Murmansk, the great seaport in far northern Russia in 1967. A person of rather average size for a hockey player, he was one of the toughest, most competitive players I have ever known. Vladdie would bring his disturbing play to the game every night and was absolutely relentless in his in-your-face attack on opposing players.

He played left defense but he grew up playing center, so he knew how forwards think and could anticipate their moves defensively. He also knew how to lead a rush. It was fun to watch opposing players coming down his wing. If they had the puck, they were looking for where he was and usually passed it off before taking a punishing hit from him. If the winger racing down the left side had just received a pass, he would either quickly pass it off, move to center, or be prepared to take a bruising body-check from him. He rarely missed getting a piece of anyone coming down his side. If they coughed up the puck and he had no one to pass to, he would generally grab the puck, race through the neutral zone into the opponent's end, and often score.

The late Steve Chiasson, Vladdie's defensive partner for more than two seasons with the Wings—and his adversary in a wild, bench-clearing brawl in the 1986 World Junior Championships—used to say that Vladimir Konstantinov was "a pain in the [expletive] to play against." Steve admitted that he loved to chop and whack away at his opponents with the best of them, but under no circumstances could he or would he do the things that Vladdie did. Konstantinov wasn't a fighter, but he was a super pest with a sharp bite.

In Europe Vladdie played tough, but because of the large rinks it wasn't as noticeable. In North America, the smaller, NHL-sized rinks were an advantage to him, allowing him to make use of his physical style. Also, he loved playing in front of the large crowds here as opposed to the 1,000–2,000 people they played in front of in Russia. Injuries that would stop other players often went unnoticed by Vladdie. When we did the exit (end-of-season) physicals after winning the Stanley Cup in 1997, a chest X-ray revealed that he had been playing with a broken rib through the last series.

His very white complexion and dull blond hair made him appear much older than he was, so his Russian teammates called him "Grandpa." Their Soviet coach, Tikhonov, was a master of discipline, dedication, and concentration, and Kónstantinov admitted he learned a lot from him. The Red Army club had very tough practices morning and evening with a soccer practice and game in the afternoon. As a Red Wing, Vladdie was instrumental in getting the Wings involved in a unique warm-up, kicking and heading the soccer ball among a circle of teammates for 10–15 minutes before they donned their uniforms for the pregame warm-up. Obviously, this did wonders for their eye-foot coordination and general relief of pregame jitters.

There are many interesting stories about Vladdie and his wife, Irena. Notable among them was how he faked cancer and the Wings bribed Russian doctors—one of them with a big Chevrolet Caprice—in order to win Vladdie's release to come to America to seek treatment. They came to us at a time when long lines existed in the food stores in Russia, and those stores would often be out of even the most essential items. After arriving in Detroit, the first time Irena went to the supermarket, she was amazed with what she saw and was afraid they were going to run out. She filled three grocery carts full of food before someone told her that it wasn't necessary, that the grocery shelves would still be full the next day.

Whenever we went to a team party, Vladdie and Irena would often ask Genevieve and me to sit with them. We had many very interesting conversations. The limo accident was a terrible tragedy, ending one of the most potentially remarkable careers in hockey. He was an athlete easily destined to become one of the greatest defensemen in the NHL and a millionaire many times over. He was struck down in the prime of his career—by guy who fell asleep at the wheel of the limo carrying the Russian contingent.

After their accident, Vladdie and Sergei Mnatsakanov always attended our team spring/Easter party. Vladdie still attends many home games, brought by his nurse-care-giver Pam Demanuel and her husband, Gary, in a van specially outfitted for Vladdie. The players always greet him enthusiastically, and they have kept his stall in the dressing room with his name above as a reminder to the team of the tragic event. He was with them for the Cup-winning game and team picture in Washington in 1998 and in Detroit in 2002.

Vladimir Konstantinov's play with The Russian Five in those Stanley Cup years was one of the proudest moments in Red Wings history—and the limo accident was one of the saddest. I truly treasured the six memorable years he played for the Wings.

Igor Larionov

Igor is one of the most talented, intelligent, and gifted players ever to play the game. The hockey-writing media used to say that "Igor Larionov" was Russian for "Wayne Gretzky." He did so many things well. Like

Gretzky, he was a thoughtful, serious, and proud player who rarely made a mistake. The great hockey experts said he was able to see the ice well and knew where to position himself to avoid injury and always make the right play. Off the ice, he wore eyeglasses slightly larger than the spectacles worn by Ben Franklin, which made him appear very studious, and he quickly became known by all he met, players and press alike, as "the Professor." Everyone loved him for his friendly manner and engaging smile.

Igor's life in Russia is hard to appreciate for those of us in North America. *Detroit Free Press* columnist Keith Gave described the Voskresensk apartment in suburban Moscow where Larionov lived as more depressing than the most depressed dwellings in Detroit. When Larionov was a boy, his grandfather was taken from his apartment by the KGB in the middle of the night and imprisoned in a forced labor camp for political dissidents for 14 years. Igor always had a very inquiring mind and as a youngster used a short-wave radio to listen to what was going on outside Russia.

He was among the first in that exodus of Russian players to the NHL, arriving in 1989 at the age of 29. That year he was named the top hockey player in all of Russia. Igor and Vancouver Canucks general manager Pat Quinn worked out a $1 million contract in the kitchen of Igor's Moscow apartment for him and teammate Vladimir "Tank" Krutov. Igor was allowed to jump to North America because players over 30 weren't as useful in the Russian system, which preferred younger players who could be more easily controlled.

Larionov was unaware of the arrangement the Russians forced upon the NHL—requiring the payment of hundreds of thousands of dollars by NHL teams as compensation for their services. When Igor learned of this, he played out his three-year contract with Vancouver and then went to Switzerland to play free of interference from the Soviet system and ending the money flow. It also gave him an opportunity to learn Italian, he says with a smile. After a year in Switzerland, he returned to the NHL, playing in San Jose for three seasons. Wings fans got to know him well when his playmaking helped the

Sharks to the monumental first-round upset of Scotty Bowman's powerful Wings in the first round of the 1994 Stanley Cup playoffs.

Originally Larionov thought he might spend three years in North America before retiring—but ended up playing 14 seasons in the NHL—and completed his sensational career resume with three Stanley Cups with Detroit. The Wings acquired him from the Sharks in October 1995 in a trade for high-scoring right wing Ray Sheppard. In Detroit, Larionov joined three elite young Russian players, Fedorov, Konstantinov, and Kozlov. Igor was just the catalyst we needed to help quarterback our team. He fit into our system of emerging elite players like a hand in a perfectly fitted glove. His ability to see the ice, make a play, carry the puck, or retreat and reload for the attack was remarkable, and our fans were treated to some beautifully structured plays when he was on the ice.

One of my fondest memories of Igor was his scoring the game-winning goal in the third overtime in Carolina against the Hurricanes in the Cup finals in 2002. The Wings subsequently won the Cup two games later in Detroit.

Rugged Swedish forward Tomas Holmstrom was in awe of Larionov when he first came to Detroit. He would rave about Igor's incredible puck-handling skills. Larionov disdained the dump-and-chase hockey favored by so many NHL teams. "He just turned around, came back, and carried the puck in," Homer said. When The Russian Five first started playing together, Chris Draper said, "Everyone on the bench was just like, 'Wow.' We couldn't believe we were playing on the same ice as they were, playing against the same guys as the rest of the team was, and yet they were so different, especially Igor with the puck."

Igor's final NHL season with the Devils, under Coach Pat Burns, was disappointing for him since their style was to throw the puck into the opposing team's end and rush into their end, recover the puck, and make a play. That style of play did not complement the artful finesse with which Larionov played the game. Igor retired after the New Jersey Devils were eliminated by the Flyers in the first round of the playoffs of 2004. Even then, Igor looked much younger than his 42 years. He is extremely conscious about his diet, though he loves exceptional wines, and in retirement has become an expert and has his own wine labels: Hat Trick and Power Play.

As his last hurrah, Igor arranged with Slava Fetisov to take a group of Red Wings and NHL legends to Moscow to play in what he described as his final hockey game. Billed as "Farewell From Moscow," the exhibition included Steve Yzerman, Sergei Fedorov, Brendan Shanahan, Nicklas Lidstrom, Ilya Kovalchuk, Martin Brodeur, Luc Robitaille, Chris Chelios, Alexander Mogilny, Sergei Gonchar, Sergei Nemchinov, and Oleg Tverdovsky along with former Red Wings coaches Scotty Bowman, Barry Smith, and Dave Lewis.

Currently, Igor resides in suburban Detroit and serves as a consultant to the KHL, Russia's Continental Hockey League, which he hopes to develop to the point where it might challenge the NHL. It is hard to find any other player who has had the combined success that Igor has had both in international play and the NHL.

Sergei Fedorov

By the late 1980s, the number of talented young European hockey players was increasing on the NHL scene, and the Red Wings were in danger of falling behind in that area. That would soon change. Nick Polano, former coach and assistant to GM Jimmy D., had many European contacts, and the team had developed a European scouting network then led by Christer Rockstrom. They were beginning to discover some high-quality though relatively unknown (at least in North America) players. It was the style of Wings management to send Nick to Europe every few months to confer with the European scouts and attend many of the European and World Cup tournaments to personally observe many of the prospects.

Sergei's father, Victor, a hockey and soccer coach, moved his family from Pskov in southwestern Soviet Union, southwest of St. Petersburg near Estonia, to an extreme northwest sub-Arctic location, Apatity, not far from the Finnish border. There, under the guidance of his father, Sergei developed from a 9-year-old youngster to a teenage player with superstar potential by practicing his skills nearly year-round.

Sergei occasionally came to our office for medical care. He would tell us about growing up playing hockey in Russia, saying they would skate on the rivers 7–8 hours each day until darkness that came early to that region. My wife, Genevieve, our office manager, asked him about the makeup of the teams, taking breaks, and keeping warm. He said they "built bonfires along the river, but you just kept skating. If you took a break and stopped, you would freeze." His mother often brought them food so they didn't have to leave the area or stop skating.

By the time he reached his teens, Sergei had become a very highly skilled, world-class player. Sergei was asked to join the elite squad of the Central Red Army team that required him to leave his family at age 15 and moving to Moscow. In 1988, he helped the Soviet National team win the silver medal at the World Junior Hockey Championships and the gold medal at the senior level World Championships the following year. He was also chosen to play in the Goodwill Games in Seattle, Washington.

A year earlier, Detroit made Sergei the highest Russian-born player ever selected in the NHL Draft in the fourth round with the 74th overall pick. At that time, Soviet players had no freedom to leave their country to play in the NHL, and he and his teammates were closely watched whenever they traveled abroad. Also, many members of the national team were soldiers in the Soviet Army, so leaving was considered desertion.

The Wings really wanted Sergei Fedorov and had no intention of waiting until the Soviets freed him to come to North America—if and when that would ever happen. So almost immediately after they drafted him, a cloak-and-dagger mission began involving a certain Russian-speaking Detroit sportswriter that led about a year later to Fedorov's successful escape from his team. Polano and Jim Lites, the former Wings executive vice president, had some experience in the defection business when they helped spirit Petr Klima out of the former Czechoslovakia in the summer of 1985. Their new ultra-secret mission was to deliver Fedorov to Detroit in time for the 1990–91 season.

Just before a team dinner on July 22, 1990, Sergei was given a prearranged signal from one of them, reading a newspaper in a Seattle hotel lobby. He slipped out of the hotel where the Soviets were staying and jumped on a plane headed for Detroit. Since he was already legally in the United States, entering with his Russian teammates a few days earlier, his departure wasn't technically a defection, though that is certainly how the Soviets described it. Fedorov, as a 20-year-old, was merely seeking to work for a company that was offering him a very good job in the country he had entered legally as a guest.

The event, naturally, created a storm of protests from Soviet officials who were tired of losing their best and brightest to the NHL with no compensation. So as a compromise of sorts, in the 1990–91 season, the NHL, (comprised then of 21 teams) agreed to play a series of games with three of the top teams in the Russian Federation. Each of those teams would play seven games against NHL opponents, guaranteeing that each NHL team would play one game against the Russians in their own building, and it would count in the NHL standings. The Fedorov "defection" angered the Soviets, and they threatened to boycott the upcoming exhibition series unless a large payment was made to them. The Wings complied, and Sergei was free to begin his NHL career.

To make sure Fedorov was comfortable and well taken care of in his new environment, the Wings had a Russian-speaking internist from Henry Ford Hospital available at all games as an interpreter to answer any medical questions he might have. Sergei lived with a young Russian-speaking couple who translated for him. Fedorov was an immense talent, gifted with speed, skating ability, strength, puck control, and a hard, accurate slap shot, all of which exceeded the ability of even most of the elite players.

Whenever he was on the ice, you could expect that exceptional events and moves were going to take place. As he became more comfortable in Detroit, he brought over his parents, Viktor and Natalia, and brother,

Fedor (actually pronounced FYO-dor). His mentor-father had Sergei employing many soccer moves using his feet with the puck to compliment his outstanding speed and skating talent. Always part of his training ritual, after a morning practice, Sergei would spend about two hours on the soccer field for exercise and for improving his eye-foot coordination. In the summer of 2006, he took part in a Soccer Aid charity event in Manchester, England, to raise money for UNICEF.

Sergei's amazing talents quickly captured the attention of the entire league and, along with Steve Yzerman, made the Wings team a serious contender. One of Natalia's best friends was the mother of 14-year-old tennis star Anna Kournikova. As she became a more accomplished tennis player, their relationship grew closer to the point where he would attend many of her matches when played outside the confines of the hockey season, including the French Open and Wimbledon.

The pair was occasionally spotted together around metro Detroit. When she was 16, she came with Sergei to our spring/Easter party. Our office treated her on several occasions during that period, and she rode with Sergei in the 1997 Stanley Cup parade. It was later reported that they had privately married. Anna won two Grand Slam doubles titles during her career that ended in 2003 following several foot injuries. During the later stages of her playing career, she became a sought-after endorsement celebrity. Forbes.com ranked her among the 100 highest-paid athletes during that time, epitomizing the stature she had acquired both in sports and advertising. Among her most famous endorsements: a sports bra. "Only the balls should bounce," she said with an impish grin.

After the 2002–03 season, the Wings went through a very tense and public attempt to sign and keep Sergei. He was a free agent, his relationship with Anna had broken off, and he apparently wanted to go to a team where he would have his own identity and not feel as though he was second fiddle to more prominent players on the team. He therefore left Detroit to join his first coach with the Wings, Bryan Murray, in Anaheim. I'm told he received the same salary he was offered by Detroit.

During the 2004–05 lockout, Brian left the Mighty Ducks for Ottawa, and the new Anaheim GM was Brian Burke, whose obvious trademark of brute force didn't afford much opportunity for a skilled player like Fedorov. Burke soon traded Sergei to Columbus where former Wings associate coach and assistant GM Doug MacLean was president of the expansion Blue Jackets, then coached by former Wings teammate Gerard Gallant. After MacLean left Columbus, the Blue Jackets traded Sergei and his high salary to the Washington Capitals, probably at the urging and consent of their Russian sensation Alex Ovechkin.

They were justly rewarded when, during the 2009 first round of the Stanley Cup playoffs, the Capitals rebounded from a 3–1 deficit to win their best-of-seven series over the New York Rangers—and Fedorov was a big part of it. With Game 7 deadlocked near the end of the third period at 3–3 and five minutes remaining, Fedorov, their oldest player at 39, did what he always did best that time of year. Relying on his extensive playoff experience, he entered the offensive zone, going one-on-one with Ranger defenseman Wade Redden and fired a blistering shot typical of his younger years with the Wings. The puck eluded Rangers goalie Henrik Lundquist short side, top shelf, a goal that will long be remembered by Capitals fans.

That would prove to be Sergei's swan song. In 2009, Fedorov left the NHL, stating that he felt the Washington Capitals did not have him in their long-term plans. His brother, Fedor, had been playing in Russia in the Kontinental Hockey League for several years with Metallurg Magnitogorsk. Sergei quickly accepted a two-year, tax-free $3.8 million contract to play there, too. Their signing was the fulfillment of a dream of their father, Viktor, who was responsible for the hockey development and training of both his sons, who were finally able to play together on a Russian team. During the Fedorov era in the NHL, No. 91 (the year Sergei entered the NHL) became synonymous with exceptional hockey-playing ability, skill, determination, and natural talent. Once back in the USSR, he retrieved his old number from his Red Army days with CCCP, No. 18. Out of respect for his brother, Fedor reversed it and wore No. 81.

Sergei loved fast beautiful cars, and he owned several world-class vehicles that brought him much pride, including a picture-perfect Ferrari. One day he came to our home because of dehydration and was given an IV. He wanted to make a call, but he said his cell phone was on the front seat of his Ferrari, red with soft, light-brown leather interior parked on the circle drive in front of our home. Genevieve offered to get it for him, but she couldn't find it since it was locked in the glove compartment. When she came back in and told him, he handed her the keys and said, "Why don't you take it for a drive?" She declined but might have been tempted; she was fascinated by its beauty.

After Detroit, Sergei made stops in Anaheim, Columbus, and Washington, but he never enjoyed the success he had with the Red Wings. And sadly, in my view, he never enjoyed the adulation he deserved in his return trips to the Joe—as former teammate Bob Probert did when he came in with the Chicago Blackhawks. Sergei left North America in 2010 to continue playing in the Kontinental Hockey League in Russia.

Viacheslav "Slava" Kozlov

Slava was the youngest of The Russian Five. He had a distinguished career in the elite league of the Soviet Union. During the days the Red Wings' Russian scout was evaluating him, Kozzie, and a fellow teammate were in a very serious head-on automobile accident, rushing to their arena to be on time for practice. His teammate was killed, and Kozzie suffered very serious facial and skull fractures. There was concern that he was not expected to live.

After several months in the hospital, he survived. Wings executive Nick Polano flew to Russia, talked to the doctors, and determined Kozlov could still play hockey—but he needed specific medical attention. He was brought to Detroit and thoroughly examined by specialists at Henry Ford Hospital. They agreed and strongly suggested that he not have any reconstructive work done, in spite of not being able to close one eyelid completely, for fear of interfering with an otherwise successful healing process.

Slava played for the Wings for 10 seasons from 1991–92 through 2000–01, moving on to Buffalo and then to former Wings assistant GM Don Waddell's team, the Atlanta Thrashers, where he remained until 2010. He then signed with his old club, CSKA Moscow, but left in February 2011 to join the playoff-bound Salavat Yulaev Ufa. He joined Dynamo Moscow, CSKA's archrival, for the 2011–12 season.

Like Sergei, Slava Kozlov learned much about playing the game from his father, an accomplished coach. Like Larionov, Kozlov grew up in the city of Voskresensk in the shadow of the massive chemical plant that dominated the "suburb" of Moscow, nearly two hours away. There was a low spot in the small yard between an apple tree and the home he grew up in where water settled in the fall and froze in the winter. It was a patch no bigger than the average American living room. It's where Slava learned to skate, as his father proudly told a visitor one day during the lockout in the fall of 1994.

Scouts described the young Slava Kozlov as a fabulous hockey player. Wings GM Jimmy Devellano remembers him being better than that. "I've seen a lot of extraordinary 14-year-old hockey players," Devellano once told the *Free Press*' Keith Gave, "including Wayne Gretzky. Slava Kozlov is the best 14-year-old player I've ever seen."

While Kozlov didn't have the kind of extraordinary success the scouts predicted for him—which may well be the result of the crash that nearly took his life—he still had some very productive seasons in Detroit. Fans will remember him for some of the huge playoff goals he scored.

Those who knew him best will tell you that Slava Kozlov was "the most Russian" of any of the other four who came from that system. Certainly no player took more pride in the accomplishments of The Russian Five than he did.

Although The Russian Five were very dedicated to their team, the city of Detroit, and to one another, the limo accident of 1997 was devastating to them. They seemed to lose their closeness. In fact, when the Stanley Cup made its first visit to Russia after the Wings won the Cup in '97, only three

The author in 1995 with the Western Conference championship trophy, the President's Cup, flanked by The Russian Five (left to right): Vladimir Konstantinov, Igor Larionov, Sergei Fedorov, Slava Kozlov, and Slava Fetisov. (Photo courtesy of Mark Hicks)

of them—Fetisov, Larionov, and Kozlov—made the trip. Vladdie, of course, was recovering from injuries sustained in the accident. But Fedorov declined to accompany his teammates and countrymen on this monumental trip.

Inevitably, the five players went in separate directions. Yet it is interesting to see how the hockey world has evolved in large part because of the impact made by this extraordinary group. In the past, Russian players had just a few certain goals—to win the Olympic gold medal and the World Championships in honor of their country. Today, young Russian players, like those in the Canada, the United States, and European countries, can grow up with some additional goals, too, such as playing with the best in the world in the NHL, and helping their teams win the Stanley Cup.

The Next Generation

So it was with Pavel Datsyuk, who led the next wave of Russian-born players to Detroit. His is a story of perseverance and luck—on the part of the Wings' scouting staff.

Hakan Andersson was the Wings' European scout under Ken Holland, when he headed their scouting staff. Holland encouraged him to stand up for players he believed in. Of course, when draft time came they had to keep Andersson under control, otherwise he would have the Wings to draft only Europeans. (And who could argue, considering the success Detroit has had drafting them?)

Like many teams, the Wings have a philosophy of drafting the best player available regardless of nationality or position, emphasizing skill and speed as opposed to size. When Andersson found Datsyuk, he was actually at the game to scout another player. But he recalls being mesmerized by the slight but skilled 19-year-old Russian playing for HC Yekaterinburg in the Russian league. Pavel Datsyuk dominated the game. Later that year, Andersson was on a plane to return to watch him. A scout from St. Louis was on the same flight that was canceled due to weather. So neither made it to the game.

Lucky for the Wings, since the result was that Hakan was the only scout to see Pavel. Although eligible for the NHL Draft in 1996 and 1997, Datsyuk went unselected, likely because of his size. In 1998, the Wings drafted him in the sixth round with the 171st overall pick. Since Datsyuk had never met or talked to anyone from Detroit, he didn't believe it when a friend told him the Wings had drafted him. He had to see it in the newspaper to be assured it was true.

The terrorist attack on the World Trade Center in New York City on September 11, 2001, occurred while the Wings were undergoing physical exams at the beginning of training camp in the Michigan resort town of

Traverse City. How difficult that was for a player who didn't speak English, who didn't know anyone, in a strange environment to understand what was going on is hard to imagine. Fortunately there were a few Russian teammates there who were able to interpret for him.

The first year Pavel attended the annual Finley spring/Easter house party, we noticed him standing alone on our sun porch while almost everyone was outside playing in the yard. We had an antique pre-WWII school map rack of the world's continents hung on one wall. I had previously pulled down the European continent map in case anyone was interested in looking at it. As Genevieve and I walked in, he said in very limited English, "This is where I am from," pointing to a city just east of the Ural mountains, likely a couple hundred miles north of the Russia-Kazakhstan border and sort of midway between Moscow and Siberia. He was so proud to be able to show us the city of Sverdlovsk.

We later learned that it was an industrial city where Pavel grew up. He lived on the fourth floor of an apartment building with no elevator. He told *Free Press* columnist Mitch Albom that climbing the stairs to the apartment is how he got his strong legs. The apartment's window overlooked a makeshift oval ice surface between his building and the next where he first learned to skate and play hockey.

Both of Pavel's parents died when he was a teenager. His greatest regret is that neither had an opportunity to see him play in the NHL. He injured his knee playing in Russia before he came to Detroit, which is when he discovered how much he really loved the game. He wants the kids in the city of Yekaterinburg, where he played, to learn some of the special skills he acquired and started a hockey school for youngsters and to show Russian minor hockey coaches other approaches to playing hockey by getting NHL coaches and players to help him.

The school's technique is to bring these youngsters through specific small-area skill stations (i.e. taking pucks off the wall, stickhandling in tight areas, stealing the puck from an opponent, wrist-shot shooting and passing). He secured Reebok to donate jerseys for the players and tracksuits (all with a white shield with big red and black PD letters on it) for the NHL instructors. He also has a mixed-martial-arts trainer who teaches them core strength and flexibility exercises they can continue to use on their own.

Pavel married his girlfriend Svetlana, whom he had known for three years before he came to Detroit, and they now have a young daughter. He is in the midst of a six-year $47 million contract.

CHAPTER 19

Spring Fling

THE ANNUAL FINLEY SPRING/EASTER PARTY.
Over the years our family had several unique opportunities to touch the lives of our players personally. With new owners and a new look to the team, it suddenly dawned on us to do something unparalleled in the lore of hockey in an effort to augment the chemistry of all team members and their families.

Here were a bunch of tough, aggressive, and sometimes mean men who played their sport with brutality and passion. What might we be able do to promote brotherly respect and admiration, to make them feel relaxed and at ease, yet continue to battle all comers for the most coveted trophy in sports, the Stanley Cup?

We decided we could have a family springtime party.

To offer a little background, one Christmas as Genevieve made dozens of cookies for our family and friends, our young pre-teen daughters, Molly and Colleen, then 10 and 8, respectively, confiscated the gingerbread men and began to decorate them. When they were finished, they had made gingerbread "Red Wings" personalized for each player on our team. Genevieve packaged them up, and I took them to the next game. After the game as Molly and Colleen waited patiently in the hallway while I finished my work, each player came out and personally thanked them for their cookies—a true testament to the kindness of each man.

On occasion, we would also invite one or two single players over for dinner. Being a true "mom," Genevieve wanted to make sure they were eating well and properly.

The Origins

In 1984, under fresh new ownership and enjoying our first trip in many years to the Stanley Cup playoffs, our daughters suggested we extend an impromptu invitation to the team's players to bring their families over to our house and let the children run around and play in our yard while the adults would relax, enjoy one another, and have lunch. A handful of players attended that year, but it seemed to grow as an event every year.

Twenty years later, it was an annual spring tradition for players, the training, medical, and dental staffs, and any visiting houseguests. Over time, it reached a point where every player came with their family entourage. They really seemed to enjoy themselves. It allowed the players to enjoy each other's company without any coaches or management staff attending. One year, a Wings forward brought his parents, grandparents, and siblings visiting from Europe—a total of eight people!

My wife and daughters always prepared the food, setting up two buffet tables for the adults and a special buffet table exclusively for the players' children. Once one of the toddlers poked his plastic fork into the back of his father's hand and yelled, "This is the kids' table! Your food is over there!"

As the years passed, every new player joined the event, usually accompanying one of the veteran players. Their reaction was always the same; the wives and children were unsure of where they were going or who we were. They usually felt a little hesitant, and more than one confessed they had plan B and only planned to stay a few minutes and be off. Many times, these players would end up being the last to leave and were gracious in thanking us for the chance to be with others in such a fun and informal way. We loved watching the children change from year to year.

We did our best, with the help of the trainers, to schedule the party before the playoffs began and often it would fall on Easter Sunday. It therefore became an Easter Brunch. Usually the weather was spring-like, and while we never had any organized games, we did have an egg hunt thanks to Lisa Colucci, wife of Dr. Tony Colucci. Each year the families played catch with the 20 or 30 tennis balls, or simply chased one another or their balloons in the yard for a few hours in between eating.

At our 1998 party, we had in attendance 73 adults and 52 children, including two newborns less than 10 days old. We are always asked how we managed to gather the children to sit together at the same time for the photo. Turns out, it was pretty easy. Colleen had made bunny cookies, and each child had to take a seat to get one. It always worked to perfection. We sent each family a copy of the photo the following Christmas, and we still hear about it. After the horrible post-Cup limo accident, Vladimir (Vladdie) Konstantinov and Sergei Mnatsakanov, even though disabled, continued to attend and were part of the party.

Some Special Memories

We had a large doghouse in the far corner of our backyard. From our extended wood deck, Bob Probert and Paul Coffey would fire tennis balls, betting each other on who could get the most into the small entrance to the doghouse.

Probie enjoyed himself and the food so much that he made Genevieve promise that if he ever got traded he would still be invited back for the party.

Another time Sergei Fedorov brought his girlfriend and budding tennis star Anna Kournikova and his teenaged brother, Fedor, with him. Fedor came up "missing" at one such gathering, and we found him in our basement, rolling around with our German Shepherd and Golden Retriever dogs. Both Anna and Fedor later became famous on their own, she on the tennis courts and he following his brother to the NHL and KHL.

At one of the parties, Chris Chelios and Brett Hull both arrived in their handsome pre–World War II autos and parked them in front of our house. Everyone attending—and our neighbors—got a big kick out of seeing those vehicles.

Homer (Thomas Holstrom) was one of the 2011 Red Wings hockey player celebrities featured at the Toast of Hockeytown wine tasting party on the Joe Louis Arena skating surface that included nearly all the team members, Coach Babcock, GM Ken Holland, many Arena officials, etc. Homer, without any prompting, said to Genevieve how much he appreciated our spring party and how grateful he was to be able to also bring along his entire visiting family here from the Swedish Arctic Circle area even though that was 15 years earlier.

Genevieve Remembers the Children's Antics

Is there anything funnier than when children's faces say "Oh, Oh?"

Our ranch house had a great floor plan, and it wasn't unusual for the little ones at our annual spring gathering to race down the hallway, through the bedrooms, and back. We wouldn't stop them as the house was pretty childproof, so we would just keep an eye on them. But once, when it was a little too quiet, I found five of them in the stall shower—with the door closed! Fortunately we found them before the oldest (a five-year-old boy) turned on the water.

Another incident we laugh about now was when two three-year-old toddlers wandered onto the taut winter cover on our 26' x 40' pool. The manufacturer promised it was strong enough to hold an automobile, but no adult had ever walked on it. No matter how much their mothers called, cajoled, and bribed them, the little girls kept going further from the edge toward the center.

I can't remember which of the hockey player/dads came over and bellowed "Do you want me to *make* you come back?" In a flash they came running. As small as they were, they respected the big tough guys!

Another time, two more adventurous boys unwound a hose on the front porch, stretched it across the driveway, and turned on the spigot. They were having the best time spraying each other. The party was always in the fenced backyard, so they were unnoticed. When the boys were discovered, their moms were good sports, saw the humor in it, and let them stay until the party was over, running around in their soggy pants and bare feet.

Usually toys were left home for this occasion, but one year a little girl brought her collection of 2" miniature dolls from McDonald's Happy

Team family fun at the Finleys! (Photo courtesy of the Finleys)

Meals. Somehow they all ended up in the toilet in the half bath in the hallway next to the kitchen. I heard some crying and found several tykes watching the toy dolls "swim" as the water swirled around from the second flush! I pulled five of them out, but the rest had been "gulped" by the "Water Fairy" never to be seen again, and we had one very sad little girl on our hands because trying to see if the dolls could swim was not her idea.

Probably the most amusing comment came from our granddaughter, Megan Straffon, who was four at the time when I introduced her to Jiri Fisher as one of the men who played hockey. She said, "Men play football, boys play hockey!"

We all laughed and had to admit we did hear a lot of "Come on, boys!" while cheering for our hockey team.

One year, John "Shaboom" Chabot phoned ahead to ask if he could bring some additional family members to our gathering.

"Sure," Genevieve said.

"How many?" John asked.

"All of them," she said.

And they came, nine of them in his party, all of them First Nation French-Canadians who didn't speak a word of English. But they seemed to enjoy themselves as much as everyone else, and that year's party was better for all because of their presence.

Obviously, a good time was had by all, and we like to think these events—which often seemed like United Nations festivities—helped to cement the relationships everyone had with one another, instilling and inspiring an even stronger team.

After I retired, we also retired the annual party—it was the end of an era. On occasion, we'll run into Red Wings' alumni, and they always mention the parties.

CHAPTER 20

A Cast of Characters

SOME OF THE MANY MEMORABLE PLAYERS AND FRIENDS ALONG THE WAY.
As tempting as it is, it would be impossible to write separate chapters on all the wonderful friends and remarkable athletes I've encountered in nearly a half-century of caring for the Detroit Red Wings and other NHL players around the league when they've visited Olympia Stadium or Joe Louis Arena. Yet I would be remiss not to make mention of at least some of the more memorable characters I've been so fortunate to get to know over the years.

Many have come and gone, leaving precious memories in their wake. Many more remain friends we see and socialize with to this day. Here are but a few of the people about whom I cannot resist sharing a story or two.

Sid "Old Bootnose" Abel
Through all our years associated with the hockey club, there was no one with whom we had a closer relationship. For more than 60 years, Sid was everything—Wings player, captain, coach, general manager, broadcaster, personal friend, and all-around great and wonderful guy.

Originally from Melville, Saskatchewan, in Western Canada, Sid had been a phenomenal left winger for the Wings beginning in the 1938–39 season through 1942–43, when they won the Stanley Cup. He was the epitome of old-time hockey. He always said, "The Red Wings are paid to play, but they would play the Toronto Maple Leafs for nothing because their interest in beating them was so entrenched." Abel was the Wings captain during the 1942–43 Stanley Cup–winning season, after which he served in the Canadian Army until the end of World War II.

Returning after the war, he was again made team captain and remained in that capacity until offered the player-coach opportunity with the Chicago Blackhawks. During that postwar period, he won the Hart Trophy (most valuable player) in the 1948–49 season and was selected by Coach Tommy Ivan to center Gordie Howe and Ted Lindsay, the trio that quickly became known as The Production Line—arguably the most famous unit in NHL history.

Everyone loved "Old Bootnose" and his wife, Gloria, who had been Jack Adams' secretary. They often had players over for an Italian dinner. Players loved and trusted him. Sid was their leader on and off the ice.

Our families grew up together. Their friends were our friends—and often our patients. Their daughter Linda was one of our first babysitters. We were among a group of seven or eight friends who went out for a bite after games and bowled together in the summer. One time, while serving as color commentator for the Wings radio broadcasts with Bruce Martyn, Abel stopped by our office to have his blood pressure checked. His health was a concern after his brother suffered from cancer. I mentioned that we hadn't seen him in a long time and suggested we do a little physical exam and some blood work. During his exam, I felt a large pulsatile mass in his mid-abdomen and sent him to the hospital for an ultrasound.

Shortly, a call came back, saying the ultrasound revealed an 8-cm abdominal aneurysm. I have to smile when Sid, not realizing the severity of his problem, quickly said that he was very relieved. He thought I was going to tell him he had cancer. He stopped traveling by air with the team for his color broadcasts since it was a couple of weeks before Christmas, and after the holidays he underwent successful surgery at the University of Michigan Hospital.

After the Abels left Detroit and retired to Florida, Sid would stop in our office each time he returned for a medical checkup.

As far as I know, he was or is the only "Bootnose" in the NHL. I love the story of how he got his nickname. It happened one night in Montreal, according to longtime Wings broadcaster and stadium announcer, Budd Lynch. Apparently Maurice Richard and Gordie Howe ran into one another one night in a game in Montreal, and the fight was on. Howe floored him. Abel skated by and looked down at the Rocket and said, "How did you like that, you Frenchman?" Rocket quickly jumped up, hit Abel, and rearranged his nose—hence the name Bootnose. Club owner Bruce Norris even named one of his horses Bootnose after him.

Sid was inducted into the Hockey Hall of Fame in 1969, and in one of the more emotional ceremonies of its kind, his No. 12 jersey was retired in 1995 when public relations man Bill Jamieson arranged a special place for it. As Abel's jersey was gliding to the rafters, Howe's No. 9 moved to the right, Lindsay's No. 7 moved to the left, and Sid's No. 12 took its place between them. The Production Line was back together, right where many Wings fans felt it belonged—up there with the sweaters of the other all-time Wings greats: Sawchuk, Delvecchio, and a bit later, Yzerman.

Sid was stricken with cancer in the late 1990s. We discovered it on one of his returns from Florida. Ted Lindsay was one of his closest friends, calling him at least once a week and visiting him every 10 days or so.

Sid passed away in February 2000 at age 81 after a courageous battle. Through it all, as he did throughout his life, Sid Abel proved he was a leader and a man above men. We all loved that guy, our beloved Bootnose.

Bill Gadsby

Another great hockey player from Western Canada—and very proud of it—was the Bill Gadsby. Being an NHL player during the Original Six days meant you had to be a gifted skater, extremely skilled stick-handler, tough with a little bit of meanness, and ready to play every day knowing you had to play through injuries. With just six teams, there were roughly 110 playing positions available in the league—and your spot was ready to be taken over by any number of likely candidates sitting in the minors, waiting for a chance to move up.

Bill learned early in his career that to earn respect, when he took someone in the corner, his "check" was sure to come out with something hurting, possibly missing a tooth, or maybe a nick or two somewhere on his body. As he put it, "I loved to rough 'em up a little." Gads felt it was an important part of the defenseman's game to make the opposing forwards aware that he was there, causing them to hurry their play or lose possession of the puck if they had experienced his unwelcoming treatment.

Bill was also frequently quick enough to retrieve the puck, jump into the play, lead the rush, and sometimes score—hardly the prototypical stay-at-home defenseman of his day. But belligerence was his calling card. The NHL referees were well aware of his tactics, and rightly so. When Bill Gadsby retired after 20 years in the league, he was the all-time penalty-minute leader.

He felt he had to stand up for himself and his teammates every night. Bill was a warrior. Every ice surface was a combat zone, every game a battle with physical confrontation between hockey players who felt they had to prove, every day, that they belonged in the NHL. And the Detroit fans adored Bill for it. In the six-team era, each team played one another 14 times each season, seven at home and seven away, so loyal fans in each arena knew who the bad guys were. Bill Gadsby was well known, and his name was reviled in every opponent's rink.

Bill's life was full of serious and potential life-threatening challenges. In 1939 when he was 12, at the start of World War II, he and his mother were returning from England on an oceanliner. Their ship was torpedoed by a German U-boat, and they spent five hours in a liferaft on the cold Atlantic before being rescued.

He contracted polio—confirmed by spinal tap analysis—while playing with the Chicago Blackhawks and was told he likely would never walk again. But he proved the doctors wrong and continued his very successful career.

In later years, he courageously overcame an alcohol problem as well as several difficult medical issues. He had exceptional support from his lovely wife, Edna, and four daughters, and he eventually wrote a book, *The Grateful Gadsby*, about his experiences in the NHL. He felt the secret to his longevity in the league, particularly during those days of the Original Six era, was his love for the game.

He admitted he even enjoyed the practices. As a 19-year-old teenager, the youngest player on the Chicago Blackhawks, he was chosen to present a gift to the Bruins' Dit Clapper, on the occasion of Dit becoming the first NHL player to play 20 years, during the 1946–47 season. Bill Gadsby and Gordie Howe became the next players to reach that milestone.

Alex "Fats" Delvecchio

Alex was one of those wonderful players who competed with some of the greatest names in hockey from the Original Six days through early league expansion. He was such a natural athlete, a skillful hockey player who appeared to do everything with incredible ease. Gordie Howe used to tell me that while he was sitting on the bench he loved to watch Alex skate. "Fats" had that unusually remarkable touch to his skating, a God-given gift that separated him from most of his peers. He did so unconsciously, and he brought it to other sporting endeavors, as well.

Since we all bowled together in the summer in what we called the "UPPA USA" league, his rare, natural coordination became far more apparent to me. Unlike the rest of the summer bowlers, when Fatty threw the ball, you would never hear it making contact with the alley, his eye-hand coordination was so incredibly perfect—and accurate. Alex's smile and calm demeanor masked his deadly competitiveness.

Alex also used a somewhat different hockey stick. It had a perfectly straight blade, not unlike those used by all professional hockey players before World War II. In all my years in hockey, I never remember seeing any other player using a perfectly straight blade. I personally have a half-dozen sticks from past Wings, and his is one of them because it was so different.

Another story about Alex took place in Toronto while the Wings were on a three-game road trip. They were in Montreal on Thursday night, Toronto on *Hockey Night in Canada* on Saturday evening, and Boston on Sunday. As was their custom after the game on Saturday evening, the players put their hockey equipment in their individual bags. They then carried them out to the landing in the basement of Maple Leaf Gardens, near the partially open steel retractable door where the bus to the airport would pick up the players and their gear.

There was always a 10–15 minute period during which some guys were doing TV, radio, and newspaper interviews while others were signing autographs and talking with friends. Suddenly, a youngster ran up, grabbed Alex's equipment bag, and was gone before anyone realized it. The whole event caused quite a dilemma. No one carried extra jerseys and pants. Those were not sold anywhere as they are today, and of course pants and skates have to be broken in. We flew commercial and had to take off when the plane was scheduled.

But more importantly, we had to figure out how to get wearable hockey gear to Alex for the Sunday game in Boston. At the time we had an AHL farm team in Glens Falls, New York, the Adirondack Wings, that had similar uniforms. Someone drove from there to Boston with the replacements. They also arranged for someone from the Detroit front office to find his practice skates in the Olympia dressing room and fly them to Boston. Delvecchio was able to get enough replacement equipment to play, and if I remember correctly, we won the game.

Marcel Pronovost

Marcel was a great skater and stick handler. His defensive style of play was principally as a stick checker, although he had developed the technique of skating backward and hitting the forward with his hip and butt just as he crossed our blue line. Bobby Hull said, "Getting hit by Marcel was like running into an oak tree because he was so strong and stable on his feet."

A Cast of Characters

In 1948–49, Marcel played junior hockey across the Detroit River in Windsor, Ontario, for the Windsor Spitfires under Coach Jimmy Skinner. At the beginning of the 1949–50 season, Marcel turned pro with Detroit and was sent to Omaha of the United States Hockey League, where he had a very successful season. Skinner again coached Marcel in Detroit from 1954–57.

Although Marcel is listed on the 1949–50 roster, he actually didn't join the team until after the start of the playoffs. Detroit had just entered the Stanley Cup semifinal playoff series against Toronto. Gordie Howe was seriously injured attempting to check Teeter Kennedy, who sidestepped and redirected Gordie into the boards head first. Defenseman Red Kelly was moved up to the forward line in Gordie's spot, and Marcel was brought in to fill Red's spot on defense.

Pronovost appeared in just nine games and had his name engraved on the Stanley Cup, the first of five times in his career, four with the Wings and one with the Maple Leafs. During the 1950–51 season, he started with Detroit's American Hockey League affiliate, Indianapolis, where he suffered a fractured cheekbone. He was then brought up to the Wings, who had a championship season, finishing in first place, but they were knocked out by the Canadiens in the first round of the playoffs.

By the time I joined the Wings' medical staff, Marcel was a well-established defenseman with a bruising hip check and an otherwise punishing game. He used to laugh about when he first came to the Wings—he spoke only French, and all the English-speaking players called it "mumbo-jumbo." But he spoke pretty good hockey. He was chosen as an NHL First Team All-Star in 1959–60 and 1960–61. In 1961, he was runner-up to Doug Harvey for the James Norris Trophy (best defenseman of the NHL).

When Gordie Howe scored his record-setting 545th goal on November 10, 1963, Marcel's younger brother, Andre, was also a member of the Wings, having been acquired from Boston for Forbes Kennedy. Another brother, Jean, had a very credible career in the NHL, scoring 391 goals, including 52 in a season (1975–76) with the Pittsburgh Penguins.

In 1965, Marcel was the key Wings man in an eight-player trade with Toronto that brought Andy Bathgate, Billy Harris, and Gary Jarrett to Detroit and sent Wings Larry Jeffrey, Lowell MacDonald, Eddie Joyal, and Aut Erickson to Toronto. Joining Bobby Baun, Carl Brewer, Tim Horton, Allan Stanley, and Larry Hillman on defense, the Maple Leafs barely made the playoffs in 1967 but went on to beat the Blackhawks and Canadiens in the playoffs, putting Marcel Pronovost's name on the Stanley Cup for the fifth time. After his playing days were over, he joined the New Jersey Devils' scouting staff and earned three more Stanley Cup rings.

Marcel spent 16 years with the Wings, including seven league championship seasons and four Stanley Cup titles. Born in Lac-a-la-Tortue and raised in Shawinigan Falls, Quebec, he was especially loved by the fans in Montreal. He was elected to the Hockey Hall of Fame in 1978, one of 56 Red Wings so honored. In 2005, Marcel's junior jersey, Windsor Spitfires No. 4, was retired in a ceremony at the Windsor Arena. In a pregame reception, Marcel said I put more stitches in him that anyone else. I responded by saying he created a lot more opponent repair work for me in return.

Terry "Ukie" Sawchuk

Terry was one of the most outstanding goaltenders of all time. Everyone questioned Jack Adams' good sense when he traded away the Wings' six-year veteran, big strong Harry Lumley, to Chicago shortly after he helped carry the Wings to the Stanley Cup in 1950. Harry was injured in January that year, and Adams brought in Sawchuk to replace Harry for a couple of games.

Having played in seven games that season, including one shutout, Terry sufficiently impressed Adams that he negotiated the biggest trade in NHL history at that time. Adams sent Lumley, premier Wings defenseman "Black Jack" Stewart, Pete Babando, who scored in the second overtime to win the Stanley Cup for the Wings, and two other forwards to Chicago. In return, the Wings acquired defenseman Bob Goldham, Metro Prystai, Gaye Stewart, and an undistinguished goaltender, Jim Henry. With Lumley gone, the 20-year-old Sawchuk began the next season in the Wings net—and that was the actual purpose of the trade, Adams later admitted.

Terry had one of the most remarkable careers of any goaltender who ever played in the NHL. Legendary New York Rangers goaltender Eddie Giacomin said Terry often wore no shoulder pads to allow him to move quickly and with greater flexibility. To me, his arm length seemed longer. One was deformed due to a baseball accident and may have increased his ability to handle shots on goal more effectively.

Originally from Winnipeg, Manitoba, Terry had a crouching goaltender style with lightning reflexes. He inherited goalie equipment from his brother who had died tragically of heart problems at age 17. Signing his first pro contract at age 17, Terry joined the minor league Omaha Knights of the USHL, a farm team of Detroit, where he won Rookie of the Year honors. He was then sent to Indianapolis of the AHL, winning the same honors there. Sawchuk arrived in Detroit, where he did the same in his rookie season in the NHL, the first player to do so in all three of the leagues he played in. On his 18th birthday, Terry was struck in the eye with a stick in Houston, and removal of his eye was contemplated. Improving overnight, he went on to a Hall of Fame career.

He used to challenge our players during practice, and he played during the Original Six days when each club carried only one goaltender, so he was responsible for playing in every game. A very confident goalkeeper, he always told his teammates, "Get me a couple of goals, and we'll win." During plane trips to playoff cities, the men either played bridge or euchre. The plane's seats could be reversed. We would spread out a blanket and "Ukie" Sawchuk, Gordie Howe, Marcel Pronovost, and I would often play Bridge the entire trip.

The goaltenders today have a great deal of protective equipment made of high-quality materials. When Terry Sawchuk played, his body shield was a half-inch cotton felt apron-like cover, worn inside the uniform. He didn't use elbow pads, and only later in his career did he try a facemask, which was merely a fiberglass face shield with openings for the eyes, nose, and mouth.

It prevented facial lacerations, but the bruising effect of being struck with the frozen hockey puck remained. Terry had such a fear of being struck in the face that even the protection of wearing the fiberglass mask gave him renewed confidence that probably extended his career about 10 years.

Once during training camp preseason play, the Wings were in Halifax, Nova Scotia, when Terry developed acute abdominal pain. He was examined by the doctors there, and they suspected a bowel obstruction. They immediately flew him back to Detroit. Our studies revealed he had become badly constipated, and no surgery was required, only bowel cleansing. The press was waiting at the hospital for the surgical report, thinking he might be lost for the season. *Detroit News* sportswriter John Walter asked for the medical report, which I gave him, but I had to smile because of the humor of the situation. He reported that after appropriate treatment, the problem was resolved and he didn't need surgery.

It was often said that Ukie was a loner, frequently troubled by personal demons. He was often the last one showered and preferred not to talk to the press. Psychiatrists and clinical psychologists tell us that one of the common signs of overwhelming stress is to seek isolation. After playing 20 seasons, and at that time with the New York Rangers, his career ended prematurely when he became involved in an altercation with a fellow Rangers teammate with whom he shared a rented home.

Being used to the hockey wars and no stranger to pain, Sawchuk suffered a hidden, undiagnosed abdominal injury to his liver during the fight and died several weeks later. Since the first NHL expansion had just occurred, I'm sure he would have been in the league several more years, extending records that Patrick Roy, Martin Brodeur, and other great goaltenders of later eras would still be chasing.

Glenn Hall

As a young resident in general surgery at Detroit Osteopathic Hospital, I was often the guest at the games of the team surgeon and assisted him in the care of the players, many of whom I had gotten to know when they came to the hospital for treatment. The goaltender at the time was Glenn Hall who had played in the Red Wings' system for their sponsored junior club, the Edmonton Oil Kings.

Typical of many goaltenders, Terry Sawchuk had a moody disposition, and likely because of that he had been traded to Boston at the end of the 1955 season. Hall was called up a couple of times when Terry was injured and couldn't play. He performed exceptionally well for a rookie, so Jack Adams knew he had a quality goaltender in the farm ranks, which made it an easy decision to trade Terry.

Glenn Hall always hated training camp, like most goaltenders. After the first NHL expansion, when playing for St. Louis, he would call into training camp headquarters, saying he would be late getting into to camp because he had to paint the barn. This seemed to happen each year. Several years later, after Glenn had retired, the son of the Blues owner, Sidney Salomon III, and Scotty Bowman were making a scouting trip through western Canada and stopped in Calgary. They decided to call Glenn and when they arrived he was sitting on his porch, so they joined him and talked for a while. Finally, Sid asked Glenn if he could see his barn. And Glenn Hall responded sardonically, "I don't have a barn."

During a reception at the time of Hall's induction into the Canadian Sports Hall of Fame, Frank Mahovlich, reminiscing with Glenn and said to him, "You know, I scored my first NHL goal against you." And Hall, with a distressed look on his face, replied, "Yes, I know, Frank. I regret that yours was a fairly common distinction."

Considered one of the most significant trades of all time, Hall, an outstanding rookie having taken Terry Sawchuk's place with the Wings, was traded to Chicago. It was thought that he sided with Ted Lindsay regarding the development of a players' union. That made him expendable with Ted. He was traded for four players headed by Johnny Wilson, who was setting the record at the time for his iron-man ability—playing more consecutive games than anyone of that era. Wilson's most remarkable record was playing in 502 consecutive games.

Garnet "Ace" Bailey

Ace played with us two years, 1972–73 and 1973–74. He was the son of the great Toronto star, Ace Bailey, who suffered a career-ending head injury after being cross-checked from behind by the rough, tough Eddie Shore of the Boston Bruins. That incident was the motivation for the first NHL All-Star game held in Toronto as a benefit for the senior Bailey. It was such a success that the league continued it every year except 1943 to honor its elite players. The original structure during the six-team era was for the Stanley Cup winner to compete against the stars from the rest of the league. After expansion, it was East vs. West.

The younger Ace, who was drafted by Boston in the third round in the 1966 amateur draft, honed his skills in Hershey and played for the Bruins for most of the 1969–70 season, scoring 11 goals on a team with such hockey greats as Bobby Orr, Johnny Bucyk, Gerry Cheevers, and Phil Esposito. GM Ned Harkness traded defenseman Gary Doak to Boston to obtain him, improving Detroit's speed, scoring ability, and toughness. Ace loved the battles in the corners.

But off the ice he was a different man with an infectious smile and charm. He seemed happy just to be playing in the NHL. We had a dismal season, but he also joined great players on our team—Marcel Dionne, Red Berenson, Alex Delvecchio, and Mickey Redmond. We missed the play-offs by a close margin to Buffalo, and afterward Harkness fired our coach, Johnny Wilson, and traded Ace, Ted Harris, and Billy Collins to St. Louis for a three-player package that included Brian Watson and Jean Hamel. The day after our last game, sensing there would soon be changes, we all went up to the Red Wings Alumni Room on the second level of Olympia Stadium and spent an hour lamenting the season and our team.

It saddened everyone when Ace was traded. Eventually, he wound up in Edmonton where he played on a line with Wayne Gretzky, who often commented on how helpful Ace was to him when he first turned pro. When his playing days ended, Ace became a scout for L.A., eventually rising to the Kings' director of pro scouting. On his visits to Joe Louis Arena,

Ace always dropped by our medical room to say hello.

Ace was on the job on 9/11, seated on United Airlines Flight 175 out of Boston when his terrorist-controled plane crashed into the World Trade Center. Knowing Ace, I'll bet he gave them a battle in the end. Everyone in the NHL felt the pain of 9/11 more for having lost one of our real heroes and a true friend.

Brian "Bugsy" Watson
Brian was one of the most memorable and beloved players the Wings ever had—and he was absolutely hated by most players, especially the elite ones on opposing teams. It was his job to shadow, harass, and impede their skills, and he did it very well. He drove Bobby Hull nuts. Bobby and many others Bugsy was responsible for checking were prone to carving him up with their sticks. He took an exceptional number of stitches, but Brian loved the battles and the intensity of the game, and he never lost his enthusiasm for it.

While in Detroit he was deeply involved with the Special Olympics. From Detroit he was traded to Washington, where he eventually retired. He bought a restaurant, a Chicago-style pizza parlor in Old Town Alexandria, Virginia, that had a picturesque bar on the second floor called the Penalty Box Lounge. The stairway is lined with photos of bleeding hockey players plying their trade.

I was president of the American College of Osteopathic Surgeons in 1990. Its central office is located in Alexandria, so we used to stop in Bugsy's Place often after our work day was over. Brian would join us, and we would talk about the great old times we shared.

Jimmy Rutherford
Jimmy was a longtime patient of ours during and after the years he tended goal for the Wings and later when he headed Compuware's amateur and professional hockey programs. He was the right-hand man and confidante of Peter Karmanos Jr. Jimmy often told me of the many frustrations Karmanos encountered trying to secure an NHL franchise. They had their

eye on Tampa Bay and were profoundly disappointed when the expansion club was given to Phil Esposito, who led a group that included financing from Japan.

Jim was a wonderful goaltender and great friend. Although he served the Wings during the 1970s, the nadir in the history of a proud Original Six team, Rutherford had some great nights. He was unbeatable one night against the Montreal Canadiens when the atmosphere in Olympia Stadium turned electric, stimulated by Jimmy's performance.

One of the stories I remember about Jim was when he was the principal goaltender under Coach Alex Delvecchio. One night, Jimmy became suddenly ill and reported to Delvecchio that he couldn't play, so Alex told Jimmy's backup that he was going in. When they took to the ice, the referee came over to the bench and told Delvecchio that he would have to start Rutherford since the coach had turned in Rutherford's name as the starting goaltender for that game; the league required him to start.

The minute the puck was dropped, the opposing team's franchise player got a breakaway on Jimmy, who stopped him cold. Jimmy looked at Alex, expecting to be taken out, but after his great save, Alex turned his back to him, avoiding responding to Jimmy's wishes. The more Jimmy pleaded, the more Alex ignored him. Jimmy played the entire game, getting stronger as the game went on, got the win, and recovered without further loss of play.

Jimmy played 13 years in the NHL, mostly with the Wings, but also Pittsburgh, Toronto, and L.A., and finally finished his career with Detroit in 1983. Karmanos, the co-founder and CEO of Compuware Corp., who had been a strong supporter of youth hockey in the Detroit area since the mid-1970s. His teams developed a tremendous rivalry with the Little Caesars teams sponsored by Mike Ilitch. After retiring from active play, Jimmy signed on with Compuware's hockey operations. One of his first duties was the purchase of the Windsor Spitfires of the Ontario Hockey League, after which he became head of the Karmanos hockey operations. During this interval, Jimmy was a frequent patient in our office, so I had a running account of the many trials and tribulations they went through while trying to secure an NHL franchise.

In 1991, when the Tampa Bay opportunity became available, they immediately submitted a bid and were optimistic that it would be approved. The bid submitted by Phil Esposito and a Japanese group he represented (after the Hyatt hotel group backed out) was accepted. I believe the size of the crowd (25,581) attending a preseason exhibition game between the L.A. Kings and Pittsburgh Penguins (Wayne Gretzky vs. Mario Lemieux) that "Espo" personally promoted enticed the bid to be awarded to his group.

As it turned out, the wealth of the foreign investors diminished considerably when the Japanese Stock Exchange lost a great deal of its value, and the Tampa Bay club playing in different temporary venues, was hemorrhaging money. After three years, the franchise was sold, and eventually wound up in the hands of Detroiter Bill Davidson, owner of the very successful NBA Detroit Pistons and well-known to NHL Commissioner Gary Bettman from his NBA days.

Jimmy said they were genuinely dejected since they felt their application was a bona-fide document that met all the financial requirements. He implied the NHL didn't seem interested in their application. They continued to keep their hat in the ring, and as the financial stability of Hartford was crumbling, the Karmanos people reentered the scene and took possession of the Whalers on the day of the 1994 Entry Draft—held that year in Hartford. It was the lone U.S. team from the former World Hockey Association to survive, while three in Canada did—Edmonton, Winnipeg, and Quebec.

They kept the team in Hartford for three more money-losing years when fan interest severely eroded. Eventually, they moved to North Carolina, playing temporarily in Greensboro while the new building, the 18,730-seat RBC Arena, was being built in Raleigh. One has to admire their courage in taking their team into an area that was the hotbed of basketball and NASCAR motor racing where little was known about hockey.

But fan support has been quite good, especially with the Hurricanes reaching the Stanley Cup finals against Detroit in 2002 and winning the Cup in 2006. Hockey seems to be well received on Tobacco Road.

Vaclav Nedomansky

One of the first moves the club made when Ted Lindsay was General Manager of the Wings under owner Bruce Norris was to look over the talent in the World Hockey Association. During a scouting trip to Cincinnati, Ted saw Vaclav Nedomansky and was impressed with his great talent, especially his ability to fire a hard, accurate wrist shot, a dying art since his Original Six days. He was able to sign Vaclav, who spent several very special years in Detroit from 1977–82. He became the first of many talented players from the former Czechoslovakia (the former country of central Europe divided in January 1993 into the Czech Republic and Slovakia.)

Vaclav was living in Prague when the Russian tanks rolled in during the Soviet-led invasion in August 1968 to halt Czechoslovakia's liberalization. Vaclav said it was the scariest moment of his life. He described the very threatening environment they lived in under the Russian regime. Being a prominent athlete, he and his wife, Vera, lived well, but they were under constant surveillance by the Communists.

During the many World Hockey tournaments and Olympic battles, Vaclav became a friend of Toronto broadcast executive John Bassett, the owner of the WHA's Toronto Toros, who enticed him to defect. This began an episode of unbelievable intrigue. Under the old Czech régime, defectors became non-entities, all of their records were purged, and their relatives were punished.

Vaclav had been the captain of the Czech national team that won the 1972 Olympic bronze medal in Sapporo, Japan, and the 1968 silver medal in Grenoble, France. It was prearranged that he would secretly disappear from the team while they were playing outside of Czechoslovakia. At precisely the same time, his wife, Vera, and their son, Vashi, would leave all their personal belongings and drive away from their apartment toward the Swiss border.

Near the border, they abandoned their car and crossed on foot until they were safely in Switzerland, where arrangements had been made to get them to North America. They rejoined one another, and Vaclav became a star in the World Hockey Association, joining former NHL great Frank Mahovlich on the Toronto team.

To understand his great athletic talent, consider that Vaclav was also a junior Davis Cup tennis player, representing the Czech Republic in those matches. Their tennis champion, Yan Kuriak, was his mentor. But after Vaclav defected, the communist government removed all of his records. Vera was also a great athlete, having won an Olympic bronze medal in cross-country skiing in Innsbruck, Austria, in 1976.

After he signed with Detroit, Vaclav and Vera moved into an old farmhouse with Vashi and new daughter, Vicki, in Franklin. Genevieve and I sponsored them for membership in our local private tennis and racquet club, the Birmingham (Michigan) Athletic Club, and both became club favorites. Vaclav took on some of our ranked tennis players who thought he would be an easy opponent, but he had little difficulty with them. Since he was at the end of his career when Mike Ilitch took control in the summer of 1982, general manager Jimmy Devellano, who was not a fan—at the time—of European hockey players, quickly dismissed him.

The contract signed between Lindsay and Vaclav was in dispute, which created a great deal of unhappiness among all parties, and it was an unpleasant parting. Vaclav later became the European scout for the L.A. Kings, and he ultimately returned to Prague to take charge of one of the country's elite hockey teams.

Genevieve and I were very close personal friends of the Nedomanskys and had many delightful times together. Their family spent Christmas dinner with us. One of the most memorable times was the evening that Vaclav called and invited us and another couple to join them for dinner. He said he had something to show us. It turned out that his Olympic medals, left behind when they defected, were secretly picked up by a police officer who was part of the group who ravaged their apartment. Years later, a shoe box containing his medals arrived at Canadian customs in Windsor. Customs officials called Vaclav, who had no idea why he was summoned—and he opened the box to find all of his and Vera's Olympic medals. To this day, he has no idea who sent them.

We had never seen an Olympic medal, so this was a real treat for us. Each medal is developed and manufactured by the host country. His bronze medal had Japanese markings on it, while his Silver was in French. As he was showing us these, Vera asked Vicki to go upstairs and bring down her medal, the bronze from Innsbruck, which had German markings on it.

Their son, Vashi, played hockey for Red Berenson at the University of Michigan. While on injured reserve, former Red Wings defenseman Jiri Fischer met Vashi in Los Angeles where he was making a video ad for Ford Motor Company in 2004, and reported that Vashi was there studying acting.

Ironically, the Wings' first foray into Eastern Europe looking for hockey players to upgrade their roster was in Czechoslovakia. They had drafted a talented left wing, Petr Klima, in the 1983 Entry Draft, and arranged his defection in the summer of 1985. Red Wings officials Jim Lites and Nick Polano spirited away the speedy Klima in a clandestine arrangement from his Czech team, racing across Germany on the Autobahn and eventually crashing and destroying their rented Mercedes Benz—driven by Klima—but successfully escaping. His wife, Irina, was smuggled out of a hotel in a laundry cart.

Petr Klima played 4½ seasons with us, 3½ with the Oilers, where he helped win a Stanley Cup, three seasons with Tampa Bay, plus short stints with the L.A. Kings and Pittsburgh before a short curtain call with the Wings in the 1998–99 season. He now makes his permanent home in Birmingham, where he built an additional home on his property. He uses it to billet young Czech hockey prospects, who come in small groups with one of the fathers of the boys who looks after them and assists in training and games.

Jimmy Devellano

When the announcement came that Jimmy D. was being honored by entry into the Hockey Hall of Fame, I couldn't help but smile.

The story of the Wings' former GM is one right out of Hollywood. He didn't apply for his first job in hockey expecting a reasonable salary. He offered to work for free. He knew what he wanted, whom he wanted to work with, and he got his initial experience right there. It was in 1967, but his remarkable story begins even before then.

I had just finished reading his book, *The Road to Hockeytown: Jimmy Devellano's 40 Years in Hockey*, in which he told of leaving school early because he couldn't master arithmetic. What a remarkable story. He sure didn't have any difficulty handling mathematical situations during his storied career in the NHL when he negotiated contracts worth tens of millions of dollars on behalf of his owners, the Ilitch family. I remember the first time we walked into the San Jose Arena in 1995, Jimmy commented how the large-access entrance portals into the arena significantly decreased the total seating capacity, therefore affecting the team's attendance income when totaled over the entire year. He saw dollar signs everywhere and recognized the importance of the bottom line by embracing—and mastering—a businessman's view of the hockey industry.

A person of small stature but strong principles, Devellano learned from watching and working with many of the NHL's iconic individuals. He was motivated by his own love and respect of the game, determination, hard work, and a big dose of good, common sense. A native of Toronto, Jimmy was inspired by Punch Imlach and Conn Smythe. He had incredible determination and confidence in his own ability and his willingness to pay the price to learn the ropes of management leadership one step at a time.

In 1967, league expansion was just beginning. Devellano had and no experience other than being a broad-based sports fan. He contacted GM Lynn Patrick of the expansion St. Louis Blues, offering to work as a non-salaried scout in Toronto-area junior games. That began his career in the NHL. Then by luck or by accident, after being released by St. Louis,

Jimmy was in Montreal where he met Bill Torrey, who was just developing the Islander team as their GM. Jimmy D. became part of their management team and scouted and brought Dave Lewis to the Islanders in 1973 where he played seven seasons.

Devellano rose through the management ranks with the Islanders, who went on to win four straight Stanley Cups starting in 1980. By this time, Devellano was a well-rounded hockey man, acquainted with the league. When Ilitch bought the Wings, he looked for an executive from a winning franchise, and he brought Devellano—then Torrey's assistant general manager—to Detroit.

Jimmy bluntly told his owners—and convinced the media—that the only way to build a sound franchise was through the draft and that it would take eight years, minimum, to build a winner. Eight years later, in 1991, the Red Wings began their current streak of 21 straight appearances in the Stanley Cup playoffs, a period during which they've won the Cup four times.

They did it Devellano's way, although curiously he continues to get little credit for the franchise's splendid success that truly began just four years into his tenure as general manager.

Scotty Bowman

What can I say about this man that is not already in print? There are not enough adjectives, not nearly enough superlatives to describe his extraordinary talents, dedication, and successes—with his teams and with his family—that make him legendary to all who knew him on or off the ice.

No matter which team he coached, Bowman had the uncanny ability to bring out the best in every player and mold that team into winners. He has the Stanley Cup rings to prove it.

Love/hate relationships abound in all professional sports, and there was never any question that Scotty was in charge, so it has been an education to get to know him on a more personal level. We had been around the rinks longer than many others in the hockey world, seen many changes, and shared many stories.

Coach Scotty Bowman raises the Cup after his final game with Detroit in 2002. (Photo courtesy of the *Detroit Free Press*)

It was fascinating to watch him through those years as coach of the opposition and very exciting when he came on board with the Red Wings. Away from the ice he was so much different than I anticipated. Of all the men I have known, there has never been anyone more devoted to his family. This was obvious when he would leave the rink immediately after weekend home games and drive over to Buffalo to be with them. Scotty is so proud of his wonderful wife, Suella, and his five children. Now grandchildren have become his greatest joy.

Getting to know Scotty and Suella has enriched our lives greatly, and to be able to share the challenges of daily living with large families and life in general is very special. We are honored to call them friends.

Shawn Burr

Shawn Burr became a Red Wing as the seventh overall pick in the first round of the 1984 draft. He made a handful of appearances with the Wings those first couple of years, but the Wings were still struggling, going through coaches Nick Polano, Harry Neale, and Brad Park. In the meantime, our youngsters were winning with our developmental farm team, the Adirondack Wings, in Glens Falls, New York.

In 1986–87, new coach Jacques Demers immediately recognized that the feisty, pesky, never-give-up defensive forward Shawn Burr was just what the Wings needed. When Brad Park came here, he told me the Wings had the reputation around the league of lacking toughness. Park was gone but the Wings had the Bruise Brothers—Bob Probert and Joey Kocur. Shawn, wearing No. 11, provided additional grit, had a nifty scoring touch, and was ranked fifth among the NHL rookies in scoring that year. He tied Adam Oates for the fifth spot in scoring on our roster.

"He's my Dougie Gilmour," Demers said, comparing Burr to the best two-way player Demers coached while with the St. Louis Blues before he bolted for Detroit. Because of his gritty playing style, Burr was always picked to check Wayne Gretsky—and he drove the Great One nuts at times. Other opponents said Burr wore them down with his relentless chatter.

Here's a guy who was always available to aid in any cause, no matter what his personal circumstance, and he always found a way to add a remarkable humorous twist to it. He spent 11 seasons with the Wings before being traded to the Tampa Bay Lightning, playing two seasons there, plus two more with San Jose, finally retiring after a brief return to Tampa Bay during his 16th year. After the trade to Tampa Bay, when Shawn saw any of our players, he would tell them to go up and kiss the side of Red Wings One, the team's official plane. Flying commercial, like the Bolts did, was brutal on a hockey team.

Noted for his wonderful sense of humor, Shawn is a highly sought-after auctioneer at Wings Alumni events. On the ice, he had three 20-goal seasons with Detroit and has the distinction of scoring two short-handed goals in a five-point three-goal game in a 9–0 win against the Minnesota North Stars. He once scored three goals in the third period in Philadelphia. He loved playing the Flyers because of their gritty style.

The media, of course, loved him as a go-to guy for postgame quotes, but players learned to give him a wide berth—even his own teammates. Bob Probert learned that the hard way. Shawn and Probie were checking an opponent against the boards one night when Shawnie missed his man and caught Pobie with a full-on body check. Bob later told me it was the hardest hit he ever took in the NHL.

After his retirement, Shawn and former Wings teammate Dino Ciccarelli became partners with the owners of the Ontario Hockey League's Sarnia Sting in their home town. Shawn also served as president of the Red Wings Alumni after his retirement. He took the opportunity to sit with Genevieve, our daughter, Colleen, and me in the Alumni Room, telling endless funny stories during a visit before a game against Boston on February 13, 2011.

Shawn confessed to feeling chronic fatigue, and one week later, after watching his daughter's soccer game, he put together a shake of pomegranate seeds his wife had purchased as a possible remedy for his weakness. Extracted from the ancient Asian fruit, it is said to have a remarkable ability to reinvigorate the body. It was her attempt to help him overcome his current challenge.

In this instance, his body rebelled. His tongue developed red spots. He began to perspire and went right to his doctor's office. Shawn was sent to the hospital's emergency department, where blood samples were drawn. Immediately, doctors recognized the gravity of his condition, acute myelogenous leukemia, and within a brief interval, Shawn was flown by helicopter from the Port Huron Hospital to the University of Michigan Medical Center's cancer treatment facility in Ann Arbor, 98 miles away. His anemic condition caused the symptoms that night in the Alumni Room, since his depleted fighter white cells were too few and unable to fight off any infection or illness he might be exposed to. It required keeping him in a sheltered, disease-free, essentially sterile environment during treatment. Recurrence required further treatment including a bone marrow transplant from a compatible donor in Toronto.

One of the cornerstones of the renaissance of the Detroit Red Wings was in trouble. As a player, he was always entertaining to watch. But on or off the ice, Shawn Burr remains on of our all-time favorite people.

Brett Hull

One of the most interesting players on our 2001–02 team—and any team he played for, truth be told—was Brett Hull. He was a wonderful addition to the Red Wings' dressing room. Being the son of one of modern hockey's greatest legends, making the grade in the big league was far more difficult than for the average entrant into the NHL.

Word was that when Brett left college (University of Minnesota–Duluth), he was too slow and poorly motivated to be successful in the NHL. Turned out, those scouting reports were all wrong. As we all know now, Brett went on to join his famous father, Bobby, in the 600-goal club. I remember repairing his first laceration in the NHL when he came into the league with the Calgary Flames, an injury that occurred in Detroit.

Brett kept everyone loose in the dressing room, including management and the media. He was chief of the one-liners with his loud raspy voice and his unparalleled wit. He was always constructive in his criticism of the way the team was playing and was a big booster of the young players on the team. He fit in perfectly with the newer members (Pavel Datsyuk, Henrik Zetterberg, and Boyd Devereaux) at the time, calling his line with Datsyuk and either of the others "two kids and a goat." Brett always gave unselfishly to aid their play and provided advice regarding where to position themselves in any given situation.

Extremely particular about his equipment, practically every night he had our masseuse and part-time equipment repairman, Sergei Tchekmarev, fashion some modification that would make his protective equipment more comfortable and suitable.

After his playing days, when his No. 16 was officially retired in St. Louis, Brett spent some time as a hockey analyst. With his glib tongue, opinionated personality, and infectious smile, he seemed destined for a great career in TV. Like his Detroit teammate Brendan Shanahan, Hull had a multitude of ideas on how to improve the game from both the spectator and player points of view, such as penalizing diving, encouraging rivalries, and nurturing the Canadian franchises.

Brett, like several of our Detroit players along with Scotty Bowman, was a classic car buff. At our Easter party in 2002, Brett and his girlfriend were the big attraction for our neighborhood when they drove up in a pre–World War II Lincoln Continental convertible with the top down. He had also shown up at the arena in a fire red classic Ford Mustang. At that time, Scotty Bowman had two classic cars—a late 1940s Chrysler Town and Country two-door woodie sedan and an early '50s Chevrolet red and white two-door sedan, both in showroom condition.

While we were playing Anaheim in the first round of the 2003 playoffs, we were staying at a hotel in Santa Monica when a woman came up to Brett with a wooden stick that was formerly used by his father, asking if he would buy it for $1,000. He did, but rather than set it aside as a memento,

Brett took it to the Pond of Anaheim that night and used it, rather effectively, in the game that night.

In 2007, a couple years after he retired, Brett admitted to a sportswriter that he had used an illegal stick for several years prior to retiring. He did it in part because he felt he had better control of his shot, but in reality moreso because he thought the rule was "stupid." According to Hull, the rule limiting the curve on the blade of the stick was instituted in the early 1980s to protect the goaltenders, who at the time were already given far more protection.

Since then, they have been allowed even more protective equipment, including huge oversized jerseys whose webbing can help make saves when a goalie lifts his arms, making their job safer for them. Therefore, he had no guilt in stretching the limit of blade curvature. Brett was to have been on the NHL's committee overseeing goaltender equipment until he rejoined the Dallas management team.

In the Stars' front office, he had a chance to see the NHL from the management side. The first thing he noticed, he said, is how much the game has changed. The players are a lot bigger, stronger, and faster, and the game is more physical. Regarding the latter, he feels there are players who think their role is to try to hurt somebody. Brett decries those kinds of individuals, warning that they are not good for the game.

While with us, he was always trying to encourage our young players to play smart hockey—how to position themselves, how they could anticipate what was going to happen next. He always said, "I hate stupid hockey players."

Sonny Eliot

One of the favorite non-hockey people in Detroit who was loved and respected by Jack and Helen Adams and everyone else was everybody's favorite weatherman, Sonny Eliot. Sonny was born and raised in Detroit, and he used his position on the weathercast to always speak fondly about the city of Detroit, its people, Michigan, and his favorite Red Wings. Prior

From left to right: Sonny Eliot, Ted Lindsay, John Finley, Bill Gadsby, and Budd Lynch on January 1, 2000. (Photo courtesy of the Finleys)

to every game he would predict the score for his radio listeners and frequently mention which player he thought would score the winning goal.

Jack Adams had great respect and admiration for this jovial weatherman. Sonny was the city's most popular TV and radio personality. Accompanied by his lovely wife, Annette, they were the commentators of the annual J.L. Hudson Thanksgiving Day parade for many years.

Sonny was a fixture at training camp. He always played goaltender in the Red Wings' celebrity games, using a special oversized goalie stick. Jack had him sign a contract worth $0.69 to complete his hockey credentials. On his oversized goalie paddle, he had the word, "HELP!"

One of our most beloved personal friends, Sonny had been a bomber pilot in World War II, flying the famous Consolidated B–24 Liberator. In that period of the war, fighter support, due to limited range, could only be given for about half the bombing runs. During his 16th bombing raid, to disable a Messerschmitt factory in northern Germany, lacking any fighter support, Sonny's squadron was attacked by German fighters and his bomber was shot down.

He parachuted safely down but was captured a couple of days later. Being Jewish made the scenario even more dangerous. He was placed in a Nazi concentration camp—Stalag Luft 1—100 miles from Berlin and about a mile south of the Baltic Sea, where he suffered their excruciating, inhumane, and humiliating treatment.

None of us can appreciate the terrible experience he was forced to go through. I have had the opportunity to meet two of his surviving fellow POWs and laugh with them about some of the incredible stories they told. They even put on theatrical shows to entertain each other. They were freed from the camp by the Russians some 15 months later.

Sonny was a favorite of Jack's. He would always come into the dressing room before the team went out for the pregame warm-up to give each player some special good luck acknowledgement, such as scuffing the blade of a player's stick, or a high-five, or a rap on the player's butt. One night, a rookie French-Canadian kid was brought in for a tryout. Unbeknownst to Sonny, Gordie Howe and Alex Delvecchio told the rookie that Sonny was homosexual, using a more pejorative term favored in the locker rooms. When Sonny gave him a rap on the butt for good luck before warm-up, the kid became obviously frightened. "No, No! Get away from me," the kid said. "I like women!" Everyone got a big laugh out of it, and it relieved some of the pregame tension.

One of the most important sports spin-offs of the golden years in Detroit from the 1950s well into the 1980s was a sports bar and restaurant, the Lindell AC, operated by Jimmy and Johnny Butsicaris and their father, Meleti. Located on the corner of Michigan and Cass, the Lindell was the city's and arguably America's first true sports bar, similar to Toots Shor's in New York City. Sonny would spend many cherished hours with Jack, a teetotaler, in the most famous sports bar in Detroit.

The legendary saloon first opened in the old second-class Lindell Hotel, a couple of blocks away in 1949, moving to its more well-known location a few years later. Johnny was a decorated World War II Air Force bomber and transport pilot, and for many years he owned a private aircraft with Sonny. Our practice occasionally cared for both of them and their spouses, and on one occasion we flew up to Boyne Mountain for lunch, an incredibly fascinating experience.

John, in addition to being a splendid saloonkeeper, was a very talented amateur photographer. A close friend and colleague of several sports photographers, he had a darkroom in the bar itself. Many of the pictures that lined the walls of his famous bar were his, from camera to chemicals to paper, and he was justifiably proud of them.

Their bar was the magnet that attracted movers and shakers, sports celebrities, stars of stage and screen, and some titans of local business and industry. Most were the "drop-in" variety, not to be seen but just to enjoy themselves and have a beer and one of their incredibly delicious burgers. Visiting sports clubs and individuals from baseball, football, hockey, wrestling, boxing, and the theater often staying in the nearby Leland House frequented the saloon, and were considered regular guys.

Because their executives and managers drank at the Leland, players looked for another place to go. Initially called a sports bar, the AC was added to the Lindell's name by the equally famous Doc Green, the celebrated sports columnist. When asked where he did a particular interview, he liked to dignify it by saying it was obtained at "the AC," implying that it was conducted at the more genteel facility, the prominent Detroit Athletic Club (DAC).

Notorious and controversial stars often made the Lindell their official home away from home, including Alex Karras, Wayne Walker, Billy Martin, Dick the Bruiser, Mark "The Bird" Fidrych, Andre the Giant, and many others. Sonny Eliot was a fixture among them, and he and Johnny B. were inseparable. The jokes and stories flowed as freely as the beer, mostly true, many exaggerated, and always in good fun. The Butsicarises treated everyone as equals and with respect. They really knew how to run a saloon.

CHAPTER 21

Distinguished Alumni

DONE PLAYING, THESE WINGS
GATHER TO CREATE MORE MEMORIES.
The original Red Wings Alumni Association, the first of its kind in the NHL, had its beginning in a meeting at Butcher's Inn restaurant in Detroit's Eastern Market in 1959, when 13 former Red Wings including Ebbie Goodfellow, Jack Stewart, Jimmy Peters, Sid Abel, Rolly Roulston, Johnny Sherf, Donnie Hughes, Normie Smith, and Larry Cain met for lunch. Their objective was to form a group of ex–Red Wings players interested in supporting the game, continuing to play as a group of so-called old-timers, and to support amateur and local community hockey.

They invited interested recently retired players, those from the 1930s and 1940s and even those who played for the teams that preceded the Wings: the Cougars, Falcons, and Detroit Olympics. The membership included the originators plus Red and Harry Doran, Stu Evans, Joe Carveth, Carl Liscombe, Leo Reise, Red Raney, Alex Motter, Scotty Bowman (the Red Wings player of the 1930s, not the coach of the 1990s), Joe Klukay (a former Maple Leaf), and associate members like broadcaster/announcer Budd Lynch, Dr. Milt Kosley, myself, team dentist Dr. Florian Muske, as well as current and former hockey writers and photographers at the time, Bill Brennan of the *Detroit News*, Jack Berry of the *Detroit Free Press*, and weatherman Sonny Eliot. Some front-office people were also included, Elliot Trumbull, former media and communications director; Linc Cavalieri, Olympia building manager under Bruce Norris;

and club attorney John Ziegler, who subsequently became president of the NHL, succeeding Clarence Campbell.

Initially the group met monthly at a downtown restaurant to plan ice time, practices, social events, and charity games. Later they rented space at Olympia Stadium in an upstairs room originally outfitted for the Olympia Club members, which was great for the wives of the coaches and staff because it gave them a comfortable place to entertain their guests before games and between periods and wait for their husbands after the games. Larry Cain, president of the Michigan Amateur Hockey Association and of his own (Thompson-Cain) meat company, provided buffet cold cuts and other nibblers that were much appreciated.

When the New York Rangers were in town, Frank Paice, their trainer, would always stop in to have a "good luck, fond memories" drink with Sid Abel's wife, Gloria, after he finished his duties in the Rangers' dressing room. Others attending the alumni meetings and playing in the early alumni games were Pete Babando, Alex Motter, Harold Jackson, George Gee, Bill Jennings, Bill Gadsby, and Jimmy "Shakey" Peters.

One of the most impressive characteristics about the alumni was the respect they had for one another. Most came from very humble backgrounds and played the game when salaries were much below the level of other major sports. They provided great memories that no one can take away from them. Every day was something different. They never took a night off. They treasured their relationships with one another. Their monthly meetings were great events, and every time a guest or friend from another club or another city dropped in, the stories flew fast and furious.

Working for the AAA Auto Club or for one of the suppliers to the automobile industry after hockey was common. Being part of the alumni gave them a chance to enjoy the game, playing with older but still talented athletes. They loved to kid around in the dressing room after practice and play euchre after the alumni meetings. As Red Wings team physicians, Dr. Milt Kosley and I served as alumni team physicians. But as the alumni's work and practice sessions increased dramatically, we were replaced by longtime friend and personal physician to many ex-Wings, Dr. Chet Boone.

The alumni's objective was two-fold: comradeship and playing exhibition games for charity, especially those aiding the disabled, against local teams such as police and fire department leagues. The alumni also played amateur teams to raise money for their clubs.

I skated in the alumni's practice sessions for eight years until my family responsibilities began to consume my time. I remain active in the Alumni Association and was always involved in the original home games against the Montreal old-timers as the physician in residence. They featured players like Jean Beliveau, Elmer Lach, Dickie Moore, Ken Reardon, and many former bitter enemies of the past who were now so very respectful of each other. Popular Red Wings alumnus and native Montrealer Jimmy Peters arranged the games.

The game was usually the night before an NHL clash between Montreal and the Wings, either in Detroit or Montreal, and usually alternated cities each year through the late 1970s and early 1980s. The games played in Montreal included former Red Wings defenseman and Montreal nightclub manager Jimmy Orlando, who was prevented from coming into the United States because of a selective service mix-up during World War II, a restriction that was later rescinded.

The games were wonderfully staged and strongly supported by the fans in each city, who loved to see and watch their hockey idols one more time, recalling their great plays from the past. Those games were the start of skating and competing alumni groups in the Original Six teams, and eventually the expansion teams, many of whom are showcased as the legends of hockey during the All-Star weekend festivities.

Originally the Detroit association's members included only those from the Red Wings family. As the playing ranks of the alumni thinned, this was later expanded to players from the NHL living in the Detroit and adjacent areas, and even later to include college players and NHL referees and linesmen. As the oldest alumni association in the NHL, the Red

Wings Alumni Association currently has nearly 150 members. They practice once a week and have a monthly business meeting during the season.

Although their bodies and legs are older and move a little slower, they all have incredible spirit and perform their basic skills. There is no body-checking, and slap shots are not allowed. However, their skating and puck-handling skills remain. They play about 20–25 games each season, have great fun, and provide a wonderful service for the community and enjoyment for their fans. The competition is in awe of their ability and skill in spite of their ages. They never lose their uncanny ability to make or receive a pass, stickhandle around opponents, and make sensational plays against typically younger rivals.

Occasionally their competition tries to take a run at one of our guys. This is particularly true when they play against a local high school team. Usually, the offending player soon learns how tough the alumni can be, and how quick they are to protect one another.

They often go to a community for a game organized by a former Red Wing or someone close to the club. Dennis Hextall is the former hockey committee chairman. John Ogrodnick, Brent Fedyk, Tom Williams, Nick Libett, Mark Hamway, Paul Ysebaert, Dino Ciccarelli, Lee Norwood, Shawn Burr, Mickey Redmond, Phil Myre, Eddie Mio, and Bill Evo are some of the well-known people on the roster. Dennis Polonich, Marcel Dionne, Bryan Watson, Reed Larson, and the late Bob Probert often returned to play with the alumni on special occasions.

From time to time, athletes from other sports skate at the practices. Some of them previously played hockey but are mostly there to join the fun and stay in condition. Former Lions and later Miami Dolphins quarterback Earl Morrall often came to practice in the 1960s during the off-season. Our son, Michael, who played high school hockey for Brother Rice in Birmingham, also skated in their practices while he was in residency training in Detroit.

The late Johnny Wilson, left winger of the 1940s and '50s and coach in the 1960s, and Joe Klukay, the former Maple Leafs star, often served as alumni coaches. John's nephew, Ron Wilson, has coached in the NHL for 18 seasons most recently with the Toronto Maple Leafs. Formerly, he coached in Anaheim, Washington (against the Wings in the Stanley Cup finals in 1998), and San Jose. Ron's father, Larry Wilson, played for the Wings in the late 1940s and early 1950s and also coached the Wings in 1976–77, as well as the Adirondack farm club in upstate New York, where he tragically died while jogging in the summer of 1979. After playing 15 years in the AHL as a player and six more as a coach, Larry was elected into the AHL Hall of Fame during its 2011 festivities in Hershey, Pennsylvania.

The first introduction of the alumni to the hockey fans of Detroit was a charity game in March 1964 against the Wings. It was a huge success at a time when our NHL team was struggling and was fighting the effects of impending league expansion and competition from the World Hockey Association. A capacity crowd paid an admission fee of $1 for any seat in the house to see our alumni face off against the current club.

Gordie Howe, still part of the Wings team until the early 1970s, joined the alumni for the game. Ebbie Goodfellow, the high-scoring center from the early 1930s later moved to defense by Jack Adams, was the alumni coach. Rolly Roulston, Wings defenseman of the mid-1930s, was the assistant coach. Joe Burt was their trainer, and I was their team physician. Others included Ford dealer Stew Evans from the 1932–33 and 1933–34 teams; Red Doran, one of the original alumni from the 1937–38 team; defenseman Ralph "Scotty" Bowman, with the Wings from 1934–40; defenseman Eddie Bush (1938–39, 1940–42); Joe Carveth (1940–46), coach of the Hamilton Wings, Detroit's sponsored junior team; Don "The Count" Grosso of the Wings' 1940s teams; goaltender Normie Smith, from the 1930s; defensemen Leo Reise, "Black Jack" Stewart, and Jimmy Orlando and forwards Carl Liscombe, Gord Haidy, George Gee, and Bill Jennings.

Detroit hockey fans loved seeing their old hockey heroes battling one another again on the ice, especially when the Production Line of Ted Lindsay, Sid Abel, and Gordie Howe was reunited. The alumni also included

The author is flanked by former Wings stars Ebbie Goodfellow and Rollie Rolston, who coached the Red Wings Alumni team in March 1964. (Photo courtesy of the Detroit Red Wings) (Photo courtesy of the Detroit Red Wings)

Jimmy Peters, Marty Pavelich, and Metro Prystai, all previously great favorites with Wings fans. Lefty Wilson was their goalkeeper, and weatherman Sonny Eliot, using a specially made enlarged goaltender's stick with "HELP" painted on the oversized blade, substituted briefly during the game.

Once, Ted Lindsay was awarded a penalty shot against Sonny. (Think Harlem Globetrotters on ice.) Flying in, he sent a rocket-like shot that was so hard Eliot never saw it, but he heard it as the puck banged off the crossbar into the stands. Sonny always claimed thereafter that he was one of the few to stop Lindsay from scoring. It was a great success and made all Detroit hockey fans aware of the alumni and their importance to the Detroit hockey scene. The game was a sellout and gave Detroit's faithful hockey fans, who had so little to cheer about during those difficult years of the 1960s–70s, something to celebrate—and remember for a lifetime.

Another early and eventful alumni charity game was the one arranged by Jimmy "Shakey" Peters, a wonderful, genuine, upbeat guy loved by all the alumni. Jimmy was originally from Montreal and played junior hockey and 2½ seasons for the Canadiens with many of the then-current Montreal alumni. He arranged the first alumni vs. alumni game against the Montreal Canadiens.

The Habs' alumni team included Elmer Lach, Ken Mosdell, Jean Beliveau, Ken Reardon, and Dickie Moore. The game was held the evening before a scheduled regular season Red Wings vs. Montreal Canadiens afternoon matinee game. The next year, a similar game was held in Montreal with a similar format—charity alumni game Friday night and a regularly scheduled Wings-Habs game the next day, plus the social event the same weekend. The game was played to benefit a Catholic charity organization at the Montreal Forum. The Cardinal attended the game just before he stepped down to go into missionary work in South America. This, too, was very successful—and players, former bitter rivals from the past, began sharing friendships that had been impossible in the six-team era.

Two years later, we went back to Montreal for the game on Friday, but the next day we traveled to the Laurentians, where everyone had a great time cross-country skiing, followed by a family-style dinner in a maple sugar mill in St. Eustache, Quebec. All were wonderful experiences that helped strengthen the alumni group of both clubs. Since then, our alumni have traveled all over the U.S.A. and Canada, playing games in nearly every Canadian province and many states. Many artifacts and remembrances of those experiences are displayed in the Red Wings Alumni Room at Joe Louis Arena.

Usually an older Red Wing, one who is no longer competing, coaches the team. Ebbie Goodfellow and Rolly Roulston were coaches for the first games. Others were Jimmy Peters, Joe Kulkay, Johnny Wilson, and Bill Gadsby. The medical fitness of the alumni players is taken very seriously. John Downs, D.O., son-in-law of Jimmy Peters and an oral surgeon on the faculty of Michigan State University College of Osteopathic Medicine, was an instrumental figure. He was deeply involved with the Michigan State hockey team and Coach Ron Mason, the MSU fitness program, and their medical assessment program.

Each year the alumni hockey players traveled to MSU to undergo a careful medical evaluation supervised by Dr. Downs before being cleared to play. He wrote a very significant medical report for the sports medicine journal in which he pointed out the importance of full facial protection for all players, including all the junior programs in North America. To his credit, the following year full facial protection was mandated for all college hockey players.

Terry Brennan, M.D., emergency room physician at South Macomb Hospital, followed Dr. Boone and has been their devoted physician, attending all practices and games.

Early in their experience, the alumni had two fatal events on the ice. One was George Gee, a Wings player from 1948–51, who after extended post–World War II experience with the Blackhawks collapsed during a game in Wyandotte of an acute coronary and died. Later, the alumni's goaltender, a former junior player named Mike Kandt, also collapsed, and in spite of being rushed to a local hospital immediately, all efforts to revive him failed.

Meanwhile, other retired players like Nick Libett have survived the pain of malignancy and continue to do very well. Players like Joe Carveth, Gary Bergman, Johnny Wilson, and Sid Abel waged extraordinary battles against the ravages of that disease and were just as courageous during their illnesses as they were on the ice in the NHL while at the top of their games.

Carl Liscombe, a sharpshooter from the 1930s and '40s, died at 89 from leukemia. He treasured his relationship with the alumni and loved to talk about his battles on the ice with other former Wings. His record for most goals in a playoff game (four) and most points in a game (seven) has been tied, but not exceeded. He played during the six-team era and frequently told of feeling the rage of Jack Adams, who constantly threatened to send Carl to the minors. If Carl had a bad game, Adams would make him spend extra time on the ice during practice sessions. One of the great things about being part of the alumni is the opportunity to relive many of the experiences that we witnessed during our tenure with the team.

Mid-1990s Alumni Club President Dennis Hextall, who played in 1976–79, continued to chair our hockey committee. He was responsible for scheduling practices, exhibition games, and most of the arrangements for each, and he does an exceptional job. Dennis is part of the famous Hextall hockey family. They include father Bryan (New York Rangers, 1937–47), brother Bryan Jr. (New York Rangers, Pittsburgh, Atlanta Flames, Red Wings 1975–76, Minnesota North Stars), and nephew Ron, the feisty Philadelphia Flyers goaltender prominent in the 1980s. Dennis came to us from Minnesota, where he played on a great team, was very productive, and scored 30 goals in a season. The Wings were floundering, but his gritty and abrasive play was one of the high spots of our club during those days. If the club was down, he would go out and stir things up and give our fans something to cheer about.

Red Wings Alumni Room
Shortly after the Wings moved from Olympia Stadium to Joe Louis Arena, the Ilitches bought the franchise and the following year they acquired the catering operation. They opened the Olympia Room dining and bar club and arranged for the alumni to have their own room, essentially as an opportunity for former players to maintain their membership while allowing them to entertain their business and social guests. This replaced the original room at Olympia Stadium. The room at Joe Louis, provided rent-free to the alumni, has its own bar and three wall television sets, allowing anyone there a chance to watch the game. In addition, the walls are decorated with some wonderful one-of-a-kind photographs.

On one wall is a large photo of the old dressing room. On another is the Production Line, and close by is a large photo of the Cougars, the original Detroit club, practicing on an outdoor ice surface. Adjacent to the bar are pictures of former teams and GM Jack Adams, while the far wall is partitioned into areas with pictures, mementoes, and team magazines in 10-year spans—the 1940s through 2000s. The entrance aisle-way displays Stanley Cup artifacts and Red Wings players on one side opposite a classic picture of Igor Larionov as a wine connoisseur.

In early summer, the alumni hold their annual golf outing, which brings out many other former Wings such as Marcel Dionne, Danny Gare, Ted Lindsay, Marty Pavelich, Leo Reise, Budd Lynch, Jack Roberts, Joey Kocur, Mike Krushelnyski, and before their deaths, Lefty Wilson, Carl Brewer, and Gary Bergman.

The alumni also contribute their celebratory status to other outings throughout the summer, especially those connected with benefits for fallen Wing Vladimir Konstantinov and team masseuse Sergei Mnatsakanov—both critically injured in the limo accident just seven days after the team's Cup title in 1997—and Detroit Lions player Mike Utley, who was paralyzed on the field of play. A devoted, kind, and sensitive fan, building contractor Ed Heike is the person behind the most prominent of these. The alumni are typically very good golfers, enjoying that great eye-hand coordination that made them world-class players on the ice.

The Ted Lindsay Foundation for Autism has an annual golf outing attended by many of the alumni. Hall of Fame broadcaster and PA announcer Budd Lynch sponsors an outing on Grosse Isle for the benefit of local downriver charities. Many alumni lend their support and participate in charity softball games.

The alumni were very fortunate to have General Motors publicist and sportswriter Bill Knight serve as their voluntary general manager. He did everything from attending practices to writing the monthly newsletter, including excerpts of newspaper articles about alumni events. Since Bill's death, that effort was assumed by one of the current alumni goaltenders,

George Bowman, golf pro at Oakhurst and grandson of a Wings defenseman from the 1930s, Ralph "Scotty" Bowman.

In the fall of 2004, without a contract settlement between the players and the NHL, the alumni had a marvelous opportunity to have a successful year of charity games. The owners indicated a willingness to give the alumni even more support than ever before. Mike Bayoff from Olympia Entertainment and Joe Louis Arena acted as liaison and volunteered the club's marketing expertise to assist in promoting their events. Games were planned with groups from Toronto, Montreal, and St. Louis. Igor Larionov's North American home was in the Detroit area, and he skated with them when he was in town. He also tried to arrange several games in Russia against retired stars from his homeland.

On February 12, 2005, the first game took place against the Toronto Maple Leafs alumni. Jacques Demers, coach in the late 1980s and the person credited with starting the Wings on their winning ways after nearly two decades of futility, came in from Hudson, Quebec. He joined former coaches Ted Lindsay, Johnny Wilson, and Alex Delvecchio as the alumni coaches. Dan Maloney and Gord Sellick served as coaches for the Maple Leafs. In the lost 2004–05 NHL season, the alumni game was great for hockey-starved fans.

For me, the game was like old home week. Eight Toronto players and two of their officials had spent some time during their careers in Detroit. Included were Andy Bathgate and Brian Conacher, the head of NHL alumni with offices in Toronto at the Hall of Fame. Brian had great fun renewing acquaintances with Red Wings Hall of Fame broadcaster Budd Lynch, who was at the height of his career when Conacher played with the Wings.

Former Wings also on the Leafs' roster for that game were Coach Dan Maloney; Walt McKechnie; forward Mark Osborne, goaltender Mark "Trees" LaForest, and Kris King; defenseman Todd Gill; and winger Wendel Clark. One of their goaltenders was Don Edwards, nephew of Wings goalie Roy Edwards.

Both teams featured many players who came long distances to compete in the game: center Garry Unger from Tulsa, Oklahoma; center Marcel Dionne from Buffalo; winger Dennis Polonich from Calgary; winger Gerard Gallant from Columbus; defenseman Rick Zombo from St. Louis; goaltender Tim Cheveldae from Saskatoon, Saskatchewan; defenseman Mark Howe from New Jersey; winger Dino Ciccarelli from Sarnia, Ontario; and forward Paul Ysebaert from Florida.

THERE WERE SEVERAL PROMINENT EARLY MEMBERS.

Larry Aurie

He's the answer to a popular trivia question often asked by fans about the mysterious missing No. 6—not worn by any Wings player in more than 50 years, yet not officially taken out of commission and retired by hanging it from the rafters with the other Red Wings greats, including Terry Sawchuk (1), Ted Lindsay (7), Gordie Howe (9), Alex Delvecchio (10), Sid Abel (12), and Steve Yzerman (19).

For much of his career in the franchise's earliest days, Larry Aurie was the most dangerous shot-maker and scorer, despite his size—5'6" and 148 pounds. A native of Sudbury, Ontario, Aurie came to the team, originally named the Detroit Cougars. He had the reputation of being a quick, fast, exceptionally aggressive, rugged right winger with an accurate shot, beloved by the fans and depended on by the team because of his scoring ability.

He led the league in scoring with 23 goals in 1936–37, leading the Wings to the Stanley Cup. This was in the era when scoring was never very high. Near the end of that season, he broke his leg in a collision with a Rangers defenseman, and although he played the following season, he never regained his previous scoring touch. Ten-plus years in the league also had taken their toll. But Aurie was highly thought of by Jack Adams. One time when Jack was ill and confined to his home, Aurie took over and ran the team at Olympia Stadium.

Aurie was publicly acknowledged by Jack Adams as the finest player he had ever coached. And when Aurie retired, Adams declared that no other Red Wing would wear that number saying, "It wouldn't seem right for anyone else to wear No. 6." Interestingly, Adams reversed that decision in my first year with the club, allowing Aurie's nephew, Cummy Burton, to wear it, quite likely with Larry's concurrence. No other player has worn No. 6, and the debate continues among hardcore fans whether it should hang alongside other team greats in the rafters at Joe Louis Arena.

Normie Smith

A very popular goaltender from 1934–39, Normie was nicknamed "Red Light." His claim to fame, in addition to winning two Stanley Cup titles, was being in goal for the longest hockey game ever played—five hours and 51 minutes—when Detroit beat the Montreal Maroons 1–0 in a Cup semi-final match in Montreal. The goal was scored by a little-used 21-year-old rookie named "Mud" Bruneteau at 16:30 of the sixth over-time period that came at 2:25 AM. The Wings went on to sweep the best-of-five series 3–0 and the Maple Leafs 3–1 in the finals to win their first-ever Stanley Cup.

This loveable raspy-voiced gentleman, like all other goalies of the day, always wore a cap to shade his eyes from the powerful overhead lights. For years Normie was a beloved member of the original Red Wings Alumni Association and its president in 1967.

In later years, he moved to Florida, where several of the alumni still meet weekly to have lunch and reminisce.

Murray Armstrong

A well-liked center of the Wings in the mid-1940s, Murray became the coach for 10 years of one of western Canada's most heralded junior hockey programs, the Regina Pats, in Saskatchewan. He loved coaching and subsequently became the coach at the University of Denver. I had known of Coach Armstrong's reputation during my early years with the Wings, when all NHL players developed out of the Canadian junior programs.

**Detroit Athletic Club Beavers luncheon on January 30, 1994.
From left to right: Gary Bergman, Ted Lindsay, Dr. John Finley, Bill
Gadsby, Bruce Martin, Dr. Florian Muske, Gordie Howe, Marty
Pavelich, Budd Lynch.** (Photo courtesy of Detroit Athletic Club Photos)

The one in Regina was among the strongest and was originally sponsored by the Montreal Canadiens. This was long before players were being
developed out of the college programs. University of Michigan Coach Red
Berenson came out of the Regina junior program and credits Armstrong as
being a strong influence on him and many other Pats players to consider a
college education rather than a junior program.

I had the distinct pleasure of meeting Murray Armstrong in the mid-
1970s and was very impressed with what a remarkable individual he was.
He had a kindly, intelligent manner, radiating a typical fatherly image. He
retired after 21 years at Denver and remains fondly remembered by the
many players whose lives were profoundly affected by his exceptional ability to mold and develop young men.

CHAPTER 22

Doctors in the House

THE ROLE OF THE TEAM/ARENA PHYSICIAN.
Although I thought competent medicine was at the doorstep of greatness when I started with the Wings, we were really just beginning to realize that greatness was beholden to it. It was prompted by the arrival of penicillin evolving in the 1930s, the aftermath of antibiotics and sulfa drugs during World War II, and the success they created, allowing us to move into a new era of medical expertise in athletic endeavors. NHL hockey was no exception. Those were the days when general surgeons did a wide scope of procedures that often included orthopedic, vascular, reconstructive, etc. Our testing procedures were limited to basic blood and bacterial evaluation, and radiological studies were limited to what the standard basic machine could give you followed by the development of photographic processing that those efforts required.

The medical people involved in athletic care would get together, sharing our talents, experiences, and intuitive ways of producing inventive techniques to improve our athletes physically and mentally to capture the most efficient result while not exceeding the limits of orthodox care. One attitude expressed by many expert physicians was that taking care of those skilled but sometimes rowdy, uncouth, and rough individuals was not considered to be worth the time and effort it required. Those of us involved were proud to be included, accepting the challenges gladly, doing our best to meet the athlete's needs expertly and efficiently, and recognizing their special time commitments by always being available.

On the Wings' bench in 1998, Coach Scotty Bowman is flanked by assistants Barry Smith and Dave Lewis. Three rows behind the bench are the author (right) and his wife, Genevieve.
(Photo courtesy of John Hartman)

It wasn't just me and our office but our entire hospital facility that was geared to assist in their care. That level of dedication is something that makes me proud to this day.

Medical care in the NHL during the Original Six days was much different from what it is today. Each club had general surgeons in attendance with the person in charge like the arena physician, as was the case in New York, Boston, and Chicago. In Toronto, the doctor in charge was a plastic surgeon, while in Montreal a gastroenterologist led the medical staff. In Detroit, a sports-minded radiologist and neighbor of Jack Adams and selected general surgeons from the Sheets/Fetzer group were charged with the general care of players.

Prior to 1976, there was little or no official medical communication between the clubs' medical staffs or with the NHL, except when an opposing player was injured and we would contact the visiting club's medical staff with all the details of what happened and the treatment provided—just as the other clubs would do with our players in their buildings. During the Original Six days, because of the limited number of players and unlimited reserves ready to take their places, team physicians had to take an inordinate period of time to try to figure out how much the player was *not* telling us about his injury rather than information about the injury itself. Professional hockey players are not like the average patient seen in regular practice. Just like those players who end up on the trainer's table, their style was always to avoid the doctor for fear of being benched because of being labeled sick or injured. Bruises, contusions, and strains were hidden as minor wounds. Superficial wounds, lacerations, and the like were repaired by suturing, initially without anesthesia, mainly to speedily return them to the ice so as not to lose their turn.

It was not at all unusual in the early days for a player to look up at me and say, "Put another stitch or two in, would you, Doc?"

"Why?"

"Because my insurance carrier pays five bucks a stitch, and I could use the extra money."

We had everything ready to immediately anesthetize and perform anatomic repair with expert results before any appreciable swelling occurred to interfere with the management of the injury. During the 70-game Original Six schedule, we encountered roughly three injuries per night and about one major injury every second game while taking care of both the home and visiting teams. Mishaps occurred every game, and during the Norris ownership we were required to look after audience injuries, as well. Those caused by fragments and splinters of broken glass panel were particularly troublesome.

During playoffs, we traveled with the team. Doug Kinnear, M.D., in Montreal and I had great respect for one another, and we were frequently confronted with injuries that required significant treatment and/or follow-up.

The medical care of all three professional sports in Detroit, the NHL Red Wings, MLB's Tigers, and NFL's Lions, was provided by members of the staff of Detroit Osteopathic Hospital. Our chief radiologist, Charles Karibo, D.O., had a special interest in evaluating sports injuries radiographically. He was a neighbor of Jack Adams and became Jack's closest friend. General surgeons from the Sheets/Fetzer group were selected to provide surgical and athletic medical care. Dr. Sheets, like many general surgeons in the late 1940s and early 1950s, practiced both general and orthopedic surgery, which made his credentials attractive to the Wings. By the 1960s, orthopedic care was provided by Dr. Robert Bailey of the University of Michigan.

In Montreal, Dr. Kinnear was a gastroenterologist who was treating the Canadiens team physician for bleeding peptic ulcer disease. When Dr. Kinnear advised the Habs' doctor that he should avoid stress, including the hockey team, that man suggested that Doug assume that role. Kinnear did, and he served in that position until the early 2000s.

The Rangers' attending physician was of Asian descent and employed by Madison Square Garden arena in the heyday of boxing, serving principally in that capacity. Myron Tremaine, M.D., the Chicago Blackhawks physician, was a member of Henrotin Hospital, not far from the Chicago Stadium that boasted the membership of a number of internationally prominent physicians of that era—medical anatomist, author, and surgeon Philip Thorek, M.D., and famous pancreatic surgeon Charles Puestow, M.D.

Most physicians for the hockey teams also looked after the other events the buildings staged—ice shows, circuses, etc. In Michigan, boxing certified and licensed its own physicians. In Chicago, Boston, and Toronto, the teams and arenas often contracted their own physicians who covered most other events, as well. The Chicago Blackhawks' trainer, Nick Garen, had the background and permission of the team to perform minor laceration repairs so that the players did not have to be sent to their team's attending physician's hospital unless it was more than an uncomplicated repair. In the Original Six days, the Toronto physician varied, one being the internist taking care of Stafford Smythe, then the plastic and hand surgeon, Jim Murray, M.D., who later was involved with the Canada Cup Games. In Boston, in the days of Bobby Orr, it was Ronald W. Adams, M.D.

Gordie Howe always said the biggest improvement in the game today is in the area of medical-care procedures available to the players. I agree. We were very fortunate in Detroit to have an outstanding orthopedic consultant from the University of Michigan working with us, Dr. Robert Bailey, who had a great interest in and authored an impressive treatise on cervical spine injuries. He had formerly been one of the team orthopedists with the University of Southern California's football medical program and had very extensive experience taking care of cervical spine fractures occurring from diving and gymnastic accidents. While he was working with us, we had two cervical spine fractures, one from a hockey accident and the other from an auto accident that occurred on the way home from a postseason team party. Neither case had associated paralysis, and both were successfully treated by Dr. Bailey with the players returning to hockey.

The orthopedic sports medicine group from the Henry Ford Health System came on board when the Ilitches bought the franchise, and currently the sports medicine group from the Detroit Medical Center has been given that responsibility. As you would expect, we have outstanding, highly competent people working with the team.

The Team Physicians Society

The genesis of this group dates to a meeting of 11 NHL team physicians called together by Clarence Campbell at the league meetings in 1976 when the drug issue surfaced as a concern of the league. But it wasn't until the mid-1980s that we got serious about organizing when a group of orthopedic hockey surgeons met during the American Orthopedic Association annual conference, which provided the impetus to organize all league physicians.

Initially, we met with the trainers in Columbus, Atlanta, and St. Louis in the early 1980s after the league schedule and playoffs were completed. On July 25, 1988, in St. Louis, we established the Society, its name, and its by-laws. We also had our first detailed discussions of steroids, AIDS, and concussions in athletics. Shortly after that, it was determined that it would be more appropriate to meet at a time when the league was meeting in order to involve representatives from the league as needed. The time selected was during the NHL All-Star break since none of the teams would be playing at that time. Gary Dorshimer, M.D., Flyers internist has served as secretary-treasurer of the NHLTPS since its formation.

The first such mid-season meeting of note for team physicians was in Edmonton during the All-Star break on February 7, 1989. There we continued our discussion on AIDS, illicit drugs, steroids, and eye injuries. We established a computerized injury form along with pre- and postseason physical documentation to standardize treatment and care. We also began serious discussion of the legal aspects regarding equipment, especially as it related to how some equipment was being altered and used by players, including some of their dated equipment like shoulder pads that may not be offering the protection they needed. In 1990 in Pittsburgh, we began to discuss in earnest the use of mouth guards and how they might offer some protection from concussions, as well as concussion protocol, drug testing, and screening.

In fact, head injuries became an almost annual agenda item as teams shared information and data of their own and from other sports on issues involving rehab protocol, equipment, neuropsychological testing, and more in an effort to protect and care for athletes who are getting bigger, stronger, and faster, making their collisions more violent with each passing year.

The Team Physicians Society now consists of more than 100 members who meet annually at the NHL All-Star break while the executive committee meets each summer. These colleagues are some of the most passionate and dedicated people associated with the National Hockey League, and the league would be smart to take seriously what they have to say regarding the well-being of these marvelous athletes.

CHAPTER 23

Reflections

FOR THE LOVE OF THE GAME, I ADMIT—IT'S PERSONAL.
In the early 1950s, metropolitan Detroit was a very dynamic place, as were the other five cities of the Original Six, each with their downtown areas being the centers of activity. The Motor City was the automotive capital of the world. There was Chrysler and its Dodge, DeSoto, and Plymouth divisions; Ford and its Mercury and Lincoln divisions; General Motors and its myriad divisions, including Fisher Body and Cadillac; and American Motors was there, now merged with Chrysler. The now-defunct Packard and Hudson Motor Corporations were going strong, and the Willys Jeep plant in nearby Toledo was operating at near capacity. Driving along Eight Mile Road (separating the city of Detroit from the suburbs), you would pass one manufacturing plant after another of varying sizes, nearly all suppliers to the massive automobile industry or in some way related to their production.

Although Detroit had always coveted its reputation of being a blue-collar town, along the shore of Lake St. Clair in Grosse Pointe, gigantic mansions overlooked the beautiful lake and downtown Detroit boasted bustling business activity centered by the J.L. Hudson Company, its iconic department store. Trolleys rolled up and down Grand River Avenue to the west and Gratiot and Jefferson Avenues to the east, and Woodward Avenue to the north.

The only expressway led directly to Willow Run Airport and the Kaiser B24 Aircraft Manufacturing Plant, a vital industry during World War II, so migration to the suburbs was very limited. Prominent world-renowned companies like U.S. Royal Tire and Parke Davis Pharmaceutical Company located to the east, Great Lakes Steel and Wyandotte Chemical to the south, the University of Michigan to the west, and Canada to the east across the Detroit River.

The businessmen's center of athletic activity was the Detroit Athletic Club. It was there that the origin of professional hockey began in Detroit in the truly roaring 1920s. The combination of great automobile business minds and their related wealth, plus the enthusiasm of the supporting athletic-minded blue-collar auto workers and the city's proximity to Windsor, Ontario, made supporting hockey across the river a natural phenomenon. Sporting events of all types were classic in Detroit. In addition to hockey, baseball, and football, the Gold Cup power boat races were held on the Detroit River next to Belle Isle, and the Detroit Boat Club hosted world-class rowing crew teams.

The Motor City Open Professional Golf Tournament was an annual event. The National Amateur Golf Tournament of 1954, won by Arnold Palmer, was held at the Country Club of Detroit in Grosse Pointe. Golf's former Masters champion Horton Smith was the very visible professional at the Detroit Golf Club, and British Open runner-up to Bobby Jones, Al Watrous, succeeded Walter Hagen as the pro at Oakland Hills Country Club in suburban Bloomfield Hills.

In the boxing arena, heavyweight champion Joe Louis and outstanding middleweight Chuck Davey, although past their competing days, lived here and were very prominent citizens. Also living in the Detroit area was baseball Hall of Famer Charlie Gehringer, and highly regarded baseball pitcher Billy Pierce's father ran his drug store a few doors down the street from our hospital. The last football lineman to win the Heisman trophy, Notre Dame's Leon Hart, was here playing for the Detroit Lions, the NFL champions, and Major League Baseball's Tigers were also very competitive, winning championships during that era. The Red Wings under the direction of the famous Jack Adams were perennially competing for the Stanley Cup. And three great daily newspapers, the *Detroit Free Press*, the *Detroit News*, and the *Detroit Times*, delivered blanket coverage and entertaining commentary with nationally renowned writers like Doc Greene and Joe Falls, among others. There was always some sports activity to keep even the most casual fan interested in and proud of our city.

Growing Up with the Game
I grew up playing hockey on the frozen outdoor rinks in the snow-belt of upstate New York and, thanks to my great sports-enthusiast father, we watched the International Hockey League's Syracuse Stars, who played in the city's New York State Fair Coliseum. Because several of the players were his patients, he would take me into their dressing room and introduce them. I watched Sid Howe play there on one occasion. During the cold Saturday evenings in Syracuse, I would join my father in my parents' second-floor bedroom and, in spite of the static, listen to Foster Hewitt broadcasting *Hockey Night in Canada* from the CBC station in Toronto. It wasn't until I was a medical student in Chicago that I realized what a talented group of athletes professional hockey players really were.

While at the Chicago College of Osteopathic Medicine, I read an article from the now-defunct *Detroit Times* newspaper written by its sports editor Lew Walters. It featured the surgery performed on Wings goaltender Terry Sawchuk by J. Donald Sheets D.O., with pictures from the operating room at Detroit Osteopathic Hospital (D.O.H.). At that time, like many general surgeons, he had skills in various surgical specialty areas, including orthopedic surgery. I was very impressed to learn about the care given by DO's to professional athletes in Detroit. Later, during my medical school senior year, I spent a three-month extern rotation at D.O.H., which stimulated my interest in surgery. After a rotating internship in Cleveland, I was pleased to be selected for surgical training in general surgery at D.O.H..

Arriving in Detroit on August 1, 1954, I began my training as a resident in general surgery at D.O.H. Due to the warm relationship our chief of radiology, Dr. Charles Karibo, had with his neighbor Jack Adams, and the interest our hospital and staff had in sports medicine, D.O.H. was providing the medical care for the Red Wings, the Tigers, and the Lions. The team physicians for each of the clubs, Drs. J. Donald Sheets and John Fetzer with the Red Wings, Drs. Russell Wright with the Tigers, and Richard Thompson with the Lions, were all members of the D.O.H. staff.

While in training, I had the opportunity to meet and assist in the care of elite professional athletes. This made me realize what terrific people they were and stimulated my interest in assisting in their care. Since the sports teams' doctors often cared for the players' immediate families, I had an opportunity to meet and know many of them on a personal basis. Dr. Sheets would often invite one of the surgical residents to accompany him to the games. Because I was single and had no other obligations, I was frequently available. While there, he would often take me into the dressing room. I remember being introduced to Ted Lindsay, and I congratulated him on the game he had just played when the Wings won. He said, "It's always a good game when you win." I thought to myself, *There is a real winner.*

Going to Olympia Stadium, the site of so many great sporting events in addition to hockey—championship boxing, figure skating, wrestling, the Harlem Globetrotters basketball, and a bevy of other extravaganzas— was a great thrill. It was the venue of so many extraordinary championship events that it created a certain aura of the ghosts of past champions.

At D.O.H., most of the residents had a great interest in everything that was going on with Detroit's sports teams because they all seemed to be competing for championships in their respective sports. We loved hockey in particular because the Red Wings had an arrangement with local TV Channel 2 to telecast the third period of each game beginning at 10:00 PM. Each hockey-game evening, we would hurry to get our work done so we could get to the residents' quarters in time to watch the third period on TV. Budd Lynch, the current Wings public address announcer, was a sports telecaster for Channel 2 and the Wings hockey play-by-play announcer at the time. Being in a city across the river from Canada, where hockey is the national sport, plus the easy availability of Canadian CBC television, gave us ample opportunity to become avid fans.

Having listened to radio broadcasts of *Hockey Night in Canada* on Saturday evenings with my father then being able to watch the games on TV and listen to Foster Hewitt was that much more rewarding—particularly when we realized that those telecasts were going across the entire Canadian continent, which at that time was an uncommon phenomenon. Having the opportunity to watch and learn more about that great sport sparked significant interest in the game in Detroit. Radio broadcasts were handled by Al Nagler, who became well known in hockey lore for calling the Red Wings' longest game in 1936 that ended at 2:25 AM.

The Red Wings' publicist was Fred Huber, a human sports encyclopedia with an inexhaustible supply of hockey and general sports facts that made him a favorite radio and television interviewee. When Fred retired to Arizona in the late 1950s, native Detroiter Elliot Trumbull took over as publicist and did an excellent job. Elliot now lives in Florida but still keeps very close ties with the Red Wings Alumni.

Elliot occasionally makes a return visit, especially for the playoffs. In 2010 he came back to enjoy the Tigers' opening game, the "Frozen Four" NCAA finals played on the NHL-owned portable ice surface at Ford Field, the NFL Detroit Lions home field adjacent to Tiger Stadium, plus the opening of the Stanley Cup playoffs at Joe Louis Arena—quite a combination in about a 10-day stretch. Elliot related how simple his PR department was in terms of preparing information to assist the press. He used to arrive at Olympia Stadium at noon on game day, take the latest information from the morning *Detroit Free Press*, add the latest scores from the wire services, update all areas, type the information on a mimeographic stencil sheet, then hand-pump the stencil fitted around an inked drum of the mimeograph machine to obtain updated information sheets to distribute to the sportswriters from the three major Detroit newspapers, two major wire services, two Windsor papers, several suburban and out-state papers, and a half-dozen or so radio and television reporters.

It was certainly some difference from today's detailed and beautifully developed information prepared by the enlarged PR department and distributed in the press lounge on the ice level near the home and visiting teams' dressing rooms and the fifth-level press box areas. Currently, the PR department's distribution also includes recent articles reprinted from both local and visiting team papers easily available on the Internet.

Getting Started

I had become very impressed with the high level of surgery and the stature of the work the Sheets/ Fetzer surgical group did, so when they offered me an opportunity to join them, I accepted in spite of having other more lucrative invitations. It was the level of medicine and the teamwork involved among the staff that was most impressive to me. I knew that staying in that atmosphere would be a continuing educational experience, so that's where I wanted to be. Working with them gave me the opportunity to continue to enhance my training, operating with very competent surgeons and assisting in the care of their patients. The Wings won the Stanley Cup two years before I joined the group. Their care was requiring more and more time, so the senior members of the group allowed Dr. Kosley and me to handle much of the work, which we gladly accepted.

Three months later in late November, my longtime sweetheart, Genevieve Keady, and I were married. Shortly after I finished my training, I became involved with our state Osteopathic organization. Those were the days when very little was taught in medical schools regarding athletic injuries and their treatment. With our skills in manipulative medicine, we were able to provide an additional modality to enhance their treatment. We then embarked upon an athletic injury seminar, bringing in nationally known experts to raise the level of expertise for members in our profession in treating those injuries.

For a period of about 10 years, we put on a weekend seminar specifically designed for those interested in enhancing their abilities in athletic medicine. The highlight of the meeting was a banquet that always featured a prominent athlete as the guest speaker. The year I was chairman of the meeting, 1936 Olympic track and field gold medal champion Jesse Owens—who outraced Hitler's "master race" athletes in the Berlin Summer Games—was our guest of honor. Sitting next to him at the head table was one of the thrills of my life. In addition to giving a very inspiring speech to everyone there, he and I enjoyed a wonderful personal conversation about the events of his training in Chicago and the people who helped mold his career. Don Faurot, the great football coach of the University of Missouri, was our guest speaker the following year.

The Detroit riots of 1967 created an atmosphere of significant uneasiness in Detroit, particularly among its urban population. About the same time, Detroit's expressway system, begun during World War II to ease transportation access to the multiple auto-related and defense plants, had matured and provided easy access to the suburbs. Much of Detroit's urban population took advantage of the opportunity for larger properties, better schools, and a safer living environment and began moving out. Since bus and rail transportation was limited, this proved to be a boom to the auto industry, whose sales increased multifold.

We moved to our first home in Southfield, which was situated on a reasonably flat 1/3-acre property that accommodated a 30' x 50' skating rink in winter and gave us the elbow room for our children to play and mature. So in more ways than one, our entire family grew up in hockey. Through the years, Michael played in Squirt, Peewee, and Junior hockey, our oldest daughter, Mary, and the next in line, Maureen, served as his goaltenders. Daughters Bridgit, Molly, and Colleen were Mike's cheering section at his games at Winter Wonderland in the amateur leagues and at Brother Rice High School.

From Southfield, we moved in the late 1960s to a four-bedroom home in Bloomfield Township, close to schools and church. The location was remarkable in that, many hockey Hall of Famers were living in the area, including Ebbie Goodfellow, Sid Abel, Ted Lindsay, Gordie Howe, Bill Gadsby, and Terry Sawchuk. What a thrill to be living in the same neighborhood and rubbing shoulders with those legends.

Making a Difference

The osteopathic medical profession, likely due to its emphasis on musculo-skeletal problems, has been deeply interested in the care of athletes. The state and national meetings always had lectures and special sessions on athletic medicine problems. Our hospital, Detroit Osteopathic Hospital, and certain members of the staff were taking care of hockey's Red Wings, baseball's American League Tigers, and the NFL's Lions. Jack Adams was a member of our hospital board.

Prominent athletes were seen every day in X-ray, physical therapy, or the out-patient department, receiving some kind of care, and as surgical residents, we were frequently involved. Having grown up in a family very much interested in sports, many of these professional athletes were the stars I had admired and respected as a teenager. The thing that impressed me most was what fine, polite, respectful gentlemen they all were and how they looked after one another.

Memories? I Have a Few

The last time I practiced with the Red Wings Old Timers was on a Saturday afternoon in December 1965. We had a great workout, and Sid Abel and a couple of others decided to stop for some refreshments on the way home. Genevieve was expecting in a week or two, so shortly after we stopped I called home. She said she didn't feel very well and was having some labor pains, but they weren't regular. We had plans to join my colleague, Dr. John Fetzer and his wife, Dorothy, and another couple for dinner in Greektown that evening. Instead, we phoned to tell them of our change in plans and the happy event of the birth of our red-headed daughter Molly, our fourth daughter and fifth child.

Three years later, we were at Olympia Stadium on a wintry Sunday night two days before Christmas, playing against the Maple Leafs. Genevieve was expecting the first week in January. Our son Michael, Mike Mahar, and his father, Judge Richard Mahar, were with us. About three

From left to right: Bridgit (Hermann), Colleen Finley, Molly
Finley (Riccio), Mary (Straffon), and Maureen (Kaplan) in 2004.
(Photo courtesy of the Finleys)

minutes before the end of the game, our goaltender, Roger Crozier, was
struck in the face with a puck and sustained a nasty laceration.

Dick took Genevieve to the hospital while I stayed and repaired Roger.
By the time Mike and I arrived at the hospital, about an hour or so later,
the newest member of the Finley family had arrived. Mike was hoping for
a brother to help even things up. On the way up to the hospital he said,
"Gee, Dad, what if it's another girl?" It was—our fifth daughter, Colleen.
We couldn't have been more pleased. I told Mike that he and I would have
to be like brothers, and that satisfied him. And by the way, we have been
ever since.

After graduation from Michigan State University, Mike entered medical school and became a third-generation graduate from Chicago College
of Osteopathic Medicine (now Midwestern University). Board certified in
internal medicine and rheumatology, he went into academic medicine and

presently is an associate dean at Western University College of Osteopathic Medicine in California.

People used to say we had two children, Michael and "the girls." However, each daughter followed her own interests to have an equally remarkable career. Both Mary and Maureen earned their engineering degrees at the University of Michigan. Mary earned her undergraduate and master's degrees in aerospace engineering and is now a project manager. Maureen earned hers in civil engineering and is an executive in Internet security. Bridgit pursued business in the medical-billing field; Molly earned a BA in English at the University of Michigan and is an advertising creative director in New York City. Colleen graduated in fine arts from Stephens College and is a director in her own Pampered Chef business.

Even though their professions and fields vary, the one constant they share is their love for hockey. From being little "rink rats" to gracious hosts at our team parties, to this day they all feel like part of the Red Wings' extended family.

The Finley family celebrating Dr. Finley's 40th year with the Red Wings. From left to right: granddaughter Lauren, Maureen, Mary, Bridgit, Genevieve, Michael Ilitch, Red Wings Alumni president Dennis Hextall, Marian Ilitch, Dr. Finley, Sergei Fedorov, Dr. Michael, Molly, and Colleen. (Photo courtesy of the Detroit Red Wings)

Glory Days

The two most significant periods in Red Wings history during my training and tenure were the early 1950s when they won three Stanley Cups championships, and the 1990s into the 2000s, when they did the same, plus one more for good measure in 2008. Both of these eras were similar in that those clubs had great chemistry. The players were close, and there was an aura of mutual respect that helped the teams of each period accomplish the ultimate goal. The teams of 1997–98 and 2002 featured a number of high-level Hall of Fame–type players.

On the contrary, the team that won the Cup in 2008 consisted of an entirely different type of team, different coach, more unknown, unheralded players, including a significant number of Europeans, the largest number from Sweden, plus Russia, the Czech Republic, and of course North America. But these players had one thing in common with those hockey greats that preceded them in the 1950s and 1990s—they were champions.

And I am forever grateful for the privilege of caring for them.

We continue to enjoy every game, and in November 2011 we celebrated our 54ᵗʰ anniversary—where else but at the Joe?
(Photo courtesy of Levi Sharp)

INDEX

282

Index

Index